HIGH/LOW
HANDBOOK
ENCOURAGING LITERACY IN THE 1990s

SERVING
SPECIAL NEEDS
SERIES

ACCEPT ME AS I AM
Best Books of Juvenile Nonfiction on Impairments and Disabilities
by Joan Brest Friedberg, June B. Mullins, Adelaide Weir Sukiennik

BOOKS FOR THE GIFTED CHILD
by Barbara H. Baskin and Karen H. Harris

BOOKS FOR THE GIFTED CHILD, Volume 2
by Paula Hauser and Gail A. Nelson

BOOKS TO HELP CHILDREN COPE WITH SEPARATION AND LOSS, 2nd Edition
by Joanne E. Bernstein

BOOKS TO HELP CHILDREN COPE WITH SEPARATION AND LOSS, Volume 3
An Annotated Bibliography
by Joanne E. Bernstein and Masha Kabakow Rudman

CHALLENGING THE GIFTED
Curriculum Enrichment and Acceleration Models
by Corinne P. Clendening and Ruth Ann Davies

CREATING PROGRAMS FOR THE GIFTED
A Guide for Teachers, Librarians, and Students
by Corinne P. Clendening and Ruth Ann Davies

HEALTH, ILLNESS, AND DISABILITY
A Guide to Books for Children and Young Adults
by Pat Azarnoff

HIGH/LOW HANDBOOK, 3rd Edition
Encouraging Literacy in the 1990s
by Ellen V. LiBretto

MORE NOTES FROM A DIFFERENT DRUMMER
A Guide to Juvenile Fiction Portraying the Disabled
by Barbara H. Baskin and Karen H. Harris

NOTES FROM A DIFFERENT DRUMMER
A Guide to Juvenile Fiction Portraying the Handicapped
by Barbara H. Baskin and Karen H. Harris

PARENTING THE GIFTED
Developing the Promise
by Sheila C. Perino and Joseph Perino

SERVING THE OLDER ADULT
A Guide to Library Programs and Information Sources
by Betty J. Turock

THIRD EDITION

HIGH/LOW
HANDBOOK™
ENCOURAGING LITERACY IN THE 1990s

Compiled and Edited by
Ellen V. LiBretto

R. R. Bowker
New York

Published by R.R. Bowker,
a division of Reed Publishing (USA) Inc.
Copyright © 1990 by Reed Publishing (USA) Inc.
All rights reserved
Printed and bound in the United States of America

Library of Congress Cataloging-in-Publication Data

High/low handbook : encouraging literacy in the 1990s / compiled and
    edited by Ellen V. LiBretto.—3rd ed.
        p.   cm.—(Serving special needs series)
    Includes bibliographical references and index.
    ISBN 0-8352-2804-5
    1. High interest-low vocabulary books—Bibliography.
2. Libraries—Special collections—High interest-low vocabulary
books.   3. Reading—Remedial teaching—Aids and devices.
4. Learning disabled youth—Books and reading.   5. Slow learning
children—Books and reading.   6. Handicapped youth—Books and
reading.   7. Libraries and the handicapped.   8. Teenagers—Books and
reading.   9. Libraries, Young people's.   10. Reading disability.
I. LiBretto, Ellen V.   II. Series.
Z1039.S5H54   1990
016.0276'63—dc20   90-35823
                                                                         CIP

ISBN 0-8352-2804-5

9 780835 228046   9 0 0 0 0

For Harriet C. Rath

Contents

viii   Contents

PART III   THE CORE COLLECTION

Preface

This third edition of *High/Low Handbook*, in Bowker's Serving Special Needs Series, is intended for teachers, librarians, and other individuals or institutions who provide easy reading material for disabled or reluctant teenage readers. This handbook cites materials with a wide range of reading levels and interest levels for the student with poor reading skills. There is also support material to assist and inspire the professional who is looking for reading material to use with teenagers who have reading problems. As used here, the term "disabled reader" refers to those teenagers who score on the fourth-grade level or below on reading tests; "reluctant readers" are those who score above the fourth-grade reading level, and therefore have some reading skills, yet lack the motivation to read.

In the decade since work was begun on the first edition of *High/Low Handbook*, I have spoken to hundreds of professionals associated with all aspects of the genre that we now call "high/low." I have watched the growth of the publishing industry and feel good about the many new publishers that are willing to take a chance on high/low materials. Also, I have worked with teachers who become excited when they see the numbers and variety of available titles that they can use as curriculum tie-ins. I have seen many small public libraries create easy-to-read sections and I have addressed many gatherings of authors who want to provide the reading disabled youngster with pertinent reading material that has an extra spark. In talks to teenagers in New York City, I have watched them eagerly seek out such titles as listed in Chapter 9, "High/Low Books for the Disabled Reader." I see more high/low books reviewed in professional journals and newsletters, making it easier for librarians and reading teachers to access these books.

All those who have been a part of the three editions of *High/Low Handbook* are true literacy pioneers. They recognize and are taking action to upgrade literacy levels of young people and are helping to stem the tide of illiteracy and school dropout rates. The media tell us that 23 million adults are functionally illiterate in the United States, many young people fail to comprehend the text on medicine bottles and maps, and 60 percent of the people in our correctional institutions are unable to read, write, or do arithmetic at the third-grade level. There are no instant cures to this national tragedy but the books, periodicals, and computer programs listed in this third edition are merely starting points for the professional to present to the low reading level and nonreading teenager. The teenagers' reaction to the material and the results have a great deal to do with the chemistry between the potential reader and the professional. Forming adult/teen reading partnerships is essential if teenagers are to find material that can match their individual needs and give them the satisfaction that comes from having read a whole book.

The primary focus here is in the selection, evaluation, and use of high interest–low reading level materials (books, periodicals, and computer software), many of them mirroring the concerns of today's youth. As in the previous editions, a number of chapters have been designed to define and demonstrate the growth in the genre and to support the core collection, which is central in enabling the practitioner to choose a sampling of material or to build a library with a wide range in interest and reading levels. *High/Low Handbook* reflects the work of contributors who have written from their own perspectives and experiences (librarians, teachers, reading specialists, and authors/publishers working in the high/low field serving teenagers) and strikes a balance between that experience and the hard core research in the field.

Part I, "Serving the High/Low Reader," begins with high/low reading material from the point of view of a small press publisher. Lyn Miller-Lachmann, who alone began a small publishing company (Square One Publishers/Stamp Out Sheep Press), focuses on material for the high/low audience and writes from this experience in Chapter 1 "Publishing and Writing for the Reluctant Reader." Miller-Lachmann also discusses the changing demographics in America and how one small press has a mission to serve the reading and survival needs of adolescents caught in this new American population. In Chapter 2, Marianne Laino Pilla highlights the growth of local and state reading initiatives that are leading the way to a National Reading Initiative. Milton Goldman and Sandra Goldman in Chapter 3, "Reading with Closed-Captioned TV," tell us how the use of the decoder on the television set can lead students to "read" their favorite television shows. Jean F. Rossman, a reading consultant, describes in Chapter 4, "The Disabled Adolescent Reader," the lives of three very different people and their reading problems. This chapter has been retained from the earlier editions of *High/Low Handbook* because the problems of those teenagers are timeless. Their reading disabilities are tied in with personal, emotional, and family problems.

Part II, "Selecting and Evaluating High/Low Materials," opens with Chapter 5, "The Promise of Computers for Reluctant Readers." Jean M. Casey and Julie M. T. Chan have revised the earlier writing in the second edition and expanded the chapter to include the latest findings in computer software for this audience. To capture teenagers' reading interest, using current material and the best visuals available today, Sandra Payne, a young adult librarian, has compiled a list of surefire periodicals in Chapter 6, "Periodicals Power: Magazines for Reluctant Readers." To meet the needs of those for whom English is a second language (ESL), Louise Spain in Chapter 7 addresses the pre-English literacy needs of adolescents in ESL programs, writing about the audiovisual approach to second language acquisition. Patsy H. Perritt has revised Chapter 8, "Readability Factors and Methods for Determining Reading Levels," with new findings in current use of readability formulas. For the nonreading specialist, this chapter clearly defines the formulas that are designed to measure the grade level of prose passages in text. (The primary emphasis is on using the Fry Readability Graph, the most popular measurement tool and the one used in evaluating the titles in Chapter 9, "High/Low Books for the Disabled Reader.")

Part III, "The Core Collection," consists of the above mentioned Chapter 9 and Chapter 10, "Books for the Reluctant Reader." Chapter 9 describes and evaluates 312 high/low books and recommends them for independent reading by the disabled teenage reader. Introducing Chapter 9 is a checklist of evaluation criteria used in selecting the titles. Only titles with first- to fifth-grade reading levels currently in print were considered for inclusion. Entries are arranged alphabetically by author and provide the following information: author, title, publisher, number of pages, price, International Standard Book Number (ISBN), fiction or nonfiction designation, subjects, reading level as determined by the Fry Readability Graph, interest grade level, and a critical annotation. The majority of the titles in Chapter 9 were published since 1985.

Chapter 10, "Books for the Reluctant Reader," is prepared by Joanne Rosario. The 100 books included range from the fourth- to eighth-grade reading level and are recommended for use with teenagers who are reluctant but moderately skilled readers.

Appendix I is a directory of publishers cited in Part III, "The Core Collection." Appendix II, "Bibliographies and Sources of Current Reviews," compiled by Patsy H. Perritt, assists the user in developing collections of professional tools and recommends review journals on the subject. A list of Contributors and an Author Index, Title Index, and Subject Index conclude the book.

I would like to thank the many people who helped in the preparation of this work. The titles selected for Chapter 9 were evaluated by many librarians who work with disabled readers and can identify areas of interest that will stimulate young people to read. Those who helped in writing the annotations for Chapter 9 are Lisa Shackelford, young adult librarian at the Central Library, Queens Borough Public Library; Ramona Koch, assistant branch library manager at the Pomonok Library, Queens Borough Public Library; and Carole McCully, educational consultant. Once again, Rosemarie Riechel, head of database searching for Queens Borough Public Library, helped with verifying statistical information. I would like to add a thank you to John Drobnicki, Office Aide I, Programs and Services Department, Queens Borough Public Library. I also thank my department heads, Joan Caruso and Kathryn Nicholas, both former young adult librarians, for much encouragement and support. In addition, thanks go to Dan Rabideau and Sara Hill from the Literacy Assistance Center, New York, for their help in supplying exciting material for Chapter 9, as well as the many publishers who sent me sample copies for review—in particular, Charles DiSanto, Creative Education; Roger Rosen, Rosen Press; Cindi Guy, New Readers Press; and Arvena Ault, Fearon Press. In addition, special appreciation to Bob Miller who built me an enormous desk; this helped me organize myself for the project.

I am grateful to Marion Sader, Publisher at R. R. Bowker, for the opportunity to compile and update this third edition of *High/Low Handbook*. I am particularly appreciative to Iris Topel, Editing Supervisor at Bowker, for her guidance in the copy editing and production stages of this book.

One of the purposes of *High/Low Handbook* is to contribute to the attainment of education as set forth by the Carnegie Council on Adolescent Development. In its publication, *Turning Points: Preparing American Youth for the 21st Century* (June, 1989, Carnegie Corporation of New York), the general goals outlined for educating American youth include creating a common core of knowledge and creating the ability to choose a healthful life-style, practice good citizenship, and think critically. Many of the teenagers for whom this material is intended have a long way to go in meeting these standards, but it is hoped that the 1990s will bring a renewed energy to America and that the 1990s will see a major reduction of illiteracy.

ELLEN V. LiBRETTO

HIGH/LOW

HANDBOOK

ENCOURAGING LITERACY IN THE 1990s

Part I
Serving the High/Low Reader

1
Publishing and Writing for the Reluctant Reader

Lyn Miller-Lachmann

I n the spring of 1988 I was asked to speak about my first novel, *Hiding Places*, to a group of students in a dropout prevention program at Far Rockaway High School, Queens, New York. It had been a typical wet spring in New York City, and on that afternoon in May it seemed as though the entire contents of Jamaica Bay were being dumped onto the Rockaway Peninsula. My talk was to be in the school library, in a space set up for 24 students. Sixty appeared. They represented some dozen countries throughout the world—blacks, whites, Hispanics, and Asians. Among them were residents of group homes and halfway houses, refugees from wars in Afghanistan and Central America, and some of the increasing numbers of youngsters in the United States who grow up in poverty.

Hiding Places is a realistic novel about a teenage runaway in New York City who must put his life together on his own while trying to come to terms with the disintegration of his family. It has been called a "problem" novel and a "high/low" novel, though I did not intend to write it as either. The language is frank, and the situations starkly portrayed. The novel does not romanticize running away, but it shows how a teenager, with the help of some very good friends, can survive and grow under the most difficult conditions.

At Far Rockaway High School, I read a passage from the novel and talked about the origins of the characters in my own experience, in the students whom I taught in two inner-city public high schools in New

York City and a private school in Connecticut, and in my reading. We discussed how characters come to life through such details as clothing, a wallet, or a meal. We compared Donald Trump's wallet with that of the neighborhood drug dealer. We were together for more than an hour on that rainy day in May, talking about reading and writing, asking and answering questions, and learning about each other's lives. The students were interested and articulate. Some of these "at-risk" youngsters had already read the book, which is more than 200 pages long. Afterward, a 16-year-old girl who had read the book, a former runaway herself, gave me a copy of a poem she had written, based on *Hiding Places* and with the same title. Her poem spoke of hiding places that "don't really hide you," because the memories one tries to escape always seem to follow.

I do not write high/low materials or anything else for the sole purpose of making money. I have worn many professional hats—teacher, librarian, political activist, writer, publisher. As a hobby, I organize concerts of Latin American popular and underground music. I have made sure that I do not have to live off my writing because I do not want to have to write anything I do not believe simply to make money. Nor do I want to gloss over or misrepresent what I feel to be the truth simply to make a sale. And that brings me to the second part of my story.

Hiding Places did not get published without a struggle. I completed the original manuscript in the spring of 1984 and quickly found it to be unpublishable, a victim of the conservative tide that brought Ronald Reagan to power in 1980. Contributors to the second edition and to this third edition of *High/Low Handbook* have already lamented the budget cuts that have devastated sales of the Skinny Books and other materials for problem readers. The cuts in library and school funding accelerated during the decade, and the principal victims have been the swelling numbers of our young people who live below the poverty line and the schools they attend. Even if those schools could afford high/low materials, new materials were increasingly unavailable. As overall sales declined, publishers cut back their programs or terminated them altogether.

The conservatism of the 1980s has affected the content as well as the supply of materials for reluctant readers. Again, the main victims have been inner-city youngsters and teenagers who belong to minority groups. Since 1983, there has been a shift away from realistic "problem" novels toward light romances and books depicting white, middle-class, relatively untroubled teens whose escapades are squeaky clean and morally uplifting. While I am not an advocate of profanity, senseless violence, or premarital sex, these are major realities in many teenagers' lives today, along with death, family breakdown, substance abuse, gangs, racism, and other problems. They are depicted in television, films, and music videos.

Why should books be the guardians of adolescent morality, and not movies, music, or television? Because of the supposed permanence of the printed word? With the advent of the video recorder and the continued use of acidified paper in books, books are now no more permanent than videotape. Because books can be reread? Tapes can be rewound and are played again more often than books are ever reread. If reading materials do not keep up with the daily experience of our adolescents, it is small wonder that teens don't read.

I do not intend to say that romances, light mysteries, and other escape literature should not be published. All teens, including reluctant readers, read to escape. However, "realistic" novels should be real. Just as it is a disservice to reluctant or problem readers to "dumb down" materials by using strict formulas for vocabulary and sentence structure, it is a disservice to water down stories of their lives to make those stories palatable to adults. Just as reluctant readers deserve the respect of authors, publishers, librarians, and teachers, so do the needs of all young people. Adolescence is a difficult time in a person's life, and it is particularly difficult today for those who do not conform to the established models of success.

With those ideas in mind, I established Square One Publishers/ Stamp Out Sheep Press in 1985. The name of the imprint originated not from a vendetta against the woolly animals but from the connotation of sheep as those who follow blindly, without thinking. At that point, my own manuscript had been abandoned by my agent, and I knew other writers outside the mainstream who faced similar problems. I defined my press as one to appeal to teens "who feel themselves to be different in some way." This did not necessarily include the reluctant or problem reader, and I followed no readability formula in publishing the Stamp Out Sheep Press novels. The original paperback books are not particularly short, nor do they have other characteristics of the traditional high/ low format—photos or illustrations on facing pages, large print, or photo covers. Nevertheless, many reluctant readers have gravitated toward the Stamp Out Sheep Press line.

I am not surprised that reluctant readers who are frequently out of the mainstream adolescent population found *Hiding Places* a novel that spoke directly to them. I have been told by many teachers and librarians that one of the press's novels is the first that a particular student actually completed. Recently, I spoke with a high school English teacher from a working-class suburb near Philadelphia. She told me that her students had grown tired of the sanitized realistic fiction on the reading list; she pointed out that with the problems her students face every day, the existing books seem inadequate. One of her students had discovered *Hiding Places* in the school library and brought it to her attention as an alternative to the outdated or overly cautious books in the curriculum.

When established, Square One Publishers/Stamp Out Sheep Press took as its mission the publishing of original paperback novels that deal with minorities in the United States, the experiences of teenagers in other countries (particularly in the Third World), teenagers who challenge traditional sex-role stereotypes, and teenagers who become involved in political and social causes. In addition to *Hiding Places*, the press brought out *Cassandra Robbins, Esq.*, by Pat Costa Viglucci, in 1987. *Cassandra Robbins, Esq.* is the story of a biracial teenager adopted at birth by a white family; it tells of the conflicts concerning her racial identity when she begins to date. While maintaining some of the structure of a teen romance, *Cassandra* deals with serious issues faced by many biracial teenagers today, with particular attention to interracial couples and racial prejudice on the part of both whites and African-Americans.

In 1988, two more novels were published—*Center Stage Summer*, by Cynthia K. Lukas, and *The Twenty-six Minutes*, by Robert Hawks. *Center Stage Summer* is about a 17-year-old girl who risks her college scholarship when she joins her older sister in protesting a nuclear power plant in her community. *The Twenty-six Minutes* portrays two teenage children of career air force officers, misfits in their military community, who become involved in a peace group and in the life of its charismatic leader.

The four Stamp Out Sheep Press novels published to date have enjoyed a fair amount of critical success. In comparison to most original paperbacks and most small press books, their critical reception has been quite remarkable. Favorable reviews have appeared in *Booklist, School Library Journal, Publishers Weekly, Voice of Youth Advocates, Emergency Librarian*, and *Kliatt*. Three of the four have been selected for the New York Public Library's "Books for the Teen Age" list. *Cassandra Robbins, Esq.* made the recommended list of the National Conference of Christians and Jews, which publishes a guide to the best multicultural books of the year. *Center Stage Summer* was chosen as a "best book" by the teenagers who form the Young Adult Advisory Board of the Enoch Pratt Free Library, Baltimore, Maryland. Individual library systems that publish reviews have given the books their highest ratings.

Libraries and schools make up about 80 percent of the market for the Stamp Out Sheep Press line. A growing number of school districts are using one or more titles for instructional purposes as well. Unlike the big presses, Square One Publishers/Stamp Out Sheep Press can survive on the school and library markets alone. One of the obstacles facing the traditional high/low series published by mainstream presses was that the titles rarely sold in bookstores. Thus, cuts in school and library budgets had a crucial impact on sales, pushing the titles into the red. Today, most large publishers concentrate on the bookstore market, and bookstores (which at times engage in joint ventures with publishers) cater to the needs and interests of middle-class, suburban teenagers (and parents) who buy books. Book-buying teenagers read fairly well, and books are part of their everyday lives. Reluctant or problem readers, on the other hand, do not generally buy books. They often live in communities where there are no bookstores and in homes where no books are owned at all. This is a double bind for large presses but allows an opening for a small press such as Stamp Out Sheep Press.

An alternative press with low overhead and a lower break-even point has another advantage. Obviously, realistic depictions of teenage life and problems, especially in inner cities and depressed rural areas, will offend some people. When the main characters are members of racial and ethnic minorities, some may say that the audience is too limited, and predominantly white, upper-middle-class readers will not be able to empathize with the characters. Books may be challenged or never purchased in the first place. Large publishers that depend on a broad national market complain that they can't locate the market for books or series with nonwhite themes. They also have more to fear from censors and more to lose if a book is deemed "special interest" than would a small press with a low break-even point and a well-defined niche.

As I see it, the signs are a lot more encouraging today than they were in 1984. Desktop publishing has become more sophisticated, lowering costs further and allowing more specialized books to reach their audience. As this trend continues, there will be a greater variety of books for young people overall, including books at various levels for reluctant or problem readers. Books that are specific to the reader's culture and community can be published, introducing a new level of realism and immediacy to the reluctant reader's experience. Desktop publishing will also permit more experimentation, including books combined with computer software to allow two-way interaction and the publication of the reader's own thoughts. A number of new small companies, such as Turman Publishing, Morning Glory Press, and Literacy Volunteers of New York, have emerged in the past few years to tap the market for high/low materials. Because of the nature of that market, I feel that the future suppliers of high/low materials will be small, lean, and innovative companies that understand the needs of the problem reader and are frequently able to combine books with nonbook resources. More in-house materials, at higher quality, may also be produced as a result of the revolution in desktop publishing.

Another encouraging sign is the increasing use of trade books in the classroom as a means of promoting lifelong reading. Adopted as an objective of the California Reading Initiative and the National Reading Initiative, using trade books in classroom instruction will provide a new market for large and small publishers at all levels, including publishers of easy-to-read materials for adolescents. In the case of materials for reluctant or problem readers, this is an especially promising development. It will make it economically feasible for publishers to enter the field with more than textbook-style materials, and some of the older favorites, now out of print, may reappear. With the new reading initiatives, reluctant readers and those who work with them will have not only more opportunities to read trade books but also more choices in the books they will be able to purchase and read.

Finally, the large presses are beginning to open up again to multicultural materials that serve a country with quickly changing demographic patterns. As one well-known writer expressed it to me in the fall of 1988, "The situation is still more restrictive than it was ten years ago, but it's better than it was five years ago."

Rita Williams-Garcia's first novel, *Blue Tights,* was one beneficiary of this change. Williams-Garcia wrote the first draft of the novel in 1979, when, as an undergraduate at Hofstra University, she had volunteered to tutor four teenage girls on Long Island. The novel's protagonist, a physically developed African-American teenager who longs for love and approval, is based on Williams-Garcia's four students; she wrote the book in the course of the semester so they would be able to read something real about themselves. When the manuscript was first submitted to publishers in the early 1980s, it was rejected everywhere as too "special interest." Making the rounds again five years later, it found a home and was finally published in 1988.

Blue Tights achieved deserved critical success and is now being used extensively as a trade book in inner-city classrooms. It is included in the core collection of books for the reluctant reader in Chapter 10 in this volume, where it receives praise for its honest portrayal of Joyce's confusion over her sexuality and the process by which she gains a sense of self-worth through dance.

Williams-Garcia is one of 38 African-American authors whose books for children or young adults were published in 1988. While a low number in comparison to the more than 1,000 juvenile books published each year, their contributions represent an improvement over the 18 juvenile books published by African-American authors in 1984. It is hoped that the pendulum will continue to swing in this direction and that mainstream publishers will begin to produce materials with diverse themes, characters, and plots for the teenagers of the 1990s.

As a publisher and an author whose books are read by reluctant readers, and as someone who has taught and spoken to inner-city teenagers, I have some observations for those who work with that group. Teachers and librarians should be aware of small presses that have emerged recently. New small press publishers of materials for reluctant readers are waiting to hear from you as well. What are the most effective aspects of their publications? What needs improvement? What suggestions do you have, based on your work in your community? We need to get past the stereotype of alternative presses as publishers of low-quality rejects from the big presses and see them as the innovative entrepreneurs that they truly are. At a time of rapid technological advances, they are best able to move quickly and respond to the needs of the market. With their lean structure, they can move into niches that are uneconomical for a large multinational corporation to fill.

The amount of realism permissible in a young adult book is a subject of debate, and as I have pointed out earlier, the boundaries have expanded and shrunk several times over the past 20 years. My own feeling is that teenagers who are looking for realistic books want them to be genuinely honest. They do not have much patience for books in which the author has obviously held back to avoid offending the mainstream market. The teenager should be able to "hear" the language in the book. An overly optimistic or hopeful ending should not be forced, lest it cause readers to doubt themselves for not attaining such a positive outcome. At the same time, the book should not sensationalize the problem, leading one to think that the writer has gone slumming to get a hot story.

Teenage characters, especially those whose experiences are out of the mainstream, deserve the respect of the author. Within the bounds of realism, the ending should not condemn the characters, and the readers by implication, to a hopelessly bleak future. It almost goes without saying (were it not for the stereotypes that still show up in books today) that the book's presentation of minority groups, foreign cultures, and global concerns must be evenhanded and free from stereotypes. Like the real teenagers who will read about them, the characters must be, above all, people and not representatives of a given ethnic or racial group. While they may have identifiable class or cultural traits (Donald Trump's wallet, as opposed to the neighborhood drug dealer's), their principal traits must be human ones. Under those circumstances, there may be many more similarities than differences (in terms of personality or as teenagers discuss the accumulation of wealth) between Donald Trump and an individual drug dealer.

Many of us have a tendency to stereotype problem readers as members of an underclass who live in inner cities. Having spoken extensively in small towns in the northern Midwest, I can testify to the existence of problem readers everywhere. I have also encountered a large number of new Asian immigrants in otherwise homogeneous communities in northern Wisconsin and Minnesota, immigrants who are struggling to acquire reading skills in a new language. Publishers, authors, teachers, and librarians need to be more aware of these new immigrants and how they are changing the school-age community by both their numbers and their cultural differences. This population will be a growing audience for high interest materials with a limited English-language vocabulary. At this point, few books exist, outside of those published by New Readers Press and Fearon Press, that deal with the circumstances of Southeast Asians, Central and South Americans, and others (such as the students from Afghanistan whom I met at Far Rockaway High School) whose numbers may be small but whose needs are great.

At the same time, we need to support authors from minority groups who have the greatest familiarity with their culture and communities and who may serve as models for their readers. Particularly in bridging reading and writing, it makes a difference when someone from the student's own community or ethnic group has succeeded in having his or her story published and read by others. Rita Williams-Garcia's experience is instructive; one of the four students she tutored went on to graduate from college.

Finally, I cannot emphasize enough the value of author visits to a group of problem readers. Every time I speak to such a group, at least one of the students tells me this is the first time he or she has met a "real live author." With students whose major experience in school is one of failure, the arrival of an author who is willing to give of his or her time and to listen is an important, memorable event. Recently, I encountered a student who, two years earlier, had heard me speak to her class; she still recalled much of what I had said then. She also told me that my talk had inspired her to submit her own writing to the school literary magazine. Though it was not published, she continues to write even today.

When planning an author visit to reluctant or problem readers, it is best to keep the group fairly small. Ask the author to read a passage from one of his or her published books or a work-in-progress. This will stimulate the teenager to read, as the passage and the context of its performance tell the teenager that the experience is real. Groups larger than 60 are intimidating for the individual who might venture a question, and it is hard to carry on a discussion with the students. Thus, large-group presentations tend to be lectures of the inspirational variety, not the most effective method of reaching the audience. A particularly good speaker may entertain, but the personal touch, the sense that someone out there is listening, is what motivates students to tackle a difficult task, such as reading a full-length book.

I would like to conclude with some observations on my own writing and why I have been considered an author of books for reluctant or problem readers, even though I have consulted no vocabulary list or readability scales. I speak extensively in secondary schools, primarily because I enjoy it and the process of writing is really too solitary for me. My most memorable and successful presentations have been to students in remedial programs. I like their questions. I am interested in their stories of their own lives. To put it bluntly, my sympathies lie with the outsiders in society; those who are on the fast track to success have plenty of advocates.

Hiding Places takes the side of a boy who feels he has been abandoned and betrayed by his well-to-do parents. My most recent work is about another outsider, an immigrant to the United States from a politically oppressive country in South America. The story is of his struggle to build a relationship with his father, who has just rejoined the family after seven years as a political prisoner in their country. When I write a novel, I consider myself an advocate for troubled teenage characters about whom I care very much; my passion and commitment drive the story. Many New York editors are shocked and appalled and won't have anything to do with my manuscripts, but even so, my file of fan letters from teenage readers is thicker than my rejection file. I would rather have readers hate my characters than not think anything of them one way or the other. Reading calls for a commitment, even for taking sides; particularly for reluctant readers, it is not an intellectual exercise but rather a means of connecting with someone else who shares the same experiences and problems. Readers of *Hiding Places* have debated with me whether the protagonist made the right decisions when on the run; a couple have even said, "I wouldn't have run away. I would have stayed and fought." Reluctant readers have strong opinions, if we only listen to them and give them a chance to think about the questions.

Writers and publishers for reluctant readers have pointed out that wanting teens to read because reading is good for them is not a sufficient motivation. Books should be enjoyable in themselves and should have the capacity to move the reader. They are not just a tool for the improvement of wayward youths. Let me take this argument one step further. Writers and publishers for reluctant or problem readers should fundamentally be on the side of the kids. Our books should contain themes that guide young people in making important decisions about their lives without preaching to them what those decisions should be. We need to understand and to represent faithfully and respectfully the diverse cultures of our young people. An author or publisher of books for adolescents, particularly for those who are reluctant readers, should never forget how he or she felt as an adolescent—chipping away at the stone walls of society, waiting for the doors to open. Those of us who have been chipping at the stone walls of mainstream publishing feel this acutely. In touch with our own experiences and committed to sharing them with our younger counterparts, we shall avoid blandness and actively seek out controversy; once confronted and engaged, our young people will amaze us with what they can accomplish.

2
Taking Notes from the California Reading Initiative: Toward a National Reading Initiative

Marianne Laino Pilla

R eading initiative" may become the buzzword for the 1990s. Since the development in 1985 of the California Reading Initiative (CRI), several imitations and numerous new programs have sprung up. This chapter explores the development of this West Coast wave that, at the time of this writing, appears to be sweeping the country with fresh ways to incorporate literature (good books) into the K–12 curriculum in the classroom and also ways for professional children's literature specialists to cooperate to promote children's books outside of it.

The California Reading Initiative has apparently led the way for such changes. Its background, the positive and negative aspects, what it has inspired, and some pitfalls to avoid are examined here. Also, the status of the "National Reading Initiative," which directly sprang from CRI, is summarized and exemplary national reading programs are highlighted. Finally, some suggestions from experts, based on an informal written and telephone survey, on important considerations when planning any type of reading initiative, whether on a local or national level, are discussed. A bibliography is presented at the end of this chapter with representative works on this topic.

THE CALIFORNIA READING INITIATIVE

Since 1985, the mandate of Bill Honig, California state superintendent of education, to encourage children to "love reading and books" has blossomed from a statewide voluntary reading initiative in school districts in California to a national presence, influencing numerous states to follow California's lead.

In a telephone interview, Mae Bungo Gundlach, consultant in language arts, from the California State Department of Education, Office of Humanities Curriculum Services, described this reading initiative primarily as a major curriculum change, an education reform since it was discovered that students had not been reading too well. The reading initiative has taken the form of revamping curriculum in seven major subject areas. To date, the English-language arts change has received the most attention, largely because of the publication of *Recommended Readings in Literature, Kindergarten through Grade Eight* in 1986, revised in 1988. In the fall of 1989, the recommended reading lists for grades 9–12 were revised. It is planned to revise the lists every three years and design a new curriculum framework every seven years.

There are four components of the CRI: staff development, upgrading tests assessments, curriculum resource development, and influencing revisions of textbooks. Presently there exists a statewide committee comprising teachers and school and children's librarians who develop lists for grades K–8 and 9–12. This reading initiative remains an option for each school district throughout the state. Each site is free to develop its own list.

There is a mixed bag of opinion regarding the success of the reading initiative, with most of the critics saying the reading initiative was poorly conceived. Lack of funds to execute the program properly has been a major drawback, especially in those school districts already underfunded and understaffed.

Whether a school district opts to participate is one thing and what its financial commitment to the program is another. There is no staff development coming from the California Department of Education and no money provided to purchase library books. One school district, the Clovis District, uses Chapter I and lottery money to assist in its literature program.

Another serious consideration is the availability of school libraries and qualified school librarians, important components in the reading initiative. The results of a 1985–1986 study, *The Crisis in California School Libraries*, commissioned by State Superintendent Bill Honig, reveal that "68 percent of schools with a library had no certified librarian on staff."[1] This study was coordinated with a nationwide study conducted by the U.S. Department of Education's Center for Statistics. The center found that "of all the 50 states, California was by far in the worst position of all 50 states in terms of having the largest percent of school libraries operating without certificated library staff."[2]

Questions of assessment procedures have surfaced. How will the students be taught and tested within this new literature-based curriculum? Numerous articles regarding this area have popped up in journals from *Reading Teacher* to *The Horn Book*. There is growing concern that the basalization of children's literature will rob the value of the work itself. For example, one editorial cited a published 100-page study guide for Eric Carle's picture book *The Very Hungry Caterpillar*: "If we misuse books, if we subject great literature to the practices of basal reading textbooks, we can get children to hate *Charlotte's Web* (Harper) and *Tuck Everlasting* (Farrar). . . . If literature in the classroom is to be at all effective, teachers must learn to trust the book to do its own teaching, and they must learn to get out of the way. . . . If we take great novels and create work sheets and drills for them, we can do infinitely more harm than good."[3]

The classroom teacher's sometimes limited knowledge of children's literature, as well as the limited availability and quality of in-service training to assist the teacher, is another drawback. The California Literature Project (CLP), offered by the State Department of Education, attempts to remedy in-service problems. During a five-week summer program, in a university setting, classroom teachers learn to implement program development in language, reading, writing, listening, and speaking.

Interagency cooperation, in particular, communication with public libraries, was an initial oversight. Public librarians were not included on the first CRI committee that chose more than 1,000 books for its first K–8 book list. The book list, as described by assistant superintendent of education Francie Alexander, is "part of a comprehensive plan that included curriculum development, staff development, test development, and resource development. These developmental efforts are the essential elements of the California Reading Initiative."[4] As a result, many libraries were unprepared when parents and students asked for books from their schools' reading lists. This situation has been rectified somewhat with the inclusion of children's librarians on the selection committee in the revision of the recommended reading lists.

THE ROLE OF BOOKSELLERS

Booksellers have been an integral part of the California Reading Initiative. According to Caron Chapman, executive director of the Association of Booksellers for Children (ABC), in a telephone interview, children's booksellers have worked very closely with teachers in getting trade books into the classrooms. They have been supplying books, doing booktalks, and other book-promotional programs throughout the state. Chapman notes: "There are 150 children's bookstores in California and they work with teachers extensively; 17 have opened up in Southern California alone in the spring of 1989." She further indicates that CRI provides "great information about children's literature which is readily accessible in these bookstores." One advantage booksellers have over children's librarians is that bookstores get advanced notice of new books and have much more current books. They also know if a book is available in paperback, which, Chapman said, is important to the CRI program.

The Association of Booksellers for Children is a growing effort to promote excellence in all aspects of bookselling and production. Established in 1985, ABC seeks to foster communication among those concerned with children's books, with the goal of promoting high standards of business practices. The 350 members include book retailers, publishers, publisher's reps, authors, illustrators, librarians, wholesalers, literary agents, manufacturers, distributors, and nonvoting staff of retail stores.

Caron Chapman cites a new trend in the children's literature field: Most of the booksellers are "professional children's literature specialists." This is a change from the past as more and more former teachers and children's librarians join the booksellers' force—and as professional children's librarians dwindle in number. This trend is having an effect on the caliber of bookstore operations, with greater emphasis on promoting children's books and reading through store programming. Chapman sums it up by saying: "In bookstores there exists the freedom to promote the highest quality children's literature as much as possible. The majority of children's booksellers have as a personal goal the desire to make available to children the best literature possible."

THE PUBLISHING ANGLE

Schools and libraries have not been the exclusive participants in the California Reading Initiative. One business/reading venture was the "Reading Is My Bag" campaign, held in October 1988, which featured ads printed on Safeway supermarket shopping bags. This event was sponsored by four book publishers and a dozen retail stores that participated by selling CRI books. Still, to date, in California, there are no substantive schemes to engage city, county, or state businesses as funders for the initiative.

It is apparent that financial gains by booksellers because of CRI have encouraged the Association of American Publishers (AAP) to create a new post, that of National Reading Initiative coordinator. Parker Ladd, director of the General Trade Publishing Division of AAP, in conjunction with the AAP Reading Initiative, has appointed its own national coordinator, Mary Sue Dillingkopski of Ripon, Wisconsin. In a telephone interview, Ladd announced: "The purpose of the National Reading Initiative officer is to reach out at the grass-roots level across the country and help interested parties, like the PTA, teachers, parents, to know how they can set up similar programs to those in California, to set up programs that teach children's literature in the classroom." It is apparent that a nationwide emphasis on literature in the classroom could open an enormous market for trade publishers.

CALIFORNIA'S SUCCESS STORIES

Ironically, one of the strongest programs exhibiting interagency cooperation is one that began more than 10 years ago. The California Young Reader Medal Award Program, for grades K–12, was formed by the California Reading Association. Currently more than 500,000 participate in selecting the best book from a list of nominated books. A 12-member committee of teachers and school and public librarians nominate the books—about 400—and these are narrowed down to 200 in June; over the summer committee members read and re-read books, getting together in September to draw up a list of five titles. Students read the books the following year and then vote. Each year's winning author is honored. Among the obvious advantages to this contest are that both professionals and students read the literature and base their selections on their reading.

An exciting new linkup involves public television working in concert with public libraries. "Vacation Video" is produced in the summer by San Francisco's public broadcasting station KQED. Alice Cahn, producer of "Vacation Video," works with Neel Parikh, coordinator of children's services, San Francisco Public Library. In a telephone interview, Cahn emphasized her excitement about working with the libraries, saying that the "best thing the public library validated was that the kids watch television and go there to get the books they've seen on television." The station produces entertaining educational programs for preschoolers to teenagers, including a children's literature series, and popular shows like "Reading Rainbow."

What makes this library/television station relationship unique is that the station contacts the children's librarians in advance of setting the programming schedule. The station sends information about summer programming during February. KQED publishes a 42-page magazine that lists programs, suggestions for books to read, and other related activities. Children can pick up a free copy of the magazine by presenting a library card at a library. In 1989, more than 70,000 copies of the publication were distributed. Milton Chen, director of instructional television at the station, explains: "By using television, which has tremendous reach and appeal to kids, the magazine is a way to lead them into activities and a whole array of community resources. . . . It's our little Trojan horse."[5]

Another area of growing networking is the relationship of booksellers and librarians. Children's librarians in the San Francisco area have a dynamic organization in the Northern California Children's Booksellers Association (NCCBA), which has been meeting monthly since 1984. One of its supporters, the *San Francisco Chronicle*, regularly publishes children's book reviews, a children's best-seller list, and articles on children's literature and literacy. NCCBA works in conjunction with the San Francisco Public Library, in particular in helping to plan Ashley Bryan's visit there last summer.[6]

Another booksellers' group, the Southern California Children's Booksellers Association (SCCBA), tied into local public library summer reading clubs. Last year it printed 250,000 bookmarks with donated funds. These bookmarks featured a coupon for a dollar off the price of any book at a local children's bookstore. At the end of the summer, each library was to receive 25 cents for every coupon redeemed.

INSPIRED STATES

The fledgling California Reading Initiative, while apparently not promoted as much within the state as outside it, has inspired other states to try similar reading initiatives. In fact, in 1987, a National Reading Initiative was formed to coordinate and promote reading and reduce illiteracy. To date, its only contributions have been the formation of a council and the publication of a paperback, *Celebrating the National Reading Initiative*, which contains activities for promoting reading. Time will tell if this effort becomes a more visible, effective campaign throughout the country.

Other states would do well to learn by California's oversights. At last count 6 states had statewide literacy initiatives and 17 states had literature-based curriculums.

The Alabama Department of Education is one that was inspired by CRI but has taken it a step farther. Alabama's program is one of the few that focus on teenagers. Many states, for example, Arizona's statewide literacy initiative, stress early elementary grades. In a telephone interview, Jane Bandy Smith, education specialist in the Student Instructional Services Division of the Alabama Department of Education, said, "When we got their literature [about CRI] we were excited about it. If we could get literature-based instruction, that would be beneficial."

About three years ago, in response to the California Reading Initiative, Alabama tried to target grades K–12 but decided to focus primarily on grades 4–6. Alabama uses new literature-based reading textbooks and includes some continuing writing programs and incorporates literature into this.

The Alabama Reading Incentive Council has been organized, an umbrella group composed of several representatives from Alabama agencies. The membership comprises the president and recent past president of the following statewide organizations interested in promoting libraries: Alabama Public Libraries Services, Alabama Library Association, Alabama Reading Association, Alabama Council of Teachers of English, Post-Secondary Reading Teachers, Alabama Congress of Parents and Teachers, and Alabama Instructional Media Association. Members of the council are "very enthusiastic about the concept," according to Smith. The honorary chairperson is the current lieutenant governor's wife, Marsha Folsom, who is very active in this cause.

Smith's Student Instructional Services Division suggests ways of encouraging literature. It had five workshops during the summer of 1989 to show teachers and librarians how to get children excited about curriculum. The programs were run by state-funded in-service centers. Participants were mostly teachers since many public librarians were involved with their own summer reading programs.

Smith summarizes their mission: "Our goal as we work through this process is to identify titles relevant to this curriculum, eventually for grades K–12; we would have a handbook of titles that would incorporate into other areas in addition to language." They encourage teaching and the use of libraries to see that this works.

COMMUNITY EFFORTS

Baltimore, Maryland, has shown that the problems of an entire state need not be tackled in order to combat illiteracy. In its exemplary program, "Baltimore Reads," initiated by Mayor Kurt L. Schmoke, a citywide literacy initiative was launched in 1988, "targeting the quantity and quality of out-of-school services and the quality of the public schools."[7] Maggi G. Gaines is the current executive director of Baltimore Reads Inc., a private nonprofit foundation founded along with Baltimore Reads. This group works with the Baltimore City Literacy Corporation, the first city agency devoted to adult literacy. Together they raise private funds and increase public awareness of literacy concerns.

Building community relations between the public and private sectors is a priority, as evidenced in the participation of 20 committee members from the television and business communities, including United Way of Central Maryland, as well as Reg Murphy, publisher of the *Baltimore Sun*, and the president of the *Afro-American Newspaper*, Frances Draper, as board members.

Funding resulted from the initial cooperative effort with United Way. Then appeals to corporations and businesses like the Fort Howard Paper Company resulted in contributions, along with a matching grants challenge from Cal Ripken, Jr., Baltimore Orioles' shortstop. The program has applied to the federal government for an Even Start grant that would enable the Baltimore public schools, Head Start, and the Community College of Baltimore to coordinate staff resources, training services, and curriculum design.[8] With this in place, participating families could receive a structured continuum of services through interagency coordination.

A central hot line to provide a database of statistics on the specific needs of the population has been planned, and the first of six one-stop adults' learning centers will open in 1990.[9] One of the program's first big events, a "Read-a-Thon," was held in the Rotunda of City Hall in July 1989, and was a great success, according to Samuel Zervitz, Office of Baltimore City Literacy Corporation, who says "networking pays." Among those participating were notables from government and business, celebrities, children, and adults—even prisoners from the city jail—who read continually for 31 days.

EXCLUSIVELY TEENS

The Friendly Place/El Sitio Simpático, the American Reading Council's former demonstration project, is currently an independent library in East Harlem, New York City. What makes this project unique is the great involvement of teenagers in the actual running of the library and its programs. Here young adults serve the public as well as participate in its services. Some are students in community service programs in their high schools and colleges; others are in subsidized youth employment programs. Their tasks range from accessioning new books, checking them out, and reshelving them to reading aloud to individuals or groups of children. An important part of their participation is their ability to reach out to potential teenage library users and other nontraditional library users.

In her 1989 *VOYA* article, Julia Reed Palmer notes that "youth workers can greatly expand the capacity for public libraries to reach new populations throughout the country. Many children are growing up at high educational risk in many of our cities where public and school libraries *could* be playing a critically important role in helping families develop literacy."[10] "What we are suggesting . . . is a major philosophical change; that of using the community to expand and enhance library services. . . . We are suggesting that by looking to young people as a creative solution to the staffing problems so many libraries face, we also find an opportunity to market the library's wares and involve many more young people in the world of books."[11] A final perk is the active participation in the library, which traditionally has difficulty luring teens into it. But "give young people the chance to practice meaningful service in a library and you will find them sold on libraries," concludes Palmer.[12]

READING INITIATIVES: WHAT SOME EXPERTS SAY

The results of an informal survey mailed to 45 professionals—among them librarians, educators, booksellers, and authors—across the country revealed similar concerns about minimal expectations of any reading initiative, whether local or national. Here are some of their suggestions.

A primary focal point is the mission of such a program. Several targeted the need to empower the reader with the belief that reading is a critical life skill but also that students should discover that it can be an enjoyable leisure-time activity—that it is a viable alternative for getting both information and pleasure.

Mary F. Lenox, dean of the University of Missouri Library School, targeted these specific components of an initiative: "It should . . . strengthen self-esteem, stimulate interest, encourage inquiry, demonstrate value, address multicultural dimensions of society . . . [it] should also encourage direct participation and strategies for obtaining feedback from participants as to their unique interests and needs."

Another major area cited by several respondents is collection development, whether strengthening existing collections or developing more current library collections. Comments urge the importance of having access not only to exemplary works but also to an abundance of materials for participants to borrow—whether print, magazines, popular adult novels (like those of Danielle Steele), or even "musical resources" to stimulate reading interest.

Which leads to the next area of concern: money. Sufficient monies should be allocated for materials, to maintain current library collections, and to create teacher-training programs to give teachers a background in literature. Beverly Kobrin, editor of *The Kobrin Newsletter*, strongly believes that funds should be provided to hire experts with the skills to train teachers to do reading lists: "You don't get the best for less." She continues, "If the money is not there for the school libraries the kids will learn that the libraries aren't important."

Other comments on this topic were that there should be a children's literature requirement for teachers with information on how to use these materials, and that principals and administrators should read these books as well. Educators should shake their "textbook bias"; kids will be "caught by better, interesting literature." School librarian Pat R. Scales, Greenville (South Carolina) Middle School, urges that there be "no testing whatsoever" in the classroom when books are involved: "Individual readers should not be made to compete with one another—minutes read by a class could be calculated—all children should be encouraged to participate whether an avid reader or a reluctant reader." And reading list requirements should be flexible and not limited to only one title or author.

For a National Reading Initiative, Betty Carter, visiting assistant professor, Department of Reading and Bilingual Education, Texas Woman's University, offers her list of critical participants:

> University reading researchers and teachers
>
> Classroom reading teachers
>
> School administrators and school board representatives
>
> School and public librarians
>
> Representatives from major professional organizations (educational, reading, library)
>
> Representatives from the business community
>
> Representatives from publishers of trade books
>
> Barbara Bush

Several respondents thought television, sports, and celebrities making public service announcements about good books through media campaigns would be a good idea. Sara Behrman, young adult coordinator at the library at Vancouver Mall, Vancouver, Washington, suggests that perhaps more attention would be paid if the American Library Association sponsored "Year of the Non-Reader" as a national reading program.

On a smaller scale, "coalitions of service providers and interested persons need to be in place at the local level and a vision statement or plan for each community should be drafted as part of any national fight against illiteracy. Perhaps the role of a member of the National Reading Initiative is to help each community define its role in the national effort," according to Behrman.

Also emphasized was the importance of educating those who work with the very young. As James Thomas, associate professor, School of Library and Information Studies, Texas Woman's University, puts it: "Backpeddling with teenagers and adults is extremely difficult." He has developed a program through which, with funding, he hopes to set up a collection of exemplary preschool materials that he would send free to every day-care facility in the country and then follow up with 15 free lectures. Others concur on the importance of reaching early childhood educators, primarily those in day-care centers, with exemplary children's materials—providing books to them. Margaret Kimmel, professor at the University of Pittsburgh, would like to "push public librarians out the door to work with them."

Pat R. Scales would "work with parents, teachers, churches, and other social agencies interested in children to acquaint them with children's books—I would teach them techniques for guiding children to books and help them realize that the love of reading is contagious— adults must be examples." And she does just this in her "Communicating through Young Adult Books" (see the bibliography at the end of this chapter). Another idea was to urge pediatricians to encourage reading among the very young.

Gretchen Wronka, senior librarian at Hennepin County Library, Minnetonka, Minnesota, emphasized the importance of politics in regional programming—the challenge of finding a leader with tremendous rapport in the community and the need for children's librarians to get more politically involved. Librarians should primarily work with superintendents and people who control the funds, not teachers, to effect lasting change. She advises: "Get people who are seen as leaders, outside the library" and to be sure to formalize the relationships so that there is continuity.

Here are some final comments to ponder:

Ultimately, serving select groups demands a perceptive mind and listening ears to the unique needs of the user.—Mary F. Lenox

I would expect that any kind of reading initiative program would value the art of reading over the mechanics of learning how to read. . . . The key to a successful reading initiative program is an excited read-a-holic . . . someone addicted to reading who is able to convey enthusiasm and excitement in the understanding of the written word.—Sara Behrman

NOTES

1. *The Crisis in California School Libraries: A Special Study* (Sacramento: California State Department of Education, 1987), p. 1.
2. Ibid.
3. Anita Silvey, "The Basalization of Trade Books," *The Horn Book* 65, no. 5 (September/October 1989): 550.
4. Francie Alexander, "California Reading Initiative," in *Children's Literature in the Reading Program*, ed. Bernice Cullinan (Newark, DE: International Reading Association, 1987), p. 151.
5. "Program Pushes Viewers to Turn Off Their Sets," *New York Times*, August 25, 1989, p. D18.
6. Lisa See, "Snapshots of the Children's Regional Booksellers Associations," *Publishers Weekly*, July 28, 1989, p. 194.
7. Barbara Prete, "Baltimore, the City That Reads," *Publishers Weekly*, August 4, 1989, p. 71.
8. Ibid., p. 72.
9. Ibid., p. 71.
10. Julia R. Palmer, "Youth Workers: What's Right with This Picture?" *VOYA* (February 1989): 275.
11. Ibid.
12. Ibid.

ASSOCIATIONS

Association of American Publishers, 220 E. 23 St., New York, NY 10010.
Association of Booksellers for Children, 175 Ash St., St. Paul, MN 55126.

BIBLIOGRAPHY

Aaron, Ira E. "Enriching the Basal Reading Program with Literature," Ch. 11 in Bernice Cullinan, ed. *Children's Literature in the Reading Program*. Newark, DE: International Reading Association, 1987, pp. 126–138.

Alexander, Francie. "California Reading Initiative," Ch. 13 in Bernice Cullinan, ed. *Children's Literature in the Reading Program*. Newark, DE: International Reading Association, 1987, pp. 149–155.

Celebrating the National Reading Initiative. Sacramento: California State Department of Education, 1988.

Cheatham, Bertha M. News (column). "Reading Initiative Program Focuses on Literacy in Arizona." *School Library Journal* (March 1988): 90.

The Crisis in California School Libraries: A Special Study. Sacramento: California State Department of Education, 1987.

Cullinan, Bernice. "Books in the Classroom." *The Horn Book* 62, no. 6 (November/ December 1986): 766–768.

———. "Latching On to Literature: Reading Initiatives Take Hold." *School Library Journal* (April 1989): 27–31.

———. "The National Reading Initiative: Outgrowth of the California Reading Initiative." *New Advocate* 2, no. 2 (Spring 1989): 105–113.

———, ed. *Children's Literature in the Reading Program.* Newark, DE: International Reading Association, 1987.

Handbook for an Effective Reading/Literature Program K–12. Clovis Unified School District, California; Ellis Vance, Coord., Language Arts/Library Programs; Support Services/District Office, 1986.

Hass, Elizabeth A. "Librarians & Booksellers: Working Together in the Year of the Young Reader." *School Library Journal* (January 1989): 24–27.

Indrisano, Roselmina, and Jeanne R. Paratore. "The Republic of Childhood and the Reading Disabled," Ch. 12 in *Children's Literature in the Reading Program,* Bernice Cullinan, ed. Newark, DE: International Reading Association, 1987, pp. 139–148.

Lamme, Linda Leonard. "Children's Literature: The Natural Way to Learn to Read," Ch. 5 in *Children's Literature in the Reading Program,* Bernice Cullinan, ed. Newark, DE: International Reading Association, 1987, pp. 41–53.

Mutter, John, and Maureen J. O'Brien. "Snapshots of the Children's Regional Booksellers Associations." *Publishers Weekly* (July 28, 1989): 194–196.

Olsen, Mary Lou. *Creative Connections: Literature and the Reading Program Grades 1–3.* Littleton, CO: Libraries Unlimited, 1987.

Palmer, Julia R. "Youth Workers: What's Right with This Picture?" *VOYA* (February 1989): 273–275.

Prete, Barbara. Literacy Matters (column). "Baltimore, the City That Reads." *Publishers Weekly,* August 4, 1989, pp. 71–72.

"Program Pushes Viewers to Turn Off Their Sets," *New York Times,* August 25, 1989, p. D18.

Recommended Readings in Literature, Kindergarten through Grade Eight. Sacramento: California State Department of Education, 1988.

Scales, Pat. "Communicating through Young Adult Books." Booklet. New York: Bantam, n.d.

See, Lisa. "Snapshots of the Children's Regional Booksellers Associations." *Publishers Weekly,* July 28, 1989, pp. 194–195.

Silvey, Anita. "The Basalization of Trade Books." *The Horn Book* 65, no. 5 (September/October 1989): 549–550.

———. "California Reading Initiative." *The Horn Book* 62, no. 5 (September 1986): 549.

3
Reading with Closed-Captioned TV

Milton Goldman and Sandra Goldman

W hat? They're watching *Family Ties* in class? *The Cosby Show,* too? Why, they get enough TV at home already. . . . What? You say they're *reading* those programs? How's that? With the sound turned off? Well, what's going on at that school? I'm getting over there to see what's going on."

This was one of many first reactions to our use of silently viewed closed-captioned television in our reading classrooms. But once parents and teachers saw our program in action, their skepticism changed rapidly to enthusiasm and encouragement.

In a time when commercial television is under attack for being a worthless time waster (Goodlad, 1984; Ravitch, 1985; Searls, Mead, and Ward, 1985), we have turned the network sitcoms into a positive educational skill builder for slow readers. The catalyst for this supplemental reading technique is the TeleCaption II decoder, manufactured by the National Captioning Institute (NCI) of Falls Church, Virginia. Hooked up to a video recorder and a 25 inch television set with a single cable, the decoder displays subtitles for a large number of prime time network shows, public TV programs, and feature films.

Originally designed for the deaf and hard of hearing, closed-captioned TV was used to experiment with teaching reading to hard of hearing elementary students (Koskinen, 1983) using *Sesame Street* and *Diff'rent Strokes.* We thought that if NCI obtained positive results with

Reprinted from the *Journal of Reading* with permission of Milton Goldman and the International Reading Association.

the hard of hearing, why not try it with students with reading problems who have normal hearing? The only difference would be that these students would watch the programs in silence, forcing them to read the subtitled dialogue. If we showed their favorite programs, how could they resist?

SKILL ACTIVITIES

At home, we recorded programs like *Amazing Stories, Family Ties, The Cosby Show, Growing Pains, Perfect Strangers, My Sister Sam, Who's the Boss?* and *Head of the Class.* By omitting commercials, we could easily fit a 24 minute program into our 55 minute teaching period once or twice weekly and allow ample time to conduct a variety of pre- and post-viewing activities to promote reading skills.

The main skill areas we addressed were sight vocabulary, comprehension, and writing. Among the previewing activities, we wrote words on the chalkboard that would be encountered in the program. Pronunciation, word analysis, and meanings were discussed and explained. Discussion topics were introduced to spark interest in the issues examined in the program, e.g., "Have you ever had a friend whose grades suddenly dropped from Bs to Ds and Fs and when you tried to find out why, you were told to get lost? Let's watch this episode of *Head of the Class* to find out why Sarah's grades upset her whole class."

At this point we ran the tape. For about 5 to 8 minutes, students had video, captions, and sound; this established the premise of the story, and more importantly captured their attention and focused their interest. Then we turned off the sound with a remote control. Of course students shouted, "Aw, c'mon, put the sound back on!" But after a few encouraging words like "Try to concentrate on the words; the more you concentrate, the easier it will get," the protests subsided and the active engagement of eyes and screen intensified. Then a few laughs emerged, assuring us that indeed, the students were reading the captions.

Sometimes we stopped programs at critical points and students discussed or wrote their own endings; these were critiqued for logic or style after viewing the actual endings. We interrupted other programs so characters could be discussed in terms of their potential actions, based on previous programs, e.g., "What kind of advice do you think Dr. Huxtable is going to give Denise?" Whenever students made judgments or inferences, these were evaluated against the actual programs.

When viewing was over, students discussed issues raised, applying their own opinions and experiences. Topics included teen and family problems, drugs, values, growing up, and many others.

Other postviewing activities included vocabulary quizzes on words from the program that were introduced earlier. They also wrote answers to literal and inferential questions and wrote summaries and critiques of the shows to test their comprehension.

We also cultivated critical viewing habits by exploring some of the structural production techniques of sitcoms. We looked at script directions and camera angles, the timing of dramatic action for commercial breaks, the ubiquitous subplot that assures participation of the show's entire cast, and the sometimes simplistic "solving" of conflict.

ENTHUSIASM AND EFFECTS

Our students' enthusiasm was high for watching captioned TV. They continually advised us when we hadn't shown "their" program for the week and they vied among themselves for a choice of program. Though we provided viewing opportunities once or twice weekly, their eagerness was so great that we set up a Closed-Caption Club, where students watched a captioned program at lunchtime every day, without comprehension activities. These showings attracted so many students from outside the reading program that we had to turn people away and begin a reservation schedule.

In terms of the measurable effects of closed-captioned TV in our remedial setting (our senior high prescriptive-tutorial program accepts students reading 2 or more years below grade level), the results are very encouraging but not conclusive. Objective comprehension test results based on the TV shows are high, rarely falling below 70% on 20 item comprehension and vocabulary checks.

Standardized testing for comprehension is a regular part of our reading program. As of this writing we have not conducted rigorous comparisons of the effects of captioned TV on standardized test results. But since we directly teach vocabulary and comprehension skills before and after viewing, we feel that some effects may be lasting. The main observable effects were the consistently high motivation of students to watch their favorite programs and their intensified concentration and focus on the task of reading the captions.

An easily measured positive effect of the viewing program was in attendance, where rates improved dramatically for many students. Some counselors were amazed at how some chronic absentees came to school regularly after we began showing the TV programs. Since program introductions began at the class bell, tardiness fell considerably, even on days when programs were not shown, since we rarely preannounced showings.

Another effect of our program was on the initially skeptical parents who observed our showings. After seeing the enthusiasm of students, many parents expressed strong interest in purchasing closed-captioned decoders for use in their homes. In addition, a few English teachers have experimented with captioned TV in their classes using book tie-ins with *Sounder, Brian's Song,* and *The Outsiders.* And all four special education teachers now use captioned TV with their advanced reading groups.

The question of rate building effects has often been raised, since it was thought that rapid left to right eye movements in reading captions might transfer to print reading. We doubt this because of two reasons. First, many studies of moving print training show that it may be psychologically and visually faulty (Moore, 1970; Spache, 1976; Wooster, 1954).

Related to this is the fact that in spite of the relative sentence shortness of TV dialogue (Liberman, 1983), captions are not always placed with particular consideration as to semantic or grammatical units or even area of the screen. Though most captions appear at the bottom, some are placed at the sides or top of the screen, depending on visual priorities; some captions consist of 1 or 2 words while others are 3 lines long.

Secondly, the angle or span of vision at normal reading distance (14 inches) is significantly different from TV viewing distance (10–15 feet). We doubt that there is a significant rate increase as a result of reading captions, despite a superficial similarity of captions to controlled reader projections. We would conjecture that if there are rate increases, they would result because of the repeated practice of motivated concentration and focus on the action of reading itself.

For us, one student summarized the value of telecaptions and commercial TV: "Just as something exciting is about to happen, the teacher turns the sound off. Then we *have* to read what's going on. It's the only way we can understand the story." Though used in the classroom as a supplementary activity, TV complements the regular program with a strong motivating force that enhances the teaching of reading skills.

REFERENCES

Goodlad, John I. *A Place Called School.* New York: McGraw-Hill, 1984, p. 42.

Koskinen, Patricia S. "Using Closed Captioned Television in the Teaching of Reading to Deaf Students." Research Report 83-2. Falls Church, VA: National Captioning Institute, August 1983.

Liberman, Michael. "The Verbal Language of Television." *Journal of Reading*, vol. 26 (April 1983), pp. 602–609.

Moore, Gladys B. "To Buy or Not to Buy." *Journal of Reading*, vol. 13 (March 1970), pp. 427–440.

Ravitch, Diane. *The Schools We Deserve*. New York: Basic Books, 1985, p. 33.

Searls, Donald T., Nancy A. Mead, and Barbara Ward. "The Relationship of Students' Reading Skills to TV Watching, Leisure Time Reading, and Homework." *Journal of Reading*, vol. 29 (November 1985), pp. 158–162.

Spache, George D. *Diagnosing and Correcting Reading Disabilities*. Boston, MA: Allyn & Bacon, 1976, pp. 313, 321.

Wooster, George F. "An Experimental Study of the Reading-Rate Controller." *Journal of Educational Psychology*, vol. 45 (November 1954), pp. 421–426.

4
The Disabled Adolescent Reader

Jean F. Rossman

The phrase *disabled adolescent reader* consists of three graphic words. As reading teachers we may immediately seize upon the word *reader*, testing pupils' skills to discover their academic deficiencies. Then, when pupils still fail to read adequately, we focus upon the first word, *disabled*. We look for auditory or visual defects, for physical or psychological disabilities which might be corrected. In this discussion, I would like to look at the middle word to ask whether in the nature of *adolescence* itself, and the adolescent experience in contemporary culture, there are further clues to what must be done to help the disabled adolescent reader.

DEFINING ADOLESCENCE

A myriad of research books have sought to define adolescence and to describe the experience of teenagers. But when I survey this literature, what generalizations can I find that are worth repeating here or that can be applied in our efforts to assist one specific disabled reader? Tanner points out that physiologically the adolescent has not changed significantly in the past five thousand years.[1] In this century, youngsters seem to be maturing sexually at a younger age, and the problems of adolescence and the impact of cultural sophistication affect many of them by

Reprinted with permission of Jean F. Rossman and the International Reading Association from Dianne J. Sawyer, ed., *Disabled Readers: Insight, Assessment, Instruction* (Newark, Del.: International Reading Association, 1980), pp. 16–29.

the ages of eleven or twelve. This fact has some bearing upon reading. Many educators and parents have thought of adolescence as a plateau, a time between childhood and adulthood when youngsters could pause to study and to learn. Some persons do seem able to delay adulthood even as they concentrate upon graduate school studies.

However, as I examine the disabled readers in the inner-city high school where I served as reading consultant for ten years, and compare them to the suburban students I now work with in a similar capacity, I find no happy plateau. Far from delaying adult emotions and involvements so that they can concentrate upon school, the disabled adolescent reader's emotional and academic problems are inseparably mixed. In the inner-city school, many disabled readers have out-of-wedlock babies, have hard drug problems, or may spend a great part of their time in courts and jails to such an extent that it seems futile to assume they will learn to read if one merely helps them attain some missing skills. Students also need help with overwhelming adolescent problems.

Perhaps the most important thing we can learn from research into adolescence is that each pupil is unique, with his or her peculiar patterns of potentiality and experience. Even physiologically students vary greatly and this has implications for reading. Some children are ready to read as young as age four, five, or six. Girls seem to develop earlier than boys, and at adolescence there is a clear pattern of relationship between physiological development and learning. Children who mature physically at an early age tend to score higher on tests of mental ability. Boys who are larger and more mature develop more self-confidence as leaders and grow faster academically. Therefore, educators and parents need to take a second look at the underachiever in school in order to understand more fully why certain children do not appear to be developing to their full academic potential. In my work with hundreds of disabled adolescent readers, I have been left with one overwhelming impression: that self-image, the faith that one can succeed, is a need which transcends all others. These youngsters lack confidence in themselves. Many of them do not try to improve their reading because they are sure they will fail. I am reminded of what Erich Fromm says in *The Practice of Love* about how essential it is for one to have faith in himself, which means being willing to take a risk even if the result is failure. I am certain that the dependence which many of my pupils have upon drugs and alcohol is rooted in this lack of self-confidence.

It is essential for me, as a high school reading consultant, to deal with these emerging young adults as they are at the moment. I must know as much as possible about the emotions, needs, desires, and problems of each disabled adolescent reader, even though what has gone on before cannot be changed. The scars will always remain, but I can help students only as they learn to come with their wounds, as they build self-confidence for the future. If I must avoid assembly line approaches and generalizations which never seem to apply to a specific case, then, as I teach, I must get well-acquainted with specific young persons.

SYLVESTER

First I want to tell you about Sylvester, who was born in an inner-city black ghetto. He was number three of seven children, the second boy. He started to go to school at the age of five and one-half, and reports from his kindergarten and his first grade teachers describe him as a quiet boy, willing to please, very small for his age. His first grade teacher indicated he was a slow learner and suggested he repeat first grade. However, such a large group of pupils entered the school the next fall that there was no room to keep him back, so Sylvester was placed in a "slower" second grade class. In other words, at age six and one-half he was already marked for failure, was moved aside from the academic mainstream with consequences not only for his academic future but also for his adolescent self-esteem. No one seems to have asked whether Sylvester was small and docile for his age because of an inadequate diet. Nor did Sylvester's second and third grade teachers add any information to his record, except to give him C and D grades.

We do not know what Sylvester was feeling and thinking as he attended four different schools between first and fifth grades. We can be certain, however, that no one teacher knew Sylvester well enough to give him the positive support and encouragement he needed; for, by fourth grade, his record shows that he was rude, a discipline problem, had no study habits, and came to school physically unkempt. Being well dressed is psychologically crucial for the inner-city child and perhaps for all children. Sylvester's fourth grade teacher did not recommend holding him back while he gained sufficient basic skills to keep up with his age level, nor is there evidence that anyone gave him special attention. By his fifth year of school, Sylvester had already been arrested twice for petty theft. Why did he steal? For clothing? For money? To bring something interesting into his unsuccessful life? In an effort to call attention to himself? Or was petty crime an area where he could demonstrate some skill, success, and accomplishment?

In these days, everyone is familiar enough with his sort of story to recognize that by the time Sylvester was in high school it was not enough to describe him as a disabled reader. He was, first of all, a disabled adolescent, a disabled person. Even if I devoted full time to him, how could I, as a reading consultant, help him read adequately unless I helped him at the same time to recover his sense of self-worth, to develop some hopes and goals in life that would motivate him to learn to read? Sylvester's reputation had preceded him to high school. He was not allowed to join the community boys' club because he was "belligerent and unmanageable." It appeared that no one had any faith in Sylvester, and he had no faith in himself. Perhaps some teachers were afraid to risk faith in him for fear he would not succeed and then they would have failed.

In the middle class suburb where I now work, I have no difficulty getting parents to come and see me to talk about how they can help their children. Indeed, I am sometimes pursued by mothers who want me to help improve the reading skills of sophomores or juniors who read on the fourteenth grade level—because mother wants her child's percentile rank increased from 90.8 to 99. But no teacher or counselor could enlist the cooperation of Sylvester's family in a plan to improve his academic skills or for anything else. His father left home when Sylvester was still in elementary school, and no one knew where he was. Sylvester's mother worked long hours to try to support seven children, and she was too tired to come to school at night. She said she had no control over Sylvester anyway.

So what sense did it make to speak of Sylvester as an adolescent? He was an adult in that he had taken control of his own life. He was making his own decisions. He had fathered an illegitimate child. He was supporting himself, albeit illegally. Perhaps it was remarkable, now that Sylvester was sixteen, that he continued to come to school at all! Newspapers reported that in a similar city nearby, 40 percent of the inner-city high school pupils are now dropping out in their junior and senior years. Why, from Sylvester's point of view, should he continue spending his time being sent out of first one class and then another? Twice, when she had been summoned to court, his mother asked the courts to "send him up" and to "get him out of her hair."

Late in his sophomore year (he was promoted along from year to year whether he had learned anything or not), the school psychologist tested Sylvester and found that although his potential seemed to be very low, he should not be classified as a special education student. So he was sent to the reading laboratory for help. Diagnostic tests showed what skills he needed, but how was he to be motivated? He was on drugs, was in and out of jail, and was drinking heavily. During the school day he slept most of the time, even in the reading class which he said he enjoyed. *He enjoyed reading class.* It was psychologically and emotionally rewarding to him to meet someone who cared about him, who gave him personal attention, who helped him establish some simple, achievable goals, and who gave him a sense of accomplishment in reaching them. In this context, it occurred to him that maybe he could get a job after all.

It is important to note that he had long ago given up any such ambition, while nevertheless secretly aspiring to find a place in life like other people. So in the process of raising his reading skill by one grade level, he was taught to fill out a job application form correctly. It was suggested that he carry a copy of the form with him in case he needed to fill out an application some time. His progress reminds us how Paulo Freire found that illiterate adults can be quickly taught to read if they begin with words which are existentially meaningful to the individual. High school students who will not read basals such as *Dick and Jane* will show an interest in a driver's manual, a book on child care, an insurance policy, or even a basic course in elementary law.

I wish I could continue this happy side of Sylvester's story, but his problems outside school and reading class were overwhelming. He got a job but lost it because he could not read the labels on cans of paint. Shortly after that he knocked down an elderly man in a robbery attempt, the victim died, and Sylvester went to jail. Because of Sylvester's court case I was most interested to read in *Psychology Today* the case of another boy in jail whose teacher went back to examine his school records to see where educators had failed him.[2] That boy was much more talented than Sylvester, had higher test scores, and was, in a sense, the victim of a system which had immediately seized upon his reading deficiency as his only problem. Teachers sought to meet his reading needs, as discovered in diagnostic testing, without examining a larger perspective of the boy's total need and emotional situation.

Blos reports research which shows that young adolescents are becoming increasingly similar in life-style to older boys or girls, as the events which formerly took place in middle or late adolescence seem increasingly to happen at younger ages.[3] Sylvester's identity development, personality consolidation, and character formation did not wait until his late teens or early twenties. To define him as a disabled adolescent suggests seeing that such formation happened early, perhaps too soon, leaving him an inadequate, disorganized, irresponsible person. On the other hand, parents and teachers may expect young people to act more adult than they are ready to be, expecting more of them than the teenagers are able to accomplish. The reverse may be equally true. Adolescents who are treated as children rebel, demanding to be recognized as emerging adults. In the case of Sylvester we see that he was thrust too soon into an adult world while at the same time being unable to accomplish (for example, read paint labels) on the level of the other adolescents at school. In these conflicts of the developing personality he was neither able to control himself nor could anyone else control him. He was both a child and an adult but was rarely an adolescent.

If we see adolescence as a time of maturing, a state of becoming as well as being, then it is clear that society failed to give Sylvester an adolescence, just as it failed to teach him to read. By the time he was in high school the two facts were inescapably intertwined. The inner-city school recognized this fact in selecting realistic materials for pupils to read, thus giving these youngsters strong meat to chew which would have been censored and forbidden to them in another time and place. Since Sylvester daily confronted raw life on the street, there was no point in trying to shelter him at school.

Sylvester's mother and teachers tended to think of him as a rebel in a time when many adults see adolescents in rebellion against authority. They complain: "He won't listen." "He won't cut his hair." "He will run away if I try to punish him." "He's useless and undependable." "Grades go down, he won't study, he is irresponsible." "It wasn't like that," they say, "when I was young." But where in Sylvester's file is there evidence that anyone ever saw things from his point of view? Fearful, insecure, lonely, powerless, restless, wounded, loosened from his moorings, if he ever had any, Sylvester—typical of a high percentage of today's disabled readers—was wounded too young to have an adolescence, to define his own personality, to establish his own identity and goals. Somehow Sylvester passed from childhood into adulthood without knowing anyone who had confidence in him, without a sense of worth, without achieving faith in himself, in others, or in society.

Yet I remember that Sylvester made a bowl in woodworking class and, after he left school, the bowl was displayed in the hall case with other objects made by students during the next term. It was so lovely that teachers asked who had made it. I'm sure it was not deliberate, withholding the exhibition of his handcraft until he was no longer in school; but what beneficial effect might this public showing have had on Sylvester if he could have heard some of the praise while he was still struggling with school?

Still, how could reading be important from his point of view? He would readily admit that unless he learned to read better he would be ill-equipped to function in the world, but what use had the world for him anyhow? Sylvester wasn't even a very good petty criminal. He always got caught.

JOSÉ

José was born in Puerto Rico where he attended elementary school through the fifth grade. His mother then sent him to Connecticut to live with his father because she had heard that the schools were much better in the States. As the eldest son, José was expected to lead the way for his younger brothers and sisters and to improve their family situation in the world. So José came with motivation and ambition, but it was difficult for a ten-year-old to fit into the new environment. Although Spanish was spoken at home, he used only English at school. It took him quite a while to make friends and to adjust himself to the new situation. Unlike Sylvester, José gave his teachers no problems. He was hard working and well behaved, so he was allowed to drift from grade to grade with his underachievement excused on the grounds that "he doesn't speak English."

When he entered high school, he was finally placed in an English as a Second Language class (even though he did not qualify since he had been in Connecticut for four years). Even so, José failed to get the attention he needed. He was so polite, well dressed, was such a "really nice kid" that teachers overlooked his failure to accomplish. They failed the pupils who were serious discipline problems and rewarded José with a passing grade because he was so well behaved. In his junior year José organized a musical group for which he played the drums. A stinging experience for him occurred when he was offered a contract for a performance by the group and he could not read it. He realized that he had to learn to read, so in his senior year he was assigned to the lowest reading laboratory in the high school—one for high school pupils reading below the fourth grade level.[4]

In the reading laboratory José became a different person, a delight to have in class, but also a student who recovered his motivation, lost his swagger, and developed a more mature self-confidence. He worked so hard in the laboratory that within four months he gained over two years on reading test scores. By March he had passed the fourth grade level and should have been moved up into the next lab, but because of his rapport with the reading consultant, he remained in a room where she could provide him with an advanced, individualized program tailored to his own needs. Perhaps the greatest moment came when his comprehension dramatically increased with the discovery that he could visualize the material he was reading. Never before had he been able to see "with his mind's eye" the picture which was being painted by the description. After that, his vocabulary and comprehension developed with speed.

On the surface, this success demonstrated the worth and methods of the reading laboratory. A boy who could hardly read at all was able to leave high school with adequate skills. But beneath the surface there is more to José's story. In spite of his earlier experience, he was able to develop self-confidence and a strong sense of who he was and where he wanted to go.

The problems of José and Sylvester were intensified by the student overload the teachers had and by the insensitivity of a system which sought to move students more or less automatically through an assembly line program which was the same for all pupils. José and Sylvester needed individualized, tailor-made programs. No matter how much one tends to blame the teachers or the educational system, it is apparent that these boys brought adolescent problems into the high school which were only partly academic. They needed reading skills, but these skills could not be learned or were almost inaccessible because of these other problems. Reading is still terribly important in our society, yet José—who as a junior in high school could not read his contract—might easily have been allowed to graduate without being able to read his diploma. He might have become increasingly bitter and hostile toward society for letting him graduate without the skills to hold a good job. Certainly, this is what happened to Sylvester. By the time he was in junior high school, Sylvester realized that the schools were failing him whether he was failing school or not.

Those of us who teach and love our work and our students can understand how these tragedies can happen. No one teacher with a full load can possibly have time to investigate thoroughly the backgrounds of all students to get complete views of their problems and needs. Counselors, too, who may have a work load of three to four hundred students, do an overwhelmingly good job on the whole. Therefore, communities must take a hard look at the expectations they have of educational systems when they realize that the problems of José and Sylvester are not unique.

ANNA MARIA

The third case I want to report comes from a far different environment. Anna Maria lived in the suburbs and attended an excellent elementary school. Her parents were both professionals who tried to do all the right things—in contrast to the parents of José and Sylvester who had no books, magazines, or even newspapers in their homes. Anna Maria was the youngest of four children and grew up in a family which had camped and traveled together, played together, and read aloud together. Anna Maria's elementary school records do not reveal many perceptive or helpful remarks by her teachers, who simply reported: "Anna Maria could do better work," or "Anna Maria should try more." When the parents visited the school, her teachers were enthusiastic, with positive comments. The parents were not aided in seeing or understanding problems which were emerging.

Anna Maria's junior high school friends were from families whose interests were largely social and whose ambitions were limited. They were interested only in dating and in getting married as soon as they were out of high school. The school environment was one in which pupils poked fun at those who were interested in reading or college. In order to fit in socially with her friends, Anna Maria quit using "large words" and hid the fact that she liked some of her subjects and teachers. She went along with her friends who were looking for fun and kicks through drugs, sex escapades, and shoplifting games—and knowing that her family disapproved made her an alien and a rebel at home. She sometimes stayed out until four o'clock in the morning on school nights and threatened to run away if her parents disciplined her. She cut school more and more until by January she was virtually a dropout.

Part of Anna Maria's real difficulty resulted from the fact that parents and school kept comparing her to her older brothers and sister who had outstanding academic records. Teachers who should have known better, often called her in to compare her poor school record with that of her siblings—which drove her further away from home and school. She decided she could never perform on the level of her brothers and sister and, therefore, was not interested in school at all. Her ambition was merely to quit school and get a job, which she did before she was sixteen. Her family could compel her to go back to school but not to learn or to succeed. By tenth grade, her reading scores had actually retrogressed until she found it difficult to read and write, even though she had read above level in fifth grade.

Put her in the reading laboratory? "Ridiculous," said school administrators. They could point to her high IQ scores, her family background, her demonstrated ability to perform in grade school. Her problem, they said, was a matter of discipline—drugs. In a sense this was true, but it was also true that she was using drugs to run away from an adolescence with which she could not cope. Other pupils might have a drug problem because they couldn't read, but surely Anna Maria had a reading problem because she was on drugs. She was placed in a drug dependence program where, as a result of personal attention, counseling, and a new sense of self-worth, she was able to solve her drug problem. But even afterwards, when she had emerged from her drug stupor, she was a disabled adolescent reader because of falling behind during her many months on drugs. Again her case shows how many adolescents must solve a wide range of personal, emotional, and familial problems before reading problems are solved.

SUMMARY

Now let me summarize some of my learning from these case studies. First, these cases reaffirm the complexity of adolescence and the variety of adolescent types. The need for an individualized program for each adolescent student is indicated. More important, the need for a much more comprehensive view of the needs and difficulties of each student is suggested. I want to express a fervent belief that more teachers must ask for and make use of information which is already available. I recognize the frustration of conscientious, caring, well-trained teachers who are staggered by the impossible load of teaching, corridor and lavatory supervision, counseling and preparation, all of which today's excellent teachers are expected to accomplish.

Often, however, when a teacher comes to me as a reading consultant to ask help with a particular student, I find the teacher has not looked at the student's personal file and has formed impressions about the student on the basis of gossip from other teachers and from superficial clues rather than tested facts. Teachers sometimes tell me that the records are there only for the use of counselors! I do not want to overlook the danger, which does exist, that an instructor will be negatively affected by a previous teacher's comments about a particular student. But how can we deal with complex adolescent problems, when many of us see a pupil only a semester or two for one period a day, if we do not trust one another's integrity and work together as a team? Competent teachers can certainly evaluate the remarks of other teachers, discriminating between prejudicial opinions and test score results.

The reading teacher must know much more than test scores. If a teacher knows, for example, that Dan is the sole support of his family and works at a job from 8:00 P.M. until 4:00 A.M., that teacher is more likely to be understanding and sympathetic—rather than sarcastic—when poor Dan falls asleep in the remedial reading laboratory. Yet I find that many teachers fail to inform themselves of such matters that do not require any research to discover.

The *Psychology Today* case of a young man who committed suicide while in jail for a crime he did not commit illustrates the complexity of the problems of the disabled adolescent reader. His family, school, and society refused to accept responsibility for various aspects of his development. The schools, of course, cannot be blamed entirely for his suicide, but, as the case unfolds through school records, it is evident that the school failed to have a complete and comprehensive view of his needs and was content with totally inadequate proposals for solving his problems. Those of us who see the interrelationships between reading disability and other adolescent problems, those of us who are concerned and care about students as whole persons, have a responsibility to help other teachers to become more involved in the development of each adolescent.

Teamwork is needed not only among teachers in dealing with the disabled adolescent but also in a larger context with other persons who have supplementary information and skills: physicians, psychologists, neurologists, oculists, speech and hearing specialists, social workers, attorneys, as well as reading specialists. The points of view and information of all such professionals must be brought together, even as early as kindergarten, for the pupil who appears to have problems. Such professionals should develop a comprehensive report, with information and treatment plans, as soon as a youngster is found to be in trouble. This is done promptly if a pupil is found to have leukemia; but if he is emotionally disabled or has fallen into delinquency or is lagging behind his peers in such academic achievements as reading, a few Band-Aids are too frequently the only applications.

Our teamwork becomes just a pooling of ignorance and confusion unless it is grounded in better information about specific pupils. The one, well-thought-of tracking system, for example, can be a major cause of reading disability if it locks a pupil into a rigid mold without taking into account the fact that a poor reader may be an excellent mathematician, an outstanding artist, or a talented mechanic.

In many ways, the most devastating fact about each of the three pupils whose cases I have cited is that their files revealed almost no information about their talents and abilities. There were negative comments like "no use suggesting college" or "a near hopeless case." But nothing was ever reported about the modest goals of Sylvester or José. Did no one note that Sylvester could make a beautiful wooden bowl? Evidently not. Did no one discover that Anna Maria was astonishingly gifted at music? No, not even her family. In both inner-city and suburban schools, teachers regularly received lists of students who were taking educational trips, playing in the band, singing in the chorus, visiting art museums, but seldom, if ever, were the names of remedial readers on these lists of students receiving such extra fringe benefits. I cannot be convinced that these disabled adolescents were never on these lists because they lacked talents or interests. Their talents, along with other facts about their personal lives which affect their reading skills, have simply not been uncovered. And, tragically, too often these students have not been considered "worth the trouble." Not encouraged to set constructive goals, they were encouraged only to fail as readers and as persons.

I'm not suggesting that there is an Einstein hidden in every José or Sylvester. More adequate perspectives on the adolescent as a person will enable teachers to value simple and realistic goals and ambitions. Girls who may never go to college, for example, who become pregnant during their high school years, can be highly motivated to improve reading skills when they are given materials about baby care and are taught how to make books for their babies so as to increase the reading ability and interests of their children. Certainly, whether one is a reading consultant, counselor, principal, or teacher, one must know when he/she has reached the limits of one's capacity to help in a particular situation. But what one learns about a student must be shared with others, so that the pupil who has special needs will not be abandoned, and everyone becomes accountable for what happens to a José, an Anna Maria, or a Sylvester. If the community has out-of-school agencies to whom a disabled adolescent can be referred, even while in school, the educational system must actively work in partnership with all who can share information and cooperate in helping solve pupil problems. If needed facilities in the community do not exist, educators have a responsibility to help develop them so that the disabled adolescent is not dropped into a great void upon leaving school.

I suppose what this means, essentially, is that we must never lose faith. Somewhere along the line everyone lost faith in Sylvester, so he lost faith in himself. At the root of most reading disabilities there is at one time or another someone's loss of faith. I feel very strongly that once teachers lose confidence in their own abilities to help pupils, or see adolescents losing confidence in themselves, the teachers must immediately get a team of people to work with the problem or turn the pupils over to someone else who can help. Most disabled adolescents lack contact with adults who believe in them, like them, have faith in them, will help them discover possible goals, and will help them gain the sense of accomplishment and self-worth which comes from success in meeting these goals.

Although we must focus on reading disability, let us not lose sight of the complexities of adolescence which lie at the heart of the phrase "disabled adolescent reader." Adolescents are individuals with their unique talents, strengths, weaknesses, dislikes, emotions, problems, and objectives. In dealing with pupils, schools and society must have clearer and more comprehensive views of them, at once particular and supportive and recognizing individuals as persons who are trying to emerge with some self-esteem, some skills, and some successes in solving problems.

Perhaps what emerges from these case studies can be framed as a question: Who is the disabled adolescent reader? Sylvester was disabled by his environment, José perhaps by the educational institution, and Anna Maria perhaps by home and peers. But each of these disabled adolescent readers needed first of all to be treated as a person who had the potential to overcome disabilities and make a unique contribution to society. No one teacher with a full load can have time to investigate thoroughly the backgrounds of all students. The problems of José, Sylvester, and Anna Maria are not unique. Less than 50 percent of learning disabilities are diagnosed early and properly.[5] Communities and school systems must take a close second look at what is demanded of teachers and disabled students and, the moment learning problems are first diagnosed, use teams of specialists to provide support for both teachers and pupils in a time when the problems of adolescence are overwhelming.

NOTES

1. J. M. Tanner, "Sequence, Tempo, and Individual Variation in the Growth and Development of Boys and Girls Aged Twelve to Sixteen." *Daedalus* (Fall 1971): 908.
2. Patricia Sullivan, "Suicide by Mistake." *Psychology Today* (October 1976): 90.
3. Peter Blos, "The Child Analyst Looks at the Young Adolescent." *Daedalus* (Fall 1971): 961.
4. Jean Rossman, "How One High School Set Up a Reading Program for 500 Students." *Journal of Reading* 20 (February 1977): 393.
5. Judy Gaylin, "Helping Learning Disabled Children." *Psychology Today* (April 1977).

RECOMMENDED READINGS

Coleman, James S. *Youth: Transition to Adulthood.* Chicago: University of Chicago Press, 1974.

Douvan, Elizabeth, and Adelson, J. *The Adolescent Experience.* New York: Wiley, 1966.

Freire, Paulo. "The Adult Literacy Process as Cultural Action for Freedom." *Harvard Educational Review* 40 (May 1970): 205.

Friedenberg, Edgar Z. *The Vanishing Adolescent.* Boston: Beacon Press, 1959.

Goodman, Paul. *Growing Up Absurd.* New York: Random House, 1956.

Gottleib, Donald, ed. *Youth in Contemporary Society.* Beverly Hills, CA: Sage Publications, 1971.

Havighurst, R. J. et al. *Adolescent Character and Personality.* New York: Wiley, 1949.

Jennings, K. K., and Niemi, R. G. *The Political Character of Adolescence.* Princeton, NJ: Princeton University Press, 1974.

Kagan, Jerome, and Coles, Robert, eds. *Twelve to Sixteen: Early Adolescence.* New York: W. W. Norton, 1972. (Includes *Daedalus* articles from Notes.)

Kandel, B. et al. *Youth in Two Worlds.* San Francisco: Jossey Bass, 1972.

Kiell, Norman. *The Adolescent through Fiction: A Psychological Approach.* New York: International Universities Press, 1959.

Maring, Gerald H. "Paulo Freire's Method of Teaching Beginning Reading." Unpublished paper.

Rice, F. Philip. *The Adolescent*. Boston: Allyn & Bacon, 1975.

The White House Conference on Youth: Report. U.S. Government Printing Office, April 1971.

Whitlock, J. K. "Causes of Childhood Disorders: New Feelings." *Social Work* 21 (March 1976).

Part II
Selecting and Evaluating High/Low Materials

5
The Promise of Computers for Reluctant Readers: A Continuing Challenge

Jean M. Casey and Julie M. T. Chan

Computers can help librarians and teachers feel more professional, and it is the professional, dedicated librarian or teacher who will create the environment in which the reluctant reader will shed his or her reluctance and experience success.

As the microcomputer becomes an accepted tool in the classroom learning environment, teachers, reading specialists, and librarians are finding it imperative to learn as much as they can about the computer in order to use it as the powerful learning tool it can be. The promise of the computer for students who are disabled and reluctant readers is great, provided its use is modeled by a knowledgeable and enthusiastic professional familiar with using the computer for his or her own purposes. Use of well-chosen appropriate software can open the door to literacy so long locked to some readers.

This chapter shows how computers may be used to set up an environment supportive of the writing and reading process, the general points to look for when selecting educational software, the specific factors to consider when selecting software for disabled and reluctant readers, and how to build a functional software collection. It clearly demonstrates the increased use of computers and software for reluctant teen readers developed since 1985. Sources for software reviews and notable programs are highlighted in this chapter.

HOW ARE MICROCOMPUTERS BEING USED?

Recent innovations in the use of microcomputers involve telecommunications and using telephone lines to transmit meaningful communication between students and their peers throughout the world. Rather than writing preassigned topic exercises in a workbook or responding to isolated drills on a computer screen, students can now communicate through FrEd Mail or other communications software on bulletin boards for kids, electronic mail systems, and conferencing systems. The power of writing to another handicapped student in Alaska about personal joys and sorrows helps students realize that they are not alone, and is one of the many exciting uses the computer offers to the disabled and reluctant reader. There is much more motivation to read a real note from a friend than a contrived message of little interest. There is public domain software available for telecommunications: Talk Is Cheap on the Apple II, Red Ryder on the Macintosh, and Procomm on IBM and IBM compatible machines.

However, the computer is also a sophisticated tool with which to write and problem solve, and as such, it empowers the reluctant reader to the same membership in the club of readers and writers that other students have long enjoyed. The ease of hitting a key to produce print, as opposed to the laboriously difficult use of the pencil, can be a key to literacy for many students. Magic Slate (Sunburst), Bank Street Writer (Scholastic), Homeword (Sierra On-Line), Milliken Writing Workshop (Milliken), and Primary Editor (IBM) are just some of the software word processors designed especially for young students.

Computers are ideal "thought" processors because ideas can be typed in, then rearranged over and over again until what one wants to say is perfected. Although most programs for idea and thought processing are called word processors, what is really being processed are the writer's thoughts and language. These language processors actually allow the language experience approach to reading to finally be implemented. In the past, teachers laboriously had to write down students' dictations of their thoughts and experiences; by using these new software programs even five year olds can record their thoughts directly on the computer. Pequeno Editor (Falcon) is a Spanish-language word processor designed especially for young Hispanic students. It is part of Falcon's Spanish Literacy Series software.

Many young children experience the element of speech when the computer can read the text typed in by the student, opening up the whole area of multisensory instruction. Talking Monsters and Make Believe (Learning Lab) is one of the newest and most exciting software programs of this kind. After hearing Maurice Sendak's *Where the Wild*

Things Are, students can create their own monsters and make them talk. They can then write a story about them that is also spoken, and print it out to make a fantastic big book with monster graphics and text all of their own creation. Talking Text Writer by Scholastic for the Apple IIe and IIGS and KidTalk (First Byte) for the IBM, Amiga, Macintosh, and Apple IIGS are two of the best software products in this area.

HOW CAN COMPUTERS BENEFIT RELUCTANT READERS?

Computers are widely used in schools to reinforce the teaching of concepts, to let students practice skills, or to provide the drill that is so necessary in developing "automaticity" in reading or math, such as in recognizing sight words or reciting math facts. They help students learn because a concept or skill can be broken down and restructured in a step-by-step sequential manner. A computer is very patient: It will wait indefinitely for a student to respond; it lets slower learners take as long as they need to work on a task; it will also let a student practice as often as is needed; it will even let a student perform a task repeatedly and present items in different combinations for interesting variations.

For nonvocal students or Down's syndrome students who need a program with ease of use especially designed to meet their needs, KeyTalk (Peal) by Laura Myers is the best software product. Myers, a linguist and researcher, also developed Exploratory Play software (Peal) that provides meaningful literacy experiences for handicapped youngsters.

With the renewed emphasis on science in the school curricula, school budgets are still limited, and it is not possible to outfit science laboratories with chemicals, flasks, and other equipment. But computers, given the right software, can become science labs. With such programs as Operation: Frog (Scholastic) or Chemistry: Series I (Focus Media), or the Science Toolkit (Broderbund), students can simulate actual science experiments, such as dissecting a frog or making a chemical solution. Students in prison schools are not permitted to handle chemicals, scalpels, and other potentially lethal instruments, but with computers these students can still conduct science experiments. Prelab Studies in Chemistry (Wiley) and Chemistry: Series I (Focus Media) not only let students perform chemistry experiments but also cause on-screen "explosions" when chemicals are mixed incorrectly. Databases like Minerals Database (Sunburst) give students access to the factual material they need when researching and writing reports on Isearch topics of their interest. Simulations such as Ecosystems (Sunburst) help students understand the crucial ecology issues so vital to our earth's future. The

Voyage of the Mimi (Sunburst) is an award-winning science and math software that includes learning American sign language and is a valuable learning tool in the curriculum.

The computer is also an instrument for creativity when used with software programs such as Songwriter (Scarborough), Magic Paintbrush (Penguin), or Movie Maker (Reston). Students who are musically inclined will be thrilled with Music Shop (Broderbund) or Music Construction Set (Electronic Arts); these programs allow students to create melodies and harmonies and then print the sheet music of their creations. Those who enjoy writing poetry can use Poetry Express (Learning Well), Electric Poet (IBM), or the Rhyming Notebook (First Byte). Rhyming Notebook gives students quick access to a 30,000-word rhyming dictionary. Its search and find capabilities allow the writer to concentrate on the creative process by letting the computer do the mechanical work of presenting rhyming word options. Remedial students can be transformed into budding songwriters, writers, and poets with this wonderful new tool. Students with an artistic bent will relish Koala Pad Touch Tablet (Koala Technologies), Power Pad (Chalkboard), Apple Mouse (Apple), and Gibson Light Pen (Koala Technologies).

Like telephones and typewriters, computers are being used in our lives as tools. Students, therefore, should learn to use and to think of a computer as a tool in the same way that a typewriter is considered a tool that aids in getting a task accomplished. Furthermore, the computer is significant because it is multipurpose. For example, a computer becomes a word processor when a word processing software program is used with it; it becomes an information manager with a database management program; it helps prepare budgets and makes forecasts with a spreadsheet program. And it can do more, much more, depending on the software program that is used. The computer can simultaneously be a word processor, database manager, and a spreadsheet generator with an integrated software program because the information from one part can be used with the other two parts. Examples of integrated software are AppleWorks (Apple) for the Apple IIe or IIC, Lotus 1-2-3 (Lotus) for the IBM personal computer, and Microsoft Works for the Macintosh and IBM.

Students can also use the computer to use and practice basic living skills, such as money management, vocational educational programs, consumer education, health and safety, job survival skills, and time management. The computer can be useful in acquiring information needed to pass certain tests to get licenses, for instance, Keys to Responsible Driving (CBS) in driver education. A fun and possibly useful software program for practicing piloting skills is Flight Simulator (SubLogic).

Publishers that specialize in software programs for basic living skills include Computer Age Education, EdMark, NTS Software, and MCE.

One of the new most exciting programs on the scene that brings it all together and is a powerful productivity tool that helps students build written communication skills and produce a variety of beautifully finished documents is The Children's Writing and Publishing Center (Learning Co.). This program allows students to easily produce their own Isearch reports with graphics and newsletters and documents that support their own personal writing and reading process.

HOW CAN COMPUTERS BENEFIT DISABLED READERS?

In the past, disabled readers were often taken out of the classroom and put in special classes to receive isolated skill practice and reinforcement. Recent research indicates that these readers are the ones who need more experience with meaningful print and reading literature and less with fragmented activities. Early attempts at producing educational software focused on what Frank Smith (University of Toronto) called "drill and kill," or electronic versions of workbook pages; these are still prevalent in large networked computer programs. However, we have found that students who end up in remedial classes tend to respond well to the visual and auditory reinforcement the computer can offer; and when they are in control of their learning, as they are in using the talking word processing programs (KidTalk, Talking Text Writer, Talking Monsters and Make Believe), they can actually construct their language in print and succeed in producing language experience books that put them firmly on the road to literacy. Very often the students who have been referred to remedial classes were chosen on the basis of their poor visual-motor coordination and auditory memory; the talking computer can help them in both of these areas. Computers can provide a tool for communication for young students who would have failed using only a pencil for writing their thoughts and ideas.

The computer is only one of many alternatives for learning—books, books on tape, videodiscs and interactive video programs, touch screen technology such as the Infowindow that IBM incorporated in its Principles of Alphabet Literacy (PALS) program and Apple uses in its Apple Early Learning Series with the Touch Screen program, tape recorders, chalkboard, and manipulatives. Computers should be used judiciously and only when they are the most effective tool for the learning involved. For example, it is much more effective to have first graders plant real seeds in dirt in milk cartons and witness the mystery and beauty of plant growth than to have them sit at a computer screen and watch a simulation of how plants grow. On the other hand, it makes sense to have students watch simulations of a volcano erupting or a heart beating when the real-life experience is too difficult to witness. The professional must always be sure that the use of the computer is appropriate and offers the student control of his or her learning that another means would not.

Computers appeal to most students, probably because computers are associated with arcade games and home computer games. This association makes students think working on a computer will also be "fun"—and it is—and learning should be fun. Furthermore, the advertising industry has made parents feel that, in order for their children to succeed, they should be able to use a computer. Thus, computers are regarded highly, and people in all walks of life need to use them today. High risk junior high and high school dropouts when enrolled in the IBM PALS program saw it as a new way to learn how to read as well as a marketable and employable skill that they could obtain after only 20 weeks of study in the computer center. The program is holistic, and at the end of 20 weeks the student can write the story of his or her life, fill out a job application, and be qualified for employment by many of the industries that use computers daily. Parents of minority and remedial students see their child's instruction on computers as a hope for providing them with a literacy tool that will enhance their chances for success in later life.

New computer programs are no longer based on predetermined skills but rather offer challenging programs to meet the needs of varied interests. A student who wants to be a playwright can work on a software program in that area (Children's Writing and Publishing Center, Learning Co.), or a student interested in music can choose from many programs in that field (Music Theory, Apple/MECC).

Students who say they can't read text in printed form are suddenly able to read when text is presented on a computer. That's because, in their opinion, reading text on a computer screen in order to play an adventure game, or to get directions in order to succeed on a computer-based task, is after all "not really reading!" Teachers are always amazed at how their nonreaders can suddenly read and their worst readers, who always balk at the thought of having to read, will do so without protest when they are at the computer. Exercises and activities that may seem to be a bore and drudgery take on new dimensions when done on a computer.

Students who have problems with dyslexia and the print moving on the page and reversals can be helped through the use of different colored screen displays. Talking Text Writer (Scholastic) includes the capability to have 13 different combinations of background and text colors. This program has been shown to help greatly students with visual perception difficulties.

The channel by which a student learns most effectively and efficiently should be taken into account more often than it is. A program such as Learning Styles Inventory (Educational Activities) can be used to determine learning modalities. The computer, as it is used today, facilitates those who are primarily visual learners, that is, those who learn best through the visual sense. Those who learn through the auditory sense are being helped with the numerous synthesized and digitized speech programs. The quality of the speech has greatly improved. Digitized speech gives almost perfect human voice sound, but it is limited by the number of words that can be spoken. Synthesized speech gives unlimited text-to-speech capabilities, but it still sounds robotic or like an uncle with a foreign accent, although it is improving daily. Kinesthetic learners, those who learn best through firsthand experience or through simulations of real experiences, seem to benefit greatly from using the computer with simulation programs such as Flight Simulator (SubLogic) or Robot Odyssey (Learning Co.).

Students' thinking styles should also be considered when computer programs are selected. Students who learn quickly by analyzing discover that the computer breaks learning into sequential steps and takes them through the learning process in an orderly and logical manner. The computer is also good at branching off to more difficult or less difficult levels. Pacing may be determined by the user. Some programs are paced according to how rapidly a student responds to presented items. The number of opportunities to practice a particular item may be increased for students who need more exposure. The computer will also move up to increasingly higher levels of difficulty in order to provide more complex items for students who learn quickly.

Intuitive learners find the computer challenging because many programs require higher-level thinking skills. There are times when answers are not immediately apparent and the big picture or concept must be attained before the parts can be put together. Programs such as Where in the World Is Carmen Sandiego? (Broderbund), Gertrude's Secrets (Learning Co.), Rocky's Boots (Learning Co.), and Robot Odyssey (Learning Co.), as well as The Factory (Sunburst) and Run for the Money (Tom Snyder Productions) are favorites.

Recent research on the use of computers for skills attainment indicates that the greatest gains are for disabled readers. As much as one to three years' growth in reading after only 20 weeks in a well-planned computer program such as IBM's Principles of Alphabet Literacy has been reported.

HOW CAN COMPUTERS SUPPORT A WHOLE LANGUAGE ENVIRONMENT?

California's new English Language Arts Framework has been a document that has launched a nationwide trend away from isolated skill teaching to a more holistic approach toward reading instruction and an integration of listening, speaking, writing, and reading. Software developers such as Teacher Support Systems have introduced a Language Experience Series to support whole language teaching. It starts with a Read A Logo program (not to be confused with Turtle Logo) to expose beginners to reading meaningful print in their environment (for example, McDonald's logo). This program is supported with digitized speech, so the learner gets multisensory feedback. To support the literature-based reading program, Teacher Support Systems has also developed Literary Sequencer, a program that will help students sequence literature they have read. It focuses on such vital story elements as character, setting, and plot. To help students with the logical organization of a story as events chronologically unfold, Timeline software (Tom Snyder Productions) is an excellent tool for putting events in order and prewriting before developing one's own story. Finally, a third program, Semantic Mapper (Teacher Support Systems), is an excellent tool for teaching mapping-webbing or clustering and fostering higher-level thinking skills and prewriting experiences. For at-risk junior high and high schoolers, Teacher Support Systems has produced Reading Realities, a program that was developed after interviewing high school students about their topics of concern and interest. Written at a second- to sixth-grade reading level it covers career preparation, jury series, and directed reading and thinking activities on such topics as drugs, alcohol, AIDS, and pregnancy.

Most reluctant readers don't read because they have never experienced success in reading. However, we have yet to meet a reluctant reader who was not literally glued to a computer and would readily read in order to succeed at Castle Wolfenstein (Muse), Zork I, II, or III (Infocom), or MadLibs (First Byte).

What's even more fun than playing an adventure game is creating their own adventure games. The excitement generated by creating an adventure game is something that every creative writing teacher would kill for. As educators, we have had years of experience guiding students through the joy of writing their own adventure game(s) through programming in the BASIC computer language. The process itself was an adventure.

At one time, adventure games could be done only by writing a program in a computer language. Today, students may use software to achieve this goal. For example, Story Tree (Scholastic) aids students in creating adventure games by having them respond to a series of questions on the screen. However, the theme, setting, characters, plot, climax, and resolution need to be thought out before coming to the computer. Options to various predicaments are typed in by the student author; these options are then presented on the screen when the game is played. Students are forced to plan carefully, to organize their work, and to think through the various options in order to provide thoughtful choices. The reward, of course, is an adventure game that everyone in the class wants to play.

Other software that enables students to be authors of an adventure game (or other subject), and which can be printed into book form, are Build a Book (Scarborough) and Playwriter (Woodbury). Build a Book displays a series of questions to which the student responds by typing in the answers. Playwriter goes one better and enables a student to plan and write the story and to build it the way a real playwright would. The end result of all three programs is a "published" book, something that most students are proud of—even if it is only printed with a dot-matrix printer.

Although the number of systematic research studies on using the computer as a means of bringing reluctant readers back to reading is still not as extensive as we would like, one of the most hopeful results has been the studies showing that early introduction of computers as problem-solving tools can enhance learning and actually decrease the number of retentions or remedial readers. Five-year follow-up studies on IBM's Writing to Read have demonstrated that an early start indeed effectively reduced the number of students being recommended for remediation. The Tulsa, Oklahoma, studies showed many positive results. Model Technology School projects like the one at Alhambra school district, California, are also gathering data on the powerful positive effects that talking word processors can have on the writing and reading development of early learners. If the computer is used well, it should provide a learning tool for the future that will dramatically reduce the numbers of students requiring remedial reading services. At the University of Virginia, in its Academic Electronic Village, a model that Thomas Jefferson would have been proud of, teachers have been integrating the use of computers with the reading of good literature. After students read a book of their interest and choice, they have an opportunity to engage in dialogue with the main character in the book via electronic telecommunications. Future research should be longitudinal and follow up the educational progress of students who have been introduced to the computer in their early years.

WHAT IS THE CRITERIA FOR SELECTING EDUCATIONAL SOFTWARE?

Guidelines, selection criteria, and checklists for evaluating educational software proliferate in the literature, as evidenced by some of the references at the end of this chapter. Regardless of the criteria chosen, it is important that those who will be using the list be involved in compiling it. The criteria should be updated periodically to reflect the changing needs of the end users (both teachers and students), as well as the advances in software technology.

The following guidelines were adopted by the Educational Technology Committee of the California State Department of Education; they are included because they make up one of the most extensive and thoughtful lists available. Items are clustered into three broad areas: educational content, technical features, and support materials. In each of these areas, criteria are classified as either essential (features that a program must have) or desirable (features considered nice but not necessary). The final section lists quality indicators, or indicators of excellence, which may be found in many educational software programs rated by reviewers as being "outstanding" or "exceptional."

These criteria, some of which are already being met by publishers, represent future directions in software development. They also represent the ideas of today; new criteria will evolve as hardware and software technology improve and instructional design becomes more sophisticated.

ESSENTIAL ATTRIBUTES

Educational Content

All content is factually accurate.

All punctuation, spelling, and grammar is correct, except when instructional strategies require the presentation of incorrect materials.

Responses to learners are appropriate, positive, and nonjudgmental.

The skill levels (reading, typing, etc.) required to operate the program are commensurate with the skill levels being taught or practiced.

Instructions are clear, concise, and complete.

The objectives of the instruction are explicitly stated or readily apparent to the learner.

Technical Features

The intended users can easily and independently operate the program.

The program is reliable in normal use.

The software is free from programming errors and runs efficiently with minimum delay time.

The program operates as specified in the instructions.

The screens are well formatted with appropriate use of color and graphics.

All sound is under the control of the teacher or the learner except when the sound is an essential element of the instructional strategy.

The pace of the program can be controlled by the teacher or by the learner unless pacing is an essential element of the instructional strategy.

Expected learner responses for program operation are consistent throughout.

Unanticipated learner input does not disrupt program operation.

Maps, graphs, and other illustrations are clear and simple to interpret.

Support Materials

All punctuation, grammar, and spelling are correct.

Documentation includes at least the following elements:
    Description of the hardware requirements
    Procedures for installing software
    Instructions for use

DESIRABLE ATTRIBUTES

Educational Content

The program contains multiple levels of difficulty, which may be selected by the learner or the teacher.

Motivational devices are appropriate to the content and skill levels being taught or practiced.

The interest level and the vocabulary are well suited to the intended learners.

The program provides useful responses to learner errors.

The learner remains in control of the program and is actively involved in the learning process.

The instructional design is based on appropriate learning strategies.

When appropriate, the program branches to harder or easier content based on learner responses.

Any game format utilized for instruction, reinforcement, or motivation is appropriate and enhances the overall instructional design.

Where simulations are used, the models and data are valid and not oversimplified.

The program represents an effective use of the computer.

Technical Features

Instructional content can be adapted to include individualized word lists, problem sets, etc.

Program operation requires minimal teacher intervention.

Content is presented in random sequence, when appropriate.

A menu allows learners to access directly specific parts of the program.

Learners can correct responses before they are accepted by the program.

Learners can access operating instructions or HELP screens from any part of the program.

Learners can bypass instructions at will.

Learners can exit from any point in the program through an established escape sequence.

Colors are selected for maximum discrimination when used on noncolor screens.

If record-keeping modules are included, they are protected from unauthorized access.

If there is a record-keeping component, a minimum of 40 students can be accommodated.

Support Materials

Documentation includes at least the following items for teacher and student use:

Content descriptions in terms of specific objectives or skills to be acquired or practiced.

Prerequisite learner skills.

Expected time needed for successful execution of the program.

Expected learner outcomes.

Suggestions for integrating the program into the curriculum.

Suggestions for use in various instructional settings.

Suggested classroom activities.

Lists of any books, equipment, or other materials required for use with the program.

Pictures of representative program screens.

Sample program runs.

INDICATORS OF EXCELLENCE

Educational Content

The program utilizes innovative approaches and encourages creativity on the part of the learner.

The learner is encouraged to use higher-order thinking skills such as application, analysis, synthesis, and evaluation, where appropriate.

Alternative methods of presenting the content are used and are based on learner response.

The program provides for open-ended natural-language responses.

The program presents material not easily provided by other methods or engages the learner in experiences not readily duplicated in the real world.

The program presents ideas and theories in a manner that makes them accessible to learners at earlier grades than the traditional curriculum would suggest.

Technical Features

The program provides for various learning modalities—auditory, kinesthetic, visual—where appropriate.

The program uses other technologies, such as speech synthesis, videotape, videodisc, or audiocassette when appropriate to enhance the learning experience.

The program makes use of alternative input devices—voice, light pen, mouse, graphics tablet, etc.—when appropriate.

The learner can exit the program from any point and return to that point directly from the beginning of the program with previous work, or record of progress, intact.

The learner can go back through the program on demand to review responses and the content.

The program includes the capability of printing appropriate instructional segments, performance records, learner-created materials, etc.

Support Materials

Teacher and student materials should:

Describe the specific learning theories employed in the instructional design.

Suggest a broad range of classroom applications.

Contain masters for transparencies and learner materials.

Include well-designed pre- and post-tests, as appropriate.

Correlate the material to standard textbook series, curriculum frameworks, and standards, as appropriate.

Describe learner outcomes obtained from field testing in a variety of settings.

Identify previous work and background qualifications of the author(s).

SPECIFIC CONSIDERATIONS IN SELECTING SOFTWARE FOR DISABLED AND RELUCTANT READERS

The following are specific features to be considered when selecting software for disabled readers. Look for software or programs that:

1. Enable specialists to develop specific hardware peripheral devices that will enable students to communicate.
2. Allow students to work independently.
3. Have future vocational applications.
4. Teach activities of daily living skills or real-life situations, such as checkbook accounting, spreadsheet budgeting, word processing, and running a business.
5. Stress basic skills in math, reading, spelling, social studies, and general information.
6. Allow students to learn by manipulating real objects, such as coins, clocks, and so on.
7. Can be run with minimal movements, such as keyboard strokes or paddles.
8. Utilize voice synthesizers and read aloud the information that is presented on the screen.
9. Incorporate voice and sound and can utilize headphones.
10. Use high-resolution graphics and large-sized print.
11. Can be used as rewards—game-type programs such as checkers, chess, board games, memory span, etc., which students can eventually use in their leisure time.

High interest software is the key to getting reluctant readers to want to read and should contain the following qualities in order to motivate them:

1. Stimulating content to capture their imagination and interests.
2. A quick pace to sustain their attention.
3. Appropriate use of color, graphics, and animation to provide visual stimulation.

BUILDING A FUNCTIONAL SOFTWARE COLLECTION

Spelling programs can be used by all students, grades K–12. Speller Bee (First Byte) is an example of a program in which the teacher can enter a weekly spelling list or, better yet, let students work with lists of words that are their own personal demons and that they need to know. It has the addition of speech technology and so in the teaching mode combines the best research in studying new words with a multisensory delivery. Students can then practice using the words in word search and scrambled word timed fun activities. Spell It! (Davidson) is another program that allows for a variety of reinforcement activities to let students practice spelling words. Whole Brain Spelling (SubLogic) capitalizes on the computer's features of color, sound, and animation. Color highlights parts of words, and prefixes or suffixes can be moved around to illustrate how affixes affect the meaning of words. The only drawback to this program is that words cannot be added to the preprogrammed list of most frequently used and misspelled words.

There is even a specialized spelling program, Spelling for the Physically Impaired (MECC); designed for special education students, this program allows control of the computer through a single-switch input (scanning) using either a game paddle or the keyboard. The cursor moves from one option to another until the student touches the keyboard or game button to select the option that is highlighted.

Because features that exist in one program (such as the ability to enter your own spelling list) may not be in another program (which may focus on a predetermined list of frequently misspelled words), it may be necessary to buy both kinds so that each may be used for different purposes and with students with different needs.

Select a word processing program that can be used by both teachers and students. Popular are Homeword (Sierra On-Line) and Milliken Word Processor (Milliken). Picture icons make these programs easy to learn and to use.

Database programs let teachers and librarians organize their instructional materials, retrieve frequently used information, and enable students to enter their research material for use in reports and projects. PFS: File (Personal Software) is popular among teachers, librarians, and administrators, while Friendly Filer (Grolier) is a database management program designed with youngsters in mind.

Teacher utility programs help teachers prepare computer-based activities, determine the reading-difficulty level of textual materials, and prepare materials for student use. Following are descriptions of some of these programs.

When budgets are tight and software is scarce, authoring programs are a good solution. Teachers (and students) can create their own computer-based activities or design customized lessons for use on the computer. Popular authoring programs include Game Show (Advanced Ideas), Square Pairs (Scholastic), Tic Tac Show (Advanced Ideas), Create (Hartley), and E-Z Pilot (Teck).

Crossword puzzles and word searches are also enjoyable and provide beneficial learning activities. Crossword Magic (HLS) and Wordsearch (Hartley) are popular and easy to use. It takes only 20 minutes to create a crossword puzzle or word search activity using a computer; it may take more than two hours done the traditional way.

In Chapter 8, on readability, Patsy H. Perritt discusses the importance of pinpointing the reading-difficulty level of materials. With computers, it is no longer necessary to perform the tedious calculations by hand. Rather, it is now as easy as locating and typing in three 100-word passages. The computer automatically processes the selections and displays on the screen the number of sentences, number of syllables, average sentence length, and the number of one-, two-, and three-syllable words.

In addition, programs such as Readability Calculations (Micro Power & Light) highlight words that should be pretaught before the students begin reading a particular selection. This program displays the Fry Readability Graph with a dot indicating the reading-difficulty level of the selection being analyzed. On a different screen display, a bar graph shows the reading difficulty as determined by seven other popular readability formulas. It's interesting to compare and contrast the reading level of a particular selection as determined by several readability formulas.

To develop reading comprehension through contextual clues, and to reinforce specific vocabulary in literature, social science, or science, for example, MadLibs (First Byte) presents cartoon stories with exciting color graphics and allows students to hear built-in stories in which they have supplied missing words and often created spoken stories with hilarious results. Cloze Plus (Milliken) is another helpful program. To prepare customized cloze activities for use on the computer, programs such as Clozemaster (SkillCorp) or Cloze Test (Softside) are a must. Teachers, instructional aides, or volunteer students merely type in a selection and instruct the computer to delete every nth word, every noun, or every specified word that is to be practiced.

The core collection is the heart of the software collection—the workhorse programs whose cost will be worth every penny invested.

To build your skills collection, start by using your district course of study, school objectives, grade-level scope and sequence, and your own classroom curriculum. This systematic analysis will enable you to get even greater use from software because it will be purchased with specific learning objectives in mind.

Because most school budgets are limited, choose only those topics or skills that cross grade levels and subject or discipline areas. Prioritize your list: The first "round" purchase should be useful to as many teachers and students as possible. For example, capitalization may be introduced in second grade, but students in all other grades could benefit from a review. Therefore, a capitalization program might be a good initial choice for your skills collection. Subsequent purchases may then focus on a specific subject area such as reading, language arts, math, or science. As your collection grows, update your collection in the same manner. This systematic, coordinated, and articulated approach should result in a functional and frequently used software collection.

Most adolescent disabled readers are able to decode words adequately. However, they have a particularly difficult time understanding and interpreting what they read. Thus, an emphasis on vocabulary development and comprehension is recommended. Although the skill may be word recognition, the content should be topics that have an immediate and direct application to adolescent interests, such as Financing a Car, Work Habits for Job Success, or First Day on the Job (all from MCE). Such programs help teenagers practice reading in a meaningful way.

Other vocabulary development programs include Vocabulary Challenge (Learning Well), Ways to Read Words (Intellectual Software), and the Vocabulary Game (J & S Software). These programs enable disabled readers to use the computer to practice those words that the class is studying.

WHAT IS THE CRITERIA FOR SELECTING EDUCATIONAL SOFTWARE?

There are two literature-based series that reluctant readers enjoy. The Newbery Series of 15 titles (Sunburst) offers four activities that help students see how well they remember what they read (comprehension); how well they understood particular words in the context of a sentence from the book (vocabulary); use of words in a crossword puzzle (word meanings); and the ability to locate words in a word search (visual discrimination/word recognition).

The Return to Reading Library (Media Basics) has 100 titles that range from science fiction to historical novels. Keeping in mind the needs of the reluctant reader, there are titles to meet varied interests, from *Lord of the Flies* to *The Outsiders*. The activities in this series require critical thinking. Incorrect responses are handled positively through coaching by providing additional information. Reluctant readers enjoy using both of these series because they receive private feedback on how well they read the book and learn ways they can use the information gained from the story.

Some programs develop critical thinking skills in a gamelike format. Examples of programs that require higher-order thinking skills include the following: for inductive or deductive reasoning skills—The Factory (Sunburst), Lost R—Reasoning (MCE), Mindbenders (Midwest), and Reasoning—The Logical Process (MCE); for problem solving—The Incredible Laboratory (Sunburst) and In Search of the Most Incredible Thing (Spinnaker); and for logic—Rocky's Boots (Learning Co.), What's My Logic? (Midwest), Mind Castles (MCE), and The Pond (Sunburst).

Effective study skills enable students to learn from text efficiently. Programs in the study skills category include Library Skills (Micro Power & Light Co.), Library and Media Skills (Educational Activities), and a series of 12 programs produced by Right On Programs (ROP) with such titles as Learning to Use an Index, Learning to Use a Table of Contents, Dictionary Skills, and Using Reference Tables in an Almanac. Both Grolier (*Book of Knowledge*) and Encyclopaedia Britannica offer software to be used with their encyclopedias to practice and reinforce research and reference skills. Programs for effective test taking, note taking, and efficient study techniques are currently being developed.

Students planning to enter the job market immediately after getting out of high school will find several series helpful: Career Directions Series (Systems Design Laboratory), Job Success Series (MCE), and World of Work (Computer Age Education).

Programs on the basic life skills for personal finance, consumer awareness, and job success are available. Titles include Tips on Buying a Used Car (Aquarius People Materials), Comparative Buying Series (MCE), Cash versus Credit Buying (MCE), and Understanding Labels (Aquarius People Materials).

The computer is the perfect tool for enriching students' learning by providing activities that extend and apply skills they have mastered. Simulations software, such as Oregon Trail, Sell Lemonade, and Sell Bicycles (all MECC), enables students to use their decision-making and mathematics skills.

There is a great need for high interest–low vocabulary software; yet these programs are few. At this time The Consumer Education Series of High Interest/Low Readability Software (MCE) is available. One solution to the scarcity of such software is one that a resourceful (and energetic) teacher can resolve. After students read high/low materials, they can use the computer with software that their teacher has created based on the materials read. This can be accomplished by using one of the authoring programs discussed at the beginning of this section.

The question of leisure versus academic software is often raised. It is important to remember that the computer is but one of many teaching tools, including textbooks, trade books (library books), magazines, and other audiovisual media such as the chalkboard, films, filmstrips, and videotape recorders. Because the computer is another medium of learning, the question of games and entertainment versus academic learning should not be a problem. Granted, many computer learning activities are contained in a gamelike format, but the purpose for using the software program should determine whether it is appropriate.

As computer technology advances, its use as a medium for teaching and learning will increase. For example, as voice technology is refined and as the price becomes affordable, students will be able to speak into the computer and see their spoken words appear on the screen. What appears on the screen can also be "read back" to the student. This is especially advantageous for those students who do not type well, for those whose first language is not English, and for those who need auditory input in their learning. Computers are primarily a visual medium at this time; thus, without sound, computers are doing only half the job.

As artificial intelligence advancements progress, computers can be used to diagnose and prescribe tasks for students as they are working on the computer. Student responses can be routinely recorded and analyzed, fine-tuned for further meaningful instructions, and generate items that challenge the student—all while the program is being used.

The ways that we are presently using computers will be considered primitive a short five years from now. In fact, by the end of the century the computer hardware and software as we know it today will not be unlike the model T in the automobile industry.

SOFTWARE REVIEW SOURCES

As software review coordinators we have found that programs that are reviewed are often chosen not because they are the best ones on the market but because the publisher has a budget that allows it to send out review copies. It is unfortunate that many worthwhile programs are not reviewed. But when review copies are not available, it's not possible to write about a program and share its merits with those who need to know.

Reviews in publications vary: *Descriptive reviews* provide details about a program without making a judgment. *Critical reviews* usually express one person's opinion about a program's merits and faults. *Evaluative reviews* rate a program according to predetermined criteria.

Some publications' policies require that a program be reviewed by a panel of experts whose composite view is expressed. Other publications' reviews are written by a single person whose name usually appears with the review. When a review is written by one person, it is important to know who the reviewer is, background, and possible biases.

Studying educational software reviews helps teachers and librarians sift through the hundreds of programs that are on the market and eliminate those that don't fit their needs. Each review provides a glimpse of a specific software product. It may not be possible to tell for sure whether a particular software program is what you want, but it is possible to eliminate those that do not seem appropriate and thus save time.

As educational software use increases, more publications will offer reviews. This can only help those who need to remain current on new software developments and products. Software reviews for reading and language arts are featured in the following publications.

Review journals and reports:

Apple Journal of Courseware Review (critical)

Digest of Software Reviews: Education (abstracts of other views)

Library Software Review (critical)

MicroSIFT Reviews (evaluative)

School Library Journal (evaluative)

Software Reports (evaluative)

Educational computing periodicals:

Access: Microcomputers in Libraries (critical)

Computing Teacher (critical)

Electronic Learning (critical)

Teaching and Computers (critical)

Reading/language arts publications:

The Journal of Reading (descriptive with critical comments)

The Reading Teacher (descriptive with critical comments)

Language Arts (critical)

Writing Notebook (creative word processing)

PUBLICATIONS

Access: Microcomputers in Libraries. DAC Publications, 3354 30 St., San Diego, CA 92104. At least one signed critical library-oriented review per issue.

Apple Journal of Courseware Review (formerly *The Journal of Courseware Review*). 20525 Mariani Ave., Cupertino, CA 95014. Available through local Apple dealers. Critical reviews by educators and instructional designers; also screen shots and cataloging information.

Computing Teacher. 1787 Agate St., University of Oregon, Eugene, OR 97403.

Digest of Software Reviews: Education. 301 W. Mesa, Fresno, CA 93704. Abstracts reviews from more than 80 educational computer journals, education journals, and computer magazines.

Electronic Learning. Scholastic, Inc., 730 Broadway, New York, NY 10003. Six critical reviews per issue written by educators.

Journal of Reading. See *The Reading Teacher.*

Language Arts. National Council of Teachers of English, 1111 Kenyon Rd., Urbana, IL 61801.

Library Software Review (formerly *Software Review*). 11 Ferry Lane W., Westport, CT 06880. Signed, extensive critical reviews.

MicroSIFT Reviews. 300 S.W. Sixth Ave., Portland, OR 97204. Teams of teachers write evaluative reviews on more than 100 programs per year. Distributed through *Computing Teacher* and other periodicals, RICE database, ERIC, and a nationwide network of educational service agencies. Includes matrix and rating scale.

The Reading Teacher and *Journal of Reading.* International Reading Association, 800 Barksdale Rd., Newark, DE 19711. For members. Two to three programs on one skill or topic are compared in critical reviews written by reading educators.

School Library Journal. 249 W. 17 St., New York, NY 10011. "Computer Software Review" section, published monthly, provides jargon-free critiques of microcomputer software intended for computer-aided instruction (K–12) based on the testing and analyses of a network of subject specialists working with the Media Evaluation Center of North Carolina's Department of Public Instruction.

Software Reports: Guide to Evaluated Educational Software. 10996 Torreyana Rd., San Diego, CA 92121. This well-organized, complete, cross-referenced buying guide and evaluative directory is a must in every school library.

Teaching and Computers. Scholastic, Inc., 730 Broadway, New York, NY 10003. Four to six critical reviews per issue written by educators.

Writing Notebook. Box 1268, Eugene, OR 97440-1268. Focuses on creative word processing in the classroom.

PROGRAM TITLES CITED IN THE TEXT

Title	Publisher	Subject
Apple Early Learning Series	Apple	Early literacy
Apple Mouse	Apple	Art/graphics
AppleWorks	Apple	Word processing
Bank Street Writer	Scholastic	Word processing
Build a Book	Scarborough	Creative writing
Career Directions Series	Systems Design Laboratory	Vocational education
Cash versus Credit Buying	MCE	Consumer education
Castle Wolfenstein	Muse	Adventure game
Chemistry: Series I	Focus Media	Simulation science
Children's Writing and Publishing Center	Learning Co.	Publishing Center
Cloze Plus	Milliken	Teacher utility
Cloze Test	Softside	Teacher utility

Title	Publisher	Subject
Clozemaster	SkillCorp	Teacher utility
CMS FrEd Mail BBS	CUE	Telecommunications; bulletin boards
Comparative Buying Series	MCE	Consumer education
The Consumer Education Series of High Interest/Low Readability Software	MCE	Consumer education
Create	Hartley	Authoring program
Crossword Magic	HLS	Authoring program
Dictionary Skills	Right On Programs	Study/locational skills
Ecosystems	Sunburst	Science
Electric Poet	IBM	Creative writing
Exploratory Play	Peal	Expressive language
E-Z Pilot	Teck	Authoring program
The Factory	Sunburst	Critical thinking
Financing a Car	MCE	Consumer Education
First Day on the Job	MCE	Vocational education
Flight Simulator	SubLogic	Simulation aviation
FrEd Mail. *See* CMS FrEd Mail BBS		
Friendly Filer	Grolier	Database management
Game Show	Advanced Ideas	Authoring program
Gertrude's Secrets	Learning Co.	Critical thinking
Gibson Light Pen	Koala Technologies	Art/graphics
Homeword	Sierra On-Line	Word processing
In Search of the Most Incredible Thing	Spinnaker	Critical thinking
The Incredible Laboratory	Sunburst	Critical thinking
Job Success Series	MCE	Vocational education
Keys to Responsible Driving	CBS	Driver education
KeyTalk	Peal	Creative writing
KidTalk	First Byte	Talking/creative writing
Koala Pad Touch Tablet	Koala Technologies	Art/graphics
Language Experience Series	Teacher Support Systems	Whole language
Learning Styles Inventory	Educational Activities	Management
Learning to Use a Table of Contents	Right On Programs	Study/locational skills
Learning to Use an Index	Right On Programs	Study/locational skills

Title	Publisher	Subject
Library and Media Skills	Educational Activities	Study/locational skills
Library Skills	Micro Power & Light Co.	Study/locational skills
Literary Sequencer	Teacher Support Systems	Whole language
Lost R—Reasoning	MCE	Critical thinking
Lotus 1-2-3	Lotus	Integrated program
MadLibs	First Byte	Comprehension/cloze
Magic Paintbrush	Penguin	Art/graphics
Magic Slate	Sunburst	Word processing
Microsoft Works	Microsoft	Integrated software
Milliken Word Processor	Milliken	Word processing
Milliken Writing Workshop	Milliken	Word processing
Mind Castles	MCE	Critical thinking
Mindbenders	Midwest	Critical thinking
Minerals Database	Sunburst	Science
Movie Maker	Reston	Art/graphics
Music Construction Set	Electronic Arts	Music
Music Shop	Broderbund	Music
Music Theory	Apple/MECC	Music
Newbery Series	Sunburst	Literature
Operation: Frog	Scholastic	Simulation science
Oregon Trail	MECC	Simulation historical
Pequeno Editor	Falcon	Spanish word processing
PFS: File	Personal Software	Database management
Playwriter	Woodbury	Creative writing
Poetry Express	Learning Well	Creative writing
The Pond	Sunburst	Critical thinking
Power Pad	Chalkboard	Art/graphics
Prelab Studies in Chemistry	Wiley	Simulation science
Primary Editor	IBM	Word processing
Principles of Alphabet Literacy (PALS)	IBM	Adult literacy
Procomm	Shareware	Communication
Readability Calculations	Micro Power & Light Co.	Teacher utility
Reading Realities	Teacher Support Systems	Comprehension
Reasoning—The Logical Process	MCE	Critical thinking

Title	Publisher	Subject
Red Ryder	Shareware	Communication
Return to Reading Library	Media Basics	Literature
Rhyming Notebook	First Byte	Talking/poetry/songs
Robot Odyssey	Learning Co.	Simulation construction
Rocky's Boots	Learning Co.	Critical thinking
Run for the Money	Tom Snyder Productions	Comprehension/ economics
Science Toolkit	Broderbund	Science experiments
Sell Bicycles	MECC	Simulation economics
Sell Lemonade	MECC	Simulation economics
Semantic Mapper	Teacher Support Systems	Concept development
Songwriter	Scarborough	Music
Spanish Literacy Series	Falcon	Spanish reading
Spell It!	Davidson	Spelling
Speller Bee	First Byte	Spelling
Spelling for the Physically Impaired	MECC	Spelling
Square Pairs	Scholastic	Authoring program
Story Tree	Scholastic	Authoring program
Talk Is Cheap	Shareware	Communications
Talking Monsters and Make Believe	Learning Lab	Talking word processor
Talking Text Writer	Scholastic	Talking word processor
Tic Tac Show	Advanced Ideas	Authoring program
Timeline	Tom Snyder Productions	Prewriting, sequence
Tips on Buying a Used Car	Aquarius People Materials	Consumer education
Understanding Labels	Aquarius People Materials	Consumer education
Using Reference Tables in an Almanac	Right On Programs	Study/locational skills
Vocabulary Challenge	Learning Well	Vocabulary development
Vocabulary Game	J & S Software	Vocabulary development
The Voyage of the Mimi	Sunburst	Science and math
Ways to Read Words	Intellectual Software	Vocabulary development
What's My Logic?	Midwest	Critical thinking

Title	Publisher	Subject
Where in the World Is Carmen Sandiego?	Broderbund	Geography
Whole Brain Spelling	SubLogic	Spelling
Wordsearch	Hartley	Authoring program
Work Habits for Job Success	MCE	Vocational education
World of Work	Computer Age Education	Vocational education
Writing to Read	IBM	Early literacy
Zork I, II, III	Infocom	Adventure game

DIRECTORY OF PUBLISHERS

Advanced Ideas, Inc.
2902 San Pablo Ave.
Berkeley, CA 94702

Apple Computer, Inc.
20525 Mariani
Cupertino, CA 95014

Apple/MECC. *See* MECC

Aquarius People Materials, Inc.
Box 128
Indian Rocks Beach, FL 34635

Bantam Books, Inc.
666 Fifth Ave.
New York, NY 10103

Broderbund Software
17 Paul Dr.
San Rafael, CA 94903

CBS Software
One Fawcett Place
Greenwich, CT 06836

Chalkboard, Inc.
3772 Pleasantdale Rd.
Atlanta, GA 30340

Computer Age Education, Inc.
1442A Walnut St., Suite 341
Berkeley, CA 94709

CUE
CUE Softswap
Box 2657
Menlo Park, CA 94026

Davidson & Associates
6069 Groveoak Place, Suite 12
Rancho Palos Verdes, CA 90274

EdMark Corp.
Box 3903, 14350 N.E. 21 St.
Bellevue, WA 98009

Educational Activities, Inc.
1937 Grand Ave.
Baldwin, NY 11510

Electronic Arts
2755 Campus Dr.
San Mateo, CA 94403

Encyclopaedia Britannica
425 N. Michigan Ave.
Chicago, IL 60611

P. Falcon International Corp.
906 Nolan
San Antonio, TX 78202

First Byte
3100 S. Harbor, Suite 150
Santa Ana, CA 92704

Focus Media, Inc.
Box 865, 839 Stewart Ave.
Garden City, NY 11530

Grolier Electronic Publishing, Inc.
95 Madison Ave., Suite 1100
New York, NY 10016

Hartley Courseware, Inc.
Box 419, 123 Bridge St.
Dimondale, MI 48821

HLS Duplication
Dist. by L & S Computerware
1589 Fraser Dr.
Sunnyvale, CA 94086

IBM Software Publishing Division
1845 S. Federal Hwy., Bldg. Harbor S.
Delray Beach, FL 33444

Infocom, Inc.
55 Wheeler St.
Cambridge, MA 02138

Intellectual Software
798 North Ave.
Bridgeport, CT 06606

J & S Software
135 Haven Ave.
Port Washington, NY 11050

Koala Technologies Corp.
3100 Patrick Henry Dr.
Santa Clara, CA 95052

The Learning Co.
6493 Kaiser Dr.
Fremont, CA 94555

Learning Lab. *See* Pelican Software

Learning Well
200 S. Service Rd.
Roslyn Heights, NY 11577

Lotus Development Corp.
161 First St.
Cambridge, MA 02142

MCE, Inc.
157 S. Kalamazoo Mall, Suite 250
Kalamazoo, MI 49007

MECC
3490 Lexington Ave. N.
St. Paul, MN 55112

Media Basics, Inc.
Larchmont Plaza
Larchmont, NY 10538

Micro Power & Light Co.
12820 Hillcrest Rd., Suite 219
Dallas, TX 75230

Microsoft Corp.
16011 N.E. 36 Way
Box 97017
Redmond, WA 98073

Midwest Publications Co., Inc.
Box 448
Pacific Grove, CA 93950

Milliken Publishing Co.
1100 Research Blvd.
Box 21579
St. Louis, MO 63132-0579

Minnesota Educational Computer
Consortium. *See* MECC

Muse Software
347 N. Charles St.
Baltimore, MD 21201

NTS Software, Inc.
141 W. Rialto Ave.
Rialto, CA 92376

Peal Software
Box 8188
Calabasas, CA 91372

Pelican Software
768 Farmington Ave.
Farmington, CT 06032

Penguin Software
830 Fourth Ave.
Geneva, IL 60134

Personal Software Co.
Box 776
Salt Lake City, UT 84110

Reston Publishing Co., Inc.
11480 Sunset Hills Rd.
Reston, VA 22090

Right On Programs (ROP)
140 E. Main St.
Huntington, NY 11743

Scarborough Systems, Inc.
55 S. Broadway
Tarrytown, NY 10591

Scholastic Software
730 Broadway
New York, NY 10003

Shareware
Cue Lab
1066 Maryland St.
Detroit, MI 48230

Sierra On-Line, Inc.
Box 485
Coarsegold, CA 93614

SkillCorp Software, Inc.
1171 McGraw Ave.
Irvine, CA 92714

Snyder, Tom, Productions, Inc. *See*
Tom Snyder Productions, Inc.

Softside Software, Inc.
305 Riverside Dr.
New York, NY 10025

Spinnaker Software Corp.
One Kendal Square
Cambridge, MA 02139

SubLogic Corp.
713 Edgebrook Dr.
Champaign, IL 61820

Sunburst Communications, Inc.
39 Washington Ave.
Pleasantville, NY 10570

Systems Design Laboratory
2612 Artesia Blvd., Suite B
Redondo Beach, CA 90278

Teacher Support Systems
1035 N.W. 57 St.
Gainesville, FL 32605

Teck Associates
Box 10732
White Bear Lake, MN 55110

Tom Snyder Productions, Inc.
90 Sherman St.
Cambridge, MA 02140

John Wiley & Sons, Inc.
605 Third Ave.
New York, NY 10158

Woodbury Software
127 White Oak Lane, CN No. 1001
Old Bridge, NJ 08857

6
Periodicals Power: Magazines for Reluctant Readers

Sandra Payne

In many ways, periodicals published for the teen market mirror those published for the reader age 18 and above. Our group, age 12 to 18, encompasses a demographic band of trendsetters, who are music conscious, sexually aware, politically aware, fashion mavens, celebrity lovers, and sports fans. Also within that band are those less sophisticated: the dreamers, the insecure, the followers, the fashion victims, the nerds, the klutzes, and the politically ignorant. In working with adolescents, we encounter teenagers who are hospitalized, institutionalized, pregnant, abused, abandoned, and physically and/or developmentally disabled. These readers need current publications offering information regarding life's choices, careers, friendship, and family relationships that are especially published for them. Periodicals publishers are beginning to fill the void between the readers of *Jack & Jill*, *Mademoiselle*, and *Gentlemen's Quarterly* with magazines in formats that teens find attractive, reassuring, informative, visually stimulating, colorful, current, and in most instances are easy to read.

Locating young adult publications is an adventure in itself. I find that I am drawn to the brightly lit magazine stands and bookstores of New York City. As I commute daily from Manhattan to Staten Island via the Staten Island Ferry, I often have the opportunity to slip into the newsstand to seek the latest young adult periodical. I am frequently surprised by the appearance of new titles that do not come to our offices by the more traditional channels. At that moment, I gleefully snap it up for preview and review. It's so much fun. As teens are generally the only buyers of these magazines, do solicit suggested titles from them. Don't be the last to know of the currently hottest publication. Do beware that like the adult periodicals market, some young adult periodicals also fall victim to a quick death. If you find that a particular publication is unavailable by subscription, perhaps consulting directly with a local newsstand, bookstore, or distributor will work to your advantage in receiving young adult periodicals in a timely manner.

It is particularly important in our work with young people to provide alternative reading choices for the reluctant readers who cannot find their primary interests in book publications for all teens. One final word about the importance of young adult periodicals for recreational readings is that in the interest of currency, magazines provide what the book industry has not or is unable to supply: up-to-date information on the latest, the greatest, the hippest of all teen interests—*What's New*—and thereby forecasting the adult interests of tomorrow. This in turn enables those who work with the reluctant and disabled readers an opportunity to combat illiteracy in the arena of their own very particular interests.

SUBJECT LIST OF PERIODICALS

This is a selected subject list of current periodicals published especially for young adults. Following the subject list is an alphabetical list of the magazines with annotations. Based on interest, appeal, and readability, they are particularly useful with the reluctant reader.

CAREERS
Careers
Scholastic Action

CELEBRITIES AND ENTERTAINMENT
Bop
Splice
Super Teen
Teen Machine
Tiger Beat

COMICS AND HUMOR
Amazing Heroes
Comics Scene
Mad

CURRENT EVENTS AND GENERAL INTEREST
News for You
Scholastic Choices
Scholastic Scope
Scholastic Update
Scholastic Voice
U.S. Express

FASHION AND BEAUTY
Sassy
Seventeen
YM

MUSIC
Black Beat
Black Sounds

Circus
Faces Rocks
Fresh!
Hit Parader
Metal Mania
Metallix
Metalshop
Power Metal
Rap Masters
Right On!/Right On Focus!
Smash Hits
Song Hits
Word Up!

SCIENCE
Science World

SCIENCE FICTION, FANTASY
Starlog

SPORTS
BMX Plus
Freestyle
Go: The Rider's Manual
Homeboy
Super BMX
Thrasher
Transworld Skateboarding Magazine
WWF

WRITTEN AND OR EDITED BY TEENS
Merlyn's Pen
New Youth Connections

PERIODICALS: AN ANNOTATED LIST

Amazing Heroes. 1800 Bridgegate St., Suite 101, Westlake Village, CA 91361. Biweekly. This comic-book format features thoughtful articles on vintage and contemporary comics. Also featured are interviews with authors and artists of graphic novels. May be somewhat difficult for some high-low readers.

Black Beat. Sterling's Magazines, 355 Lexington Ave., New York, NY 10017. Monthly. The spectrum of black music is covered ranging from rap and reggae to urban contemporary featuring interviews and color pinups.

Black Sounds. Music Magazine Co., Inc., 7080 Hollywood Blvd., Suite 415, Hollywood, CA 90028. Quarterly. Black urban contemporary music and musicians are featured in interviews and color pinups.

BMX Plus. Hi-Torque Publications, Inc. 10600 Sepulveda Blvd., Mission Hills, CA 91345. Monthly. Devoted primarily to competition news and views in the world of freestyle bicycling; also features product evaluation and safety.

Bop. Laufer Publishing Co., 3500 W. Olive Ave., Suite 850, Burbank, CA 91505. Monthly. Younger teens will find current film television and music celebrities airbrushed to cuddly cuteness among short interviews, gossipy news, and pen pals.

Careers. E. M. Guild, 1001 Ave. of the Americas, New York, NY 10018. Triquarterly, controlled circulation. Especially targeted toward high school seniors, focuses on the world of work and higher education. Inspirational and upbeat.

Circus. Circus Enterprises Corp., 3 W. 18 St., New York, NY 10011. Monthly. More than 20 years in print, this rock 'n' roll monthly remains ever popular and requested.

Comics Scene. Comics World Corp., 475 Park Ave. S., New York, NY 10016. Bimonthly. For comic enthusiasts of books, film, and television; fascinating interviews with artists, writers, and filmmakers.

Faces Rocks. Faces Magazines, Inc., 63 Grand Ave., Suite 230, River Edge, NJ 07661. Monthly. Heavy metal musicians are presented as polished performers and professionals. The publication is not as visually arresting as are similar publications.

Freestyle. Challenge Publications, Inc., 7950 Deering Ave., Canoga Park, CA 91304. Bimonthly. Step-by-step freestyle bicycling tricks and safety techniques are featured with competition listings and product evaluations.

Fresh! Ashley Communications, Inc., 1943 Business Center Dr., Northridge, CA 91324. Every 3 weeks. Black film and television stars, sports celebrities, and popular musicians are featured in interviews and color pinup photographs.

Go: The Rider's Manual. Wizard Publications, Inc., 3882 Del Amo Blvd., #603, Torrance, CA 90503. Monthly. Features freestyle bicycle riding. Focuses on safety, skill, and competition listings; the highlight of each issue is the photography.

Hit Parader. Charlton Publications, Inc., Box 158, 60 Division St., Derby, CT 06418-0158. Monthly. Devoted to heavy metal music, this publication offers a look at the music and its creators.

Homeboy. Wizard Publications, Inc., 3882 Del Amo Blvd., #603, Torrance, CA 90503. Monthly. Though this is not a technical how-to for freestyle bikers and skateboarders, the numerous photographs translate the pure joy and thrill of defying gravity. The visuals reflect graffiti's influence.

Mad. E. C. Publications, Inc., 485 Madison Ave., New York, NY 10022. Monthly. The old granddad of humor and satire still remains a teen favorite.

Merlyn's Pen. Box 1058, East Greenwich, RI 02818. Quarterly. Aspiring writers in grades 7–10 may wish to approach this publication, which features the work of students.

Metal Mania. Tempo Publishing Co., 475 Park Ave. S., Suite 2201, New York, NY 10016. Bimonthly. The spectrum of metal music's personalities is presented in interviews, reviews, and pinups.

Metallix. Pilot Communications, 25 W. 39 St., New York, NY 10018. Monthly. Great graphics and all color photographs separate this publication from the many others featuring metal music.

Metalshop. Sterling's Magazines, 355 Lexington Ave., New York, NY 10017. Bimonthly. Closer in spirit to teen celebrity fanzines, this publication features contests, reviews, and interviews with metal music's stars.

New Youth Connections. Youth Communications, 135 W. 20 St., New York, NY 10011. 8 issues yearly. Written and edited by New York City teenagers, this hard-hitting paper features on-the-spot interviews and in-depth feature articles on subjects as current as today's news. A model for student journalists, this publication could have national appeal.

News for You. New Readers Press, Box 131, Syracuse, NY 13210. Weekly. Tabloid format. This weekly covers national and international news events. Photos and maps append easy-to-read articles.

Power Metal. Charlton Publications, Inc., Box 158, 60 Division St., Derby, CT 06418-0158. Bimonthly. Though its look is gritty, it is a serious look at the world of heavy metal music and musicians.

Rap Masters. Word Up Publications, Inc., 63 Grand Ave., Suite 230, River Edge, NJ 07661. Monthly. Rap music and only rap is the featured star with interviews, lyrics, and color pinups.

Right On! D. S. Magazines, Inc., 1086 Teaneck Rd., Teaneck, NJ 07666. Monthly. Popular black entertainers from the worlds of film, television, and music are featured in interviews and color pinups. Its sister publication, the bimonthly *Right On Focus!* features in-depth subject presentations.

Sassy. Matilda Publications, Inc., One Times Square, New York, NY 10036. Monthly. Provocative feature titles may at first disguise the clear, helpful responsible tone of this publication for girls. Also features fashion, beauty, current events, advice, and celebrity interviews.

Scholastic Action. Scholastic, Inc., 730 Broadway, New York, NY 10003. 14 issues/yr. English skills at an easy-reading level for the slow reader. Interest/grade level: 7–9; Reading level: 2–4.

Scholastic Choices. Scholastic, Inc., 730 Broadway, New York, NY 10003. 8 issues/yr. Life-style and home economics magazine for seventh- through twelfth-grade students (ages 14–18). Covers relationships, career goals, consumerism, and health.

Scholastic Scope. Scholastic, Inc., 730 Broadway, New York, NY 10003. 20 issues/yr. English skills for the poor reader; encourages finer points of literacy. For grades 8–12 reading at grade 4–7 level.

Scholastic Update. Scholastic, Inc., 730 Broadway, New York, NY 10003. 16 issues/yr. Covers social studies and current events; intelligent yet easy-to-follow reading.

Scholastic Voice. Scholastic, Inc., 730 Broadway, New York, NY 10003. 16 issues/yr. Language arts for eighth- through twelfth-grade readers.

Science World. Scholastic, Inc., 730 Broadway, New York, NY 10003. 16 issues/yr. Science magazine for seventh through tenth grades (ages 12–15). Issues include articles about developments in science and technology as well as experiments, crossword puzzles, and television reviews.

Seventeen. Triangle Publications, 850 Third Ave., New York, NY 10022. Monthly. Still popular, this publication continues to feature timely articles, fashion, beauty, celebrities, advice, and entertainment news.

Smash Hits. Pilot Communications, 25 W. 39 St., New York, NY 10018. Monthly. Snappy, colorful graphics and photographs highlight contemporary music's personalities and the lyrics to current hits.

Song Hits. Charlton Publications, Inc., Box 158, 60 Division St., Derby, CT 06418-0158. Bimonthly. Metal music's lyrics make this publication unique. Also features record, concert, and video reviews.

Splice. Jannis Communications, Inc., 10 Columbus Circle, Suite 1300, New York, NY 10019. Bimonthly. An overall look at the entertainment scene, especially appealing to younger teens.

Starlog. Starlog Press, 475 Park Ave. S., New York, NY 10016. Monthly. Featuring science fiction, fantasy, and special effects on film and television.

Super BMX. Challenge Publications, Inc., 7950 Deering Ave., Canoga Park, CA 91304. Monthly. News from the world's bike tracks, featuring cyclist celebrities, motivational techniques, training, equipment, and safety.

Super Teen. Sterling's Magazines, 355 Lexington Ave., New York, NY 10017. Monthly. "Exclusive" interviews, dreamboat trivia, color pinups, and advice from teen superstars make this appropriate fantasy and crush material.

Teen Machine. Sterling's Magazines, 355 Lexington Ave., New York, NY 10017. Bimonthly. Published now for over a decade, its specialty has remained teen celebrities and all you wish to know about them.

Thrasher. High Speed Publications, Box 884570, San Francisco, CA 94188-4570. Monthly. Bold graphics, photographs of airborne youth, and interviews with skate boarding's celebrities. Music reviews make this the number one requested publication of skaters.

Tiger Beat. D. S. Magazines, Inc., 1086 Teaneck Rd., Teaneck, NJ 07666. Monthly. Film and television celebrities appealing to the younger teens remain the staple of this now "venerable" publication.

Transworld Skateboarding Magazine. Imprimatur, 1016 S. Tremont, Oceanside, CA 92054. Monthly. Action photographs and interviews with teen skaters, semi-professionals, and professionals are featured among step-by-step tricks and safety tips.

U.S. Express. Scholastic, Box 3710, 2931 McCarty St., Jefferson City, MO 65102. Biweekly. Full-color photos complement articles on contemporary teen issues that meet the needs of young people who are learning English as a second language.

Word Up! Word Up Publications, Inc., 63 Grand Ave., Suite 230, River Edge, NJ 07661. Monthly. Rap music's stars are the primary focus, though some nonrap performers are featured. Interviews and full-page color photographs are appealing to fans of the urban beat.

WWF. Titan Sports Publications, Inc., 1055 Summer St., Stamford, CT 06905. Monthly. Would you believe a wrestling magazine lacking blood? This one does. The titans of the World Wrestling Federation are presented in this periodical published for young teens.

YM. Gruner & Jahr U.S.A. Publishing, 685 Third Ave., New York, NY 10017. Monthly. Formerly *Young Miss*. YM has recently undergone a face-lift featuring inviting graphics and more color photographs, but it has sustained its editorial tone, keeping its emphasis on fashion, beauty, advice, and entertainment.

The following is a selected list of periodicals published for the adult market, but finding some appeal among teenagers.

Analog Science Fiction-Science Fact	*GQ (Gentlemen's Quarterly)*
Baseball Digest	*Hot Rod Magazine*
Basketball Digest	*In Fashion*
Beckett Baseball Card Monthly	*Life*
Bicycling	*Mademoiselle*
Black Hair Care	*National Geographic Magazine*
Car and Driver	*People*
Chess Life	*Premiere*
Creem	*Pro Wrestling Illustrated*
Ebony	*Road and Track*
Ebony Man	*Rolling Stone*
Elle	*Spin*
Essence	*Sports Illustrated*
Glamour	*US*

PERIODICALS PUBLISHERS

The following is a selected list of publishers whose periodicals frequently find appeal among teenagers.

Ashley Communications, Inc.
1943 Business Center Dr.
Northridge, CA 91324

High Speed Publications
Box 884570
San Francisco, CA 94188-4570

Challenge Publications, Inc.
7950 Deering Ave.
Canoga Park, CA 91304

Hi-Torque Publications, Inc.
10600 Sepulveda Blvd.
Mission Hills, CA 91345

Charlton Publications, Inc.
Box 158, 60 Division St.
Derby, CT 06418-0158

Imprimatur
1016 S. Tremont
Oceanside, CA 92054

D. S. Magazines, Inc.
1086 Teaneck Rd.
Teaneck, NJ 07666

Jimmijack Publishing Co.
807 Vivian Court
Baldwin, NY 11510

Gruner & Jahr U.S.A. Publishing
685 Third Ave.
New York, NY 10017

Laufer Publishing Co.
3500 W. Olive Ave., Suite 850
Burbank, CA 91505

L.F.P., Inc.
9171 Wilshire Blvd., Suite 300
Beverly Hills, CA 90210

McFadden Holdings, Inc.
215 Lexington Ave.
New York, NY 10016

Matilda Publications, Inc.
One Times Square
New York, NY 10036

New Readers Press
1320 Jamesville Ave.
Syracuse, NY 13210

O'Quinn Studios
455 Park Ave. S.
New York, NY 10016

Petersen Publishing Co.
8490 Sunset Blvd.
Los Angeles, CA 90069

Pilot Communications
25 W. 39 St.
New York, NY 10018

Scholastic, Inc.
730 Broadway
New York, NY 10003

Starlog Press
475 Park Ave. S.
New York, NY 10016

Sterling's Magazines
355 Lexington Ave.
New York, NY 10017

Tempo Publishing Co.
475 Park Ave. S., Suite 2201
New York, NY 10016

Triangle Publications
850 Third Ave.
New York, NY 10022

Wizard Publications, Inc.
3882 Del Amo Blvd., #603
Torrance, CA 90503

Word Up Publications
63 Grand Ave., Suite 230
River Edge, NJ 07661

7
The International High School at LaGuardia Community College: An Audiovisual Approach to Second Language Acquisition

Louise Spain

INTRODUCTION: A BRIEF HISTORICAL BACKGROUND

LaGuardia Community College of the City University of New York is one of 21 public institutions of higher education serving the academic needs of the multicultural, urban population of New York City. From its founding in 1971, LaGuardia has actively sought innovative techniques for solving such educational problems as the following:

1. Many students were dropping out of public high schools.
2. New college students were academically unprepared and needed to take courses in basic reading, writing, mathematics, and oral skills.
3. Immigrants seeking the "American dream" were pouring into New York City from various countries of the world.

The introduction to this article was contributed by Ngozi P. Agbim, chief librarian of the Library Media Resources Center at LaGuardia Community College, whose longtime tenure at the college and in-depth knowledge of its history have given an invaluable perspective. Thanks also to Cecilia Cullen, principal of Middle College and International High Schools; Eric Nadelstern, assistant principal-in-charge; and Ruthellyn Weiner, administrative assistant, whose unstinting cooperation and support are deeply appreciated.

In 1972 a Carnegie Foundation Report suggested the "establishment of a new educational unit covering the last two years of high school and the first two years of college as a means of providing the necessary continuity for nurturing the coherent, common sets of attitudes and educational needs of late adolescence."[1] LaGuardia Community College responded by establishing the Middle College High School on its campus, combining the last two years of high school with the first two years of college. Begun in 1974, this special experimental high school enrolled only high risk students referred to it by local junior high schools. "Because of their poor academic records, high rates of absenteeism, and home/emotional problems, these students [were] all targeted as potential dropouts."[2]

The partnership between LaGuardia Community College and the New York City Board of Education (responsible for the city's public high schools) resulted in several exciting and rewarding outcomes: The dropout rate at Middle College High School was reduced to less than 10 percent compared to 45 percent citywide; and 85 percent of the graduates went on to college.[3] In recognition of the resounding success of the Middle College High School program, a second public high school—the International High School—was opened on LaGuardia Community College's campus in 1985. It offered admission to all foreign-born New York City residents of high school age or eligibility whose English proficiency was below a certain level as determined by a test score and who had been in the United States for less than four years.[4]

What is noteworthy about these two experimental high schools is that they are both located at LaGuardia's campus. They share all the college resources, including the library, media services, and the television studio, as well as the library/media services personnel.

AN AUDIOVISUAL APPROACH TO
SECOND LANGUAGE ACQUISITION

The mission of the International High School (IHS) is "to enable each of our students to develop the linguistic, cognitive and cultural skills necessary for success in high school, college and beyond." This simple statement of purpose provides the framework for a sophisticated and complex learning environment, which for four years has been successfully assimilating some of the most at-risk students in American society today—the foreign-born adolescent immigrant.

These students must learn English at the same time that they follow the traditional American four-year high school curriculum. For them, as well as their American teachers, this is hardly an easy task. One imagines the entering class as a veritable Tower of Babel, represented by many different native languages, ages, and English-language abilities and varying levels of education. Some of the students have grown up in simple villages or have only recently arrived in New York City. They may be troubled refugees of war, politics, or economic upheavals, or shy and unassertive as a result of cultural upbringing. What must emerge at the end of their four years in high school is a group of Americanized, English-speaking, college-ready graduates—and it does!

In its first three years of operation, IHS's success rate has been astounding. According to a three-year status report, 90 percent of the 1985 intake (54 of 60) went on to graduate in June 1988. One hundred percent of those first graduates were accepted at colleges. Compare this to a report that cites Hispanic students dropping out of school at a rate of 80 percent "due to their limited English proficiency, cultural isolation and low socioeconomic status. These factors often result in pressure to drop out of school and find a job."[5]

The current IHS enrollment has increased to 400 students, representing 45 countries and more than 30 languages. Its unique program has attracted first-rate teachers who have clearly contributed to its success. Under an innovative and activist administration, IHS teachers are free to let their imaginations roam. However, the educational philosophy of the school provides them with a basic structure within which learning is directed. Some of the significant points of this philosophy are "learning language skills in context and embedded in a content area; learning the way in which adolescents learn best, that is, from each other; and using career education as a significant motivation factor for adolescent learners."[6]

I explored the methods of four IHS teachers who have been particularly active in using the LaGuardia Library's Media Services Department that I direct: career education teacher Kathy Fine, English teacher Marcia Slater, social studies teacher Stacia Robbins, and integrated learning skills teacher Simon Cohen. For each of these four teachers, one way of facilitating language acquisition is using audiovisual materials and methods. The common threads in their use of AV are to motivate the students and engage their attention, illustrate concepts that are not easily verbalized, and generate activities that require speech and the speaking of English.

Career education includes a unit on personal development, which is a study of maturation and adult behavior. These qualities prepare the students for the career internships (unpaid work training experiences) that are a graduation requirement. The teacher calls it an "experiential" class because of the use of exercises, role play, and collaborative learning (students working cooperatively in groups, talking and interacting with each other).

Kathy Fine and her colleagues often develop teaching ideas spontaneously, creating new activities based on what happens from moment to moment. For example, when her students were working excitedly in groups on the concept of budgets, Fine thought, "This is engaging." And then, "Engaging? Engagement!" She spontaneously proposed to the group that they play a game and pretend they were getting married in class. They went wild over the idea. The teacher immediately integrated it into the personal development course, having them pair off, find common interests, go on a date, hunt for an apartment, look for a job, and set up a budget, using newspapers, books on survival skills, and periodicals. The students wrote scripts, performed short sketches based on their activities, and eventually had to decide whether to get married, live together, be friends, or separate.

Those who "got married" did so in a mock ceremony that was videotaped. The students dressed up, rehearsed, invited other students and teachers as guests, and held a wedding reception. The tape speaks for itself in recording the joyous emotions. In the course of the project most of the young people underwent deep changes in their relationships with the opposite sex, attitudes toward career and life planning, and their ability to gather information through the use of standard reading materials.

Although the video was mainly of value as a record, Fine also uses commercial tapes, such as a documentary on Martin Luther King, as part of her career education curriculum. She was able to connect the material on King to the Equal Employment Opportunities Act and to such issues as racism in the workplace. "For students who have no American historical or cultural context, who don't know anything about the civil rights movement, Martin Luther King means nothing to them without some visuals to back it up. Pictures and action are very important to them."

A tape made in-house at LaGuardia to illustrate the job interview process was also very useful for career education. The tape showed two interviews, one good and one bad, and effectively and very directly demonstrated the concepts Fine was trying to get across.

Hollywood feature films are also shown in class, such as *Moscow on the Hudson*, which humorously illustrates the problems of employment for immigrants. Other titles that have workplace themes are *Nine to Five*, *Working Girl*, and *The Secret of My Success*.

When the class expressed an interest in music videos, Fine created a project in which they selected the one they liked the best and wrote down the words to the song while watching the video. It then became a listening exercise, enabling the students to make connections from the action and scenery to the words of the song. Traditional American folk and country music about work serves a similar purpose: songs about labor unions, railroads, coal mining, canal boating, and factory closings.

In general, Fine relies heavily on the use of material that is suggested by the students. Each cycle may be different as she explores their interests and experiences and then uses them as a starting point to find material with a career or workplace theme.

Marcia Slater's task of teaching literature is made more difficult by the students' vastly diverse educational backgrounds, ranging from those who are illiterate to those who read brilliantly in their native languages. One method she uses to bridge this gap is to show a video based on a novel or story. She finds that video is a means of conveying the human element of literature to the students, who view it before they read, while they are reading, and after they read. "Video gives so much information in one frame—on costumes, on setting, on the whole period, that you can't get from words." And she feels the images convey much more of the context than do the words by themselves.

Listening to standard English speech also helps students to model their own use of the English language. Even if they do not understand every word, they absorb the accent, intonation, gestures, and body language—all of which may differ from those of their own culture. Listening/viewing activities provide an alternative activity and take some of the pressure off students who have to function hour after hour in a different language. Slater also feels that the entertainment value of film and video provides a change of pace and alleviates boredom.

New students start out with the Longman taped books that they listen to while reading along, stopping the tape to ask questions and make notes for writing activities. But textbooks in the English class are used mostly as supplementary material, with preference given to something brought in from home or made up in class. Video provides the English teacher with extraordinary flexibility, such as the ability to videotape students as they conduct interviews with each other or make presentations that are then shown to other classes. A lesson on prejudice included a screening of *West Side Story*, after which the students were required to write from the point of view of different characters and explain how they felt and why they acted the way they did. A rich source for teaching poetry is recordings of American folk songs, as everyone enjoys singing along with the words visible on an overhead projecter.

Stacia Robbins, the social studies teacher, uses such techniques as collaborative learning and what she calls preteaching, which involves prescreening the film or tape she intends to use and targeting particular words, ideas, and idioms to explain before showing the film. She believes that teenagers of the television age are not as media aware as they are thought to be, but have to be taught to analyze, evaluate, and focus on what they are viewing. This is particularly true for students who are struggling with language; by prescreening, the teacher can help them to focus on various aspects of the film.

Robbins has reasons similar to those of her colleagues for teaching with video and film: "You see something moving and alive; you see people really doing something, history unfolding. It's much more alive than just the words on the page." Reading is particularly hard for second language students, and she will choose to show a video of *Red Badge of Courage* (Stephen Crane's novel about the Civil War) in order to illustrate visually "the personal cost, the clothing, the time period, the kind of war. It doesn't come through by just reading a dry text, and when you're going through a lot of historical and cultural information for kids who are not American, there's not enough time to read books on every time period we teach."

Robbins shows the film in small sections, stopping at an exciting moment, and then discussing the action that students must write about in film logs. Rather than a summary, she asks them to describe their emotional reaction to a character or scene. She selects material mainly based on content, even if the level of difficulty is beyond their abilities. For example, she showed *Controlling Interests*, a film about multinational corporations' exploitation of the Third World, combined with a chapter from *Food First*, a book about the Nestle Company's marketing of baby formula in Third World countries. With intensive discussions, the students were able to understand, even though the film itself was beyond their level.

Another interesting activity came out of the students' own positive reactions to media as a teaching/learning tool. When asked to speak on such subjects as immigration, urbanization, civil rights, war, and women's history, the students were encouraged to use a combination of visuals and books as their source material. On their own initiative, many of them came to the library's media center and selected such tapes as *Dreams of Distant Shores* (about immigration to the United States), *Hiroshima/Nagasaki* (two Japanese cities on which the atomic bomb was dropped), *Hearts and Minds* (about Vietnam), and *Eyes on the Prize* (a series on the civil rights movement). They previewed and selected sections to show in class, inspired by their newly found media awareness.

The teacher of integrated learning skills (the English as a Second Language component of the curriculum) is one of the most prolific and proficient users of Media Services. Simon Cohen, like his colleagues, stresses engagement, promoted by a demonstrated need or interest of the student. He uses video to achieve this goal because "it presents analogies to their lives, presents events that are very close to them, on a small enough screen so that they can make the emotional connections, without feeling threatened. Video offers a way to see a world that they might not normally see."

The traditional use of textbook exercises, in his opinion, "is outdated and needs to be buried." Instead, Cohen uses material that presents itself spontaneously, which provides "something to spark, to hook, to catch them each day." For example, an unfamiliar piece of equipment or a visitor to the classroom might serve as an instant source of information and instruction. Media material also serves the purpose of enlarging their worldview, for example:

A Japanese samurai film that counteracts a stereotype in that the lovers in the film are from different cultures while the enemies are from within the same culture. Normally, his students expect the opposite to be true, and they are astounded to see a multiethnic group connecting in a positive way.

A film called *Maricella*, about an immigrant girl with whom students could strongly identify.

Laurel and Hardy's *The Music Box*, to generate discussions about friendship.

Chaplin's silent shorts, such as *The Immigrant*, to focus on expression and gestures representative of American culture.

West Side Story, for its cross-cultural theme.

El Norte, a story of Hispanic immigrants.

Stand and Deliver, because it deals with relevant student issues and problems.

Most of these titles are available in the Media Services collection, but tapes are also rented from local video stores or taped off the air (sources that are legal within certain limitations).

Cohen's other uses of video range from simply freezing the frame at a point where there is expression on a character's face so that students can describe the feelings that are revealed to complex projects involving complete video pre- to postproduction. By taping plays and sketches dealing with their immigration experience, students get involved in a more active way, not only sharing but overcoming shyness and fear of appearing on camera. His class has created a music video on immigration—writing words to a song, developing the action to go with it, and adding scenes of the school in action. The editing was done in the television studio with the assistance of Media Services staff.

The students have also created an informational tape for new teachers showing school events and activities; a tape for new students called *Internship: What Is It?* which uses footage of students at their work site demonstrating and talking about their activities; and a tape illustrating IHS teaching/learning techniques that will be shown at conferences. Other tapes simply record a class period for the teacher to review and study his or her own style and teaching techniques.

Most of these activities come out of no set curriculum; the ideas come organically out of issues that are raised at the moment. The benefits of giving this prodigious amount of class and personal time to video production include developing the students' technological and artistic skills, reasoning ability, and imagination. But Cohen places motivation at the core of it all: "Without the engagement, without the involvement, nothing is going to occur. The root is the human relationship, the involvement, the engagement, and then all things are possible."

Each of these teachers, as well as their other colleagues within the International High School, uses highly creative methods for teaching students of limited English reading and speaking ability, but none that could not be duplicated by any dedicated instructor in almost any secondary school, anywhere in the world. It's tempting to use words such as "gifted" and "outstanding" to describe these talented individuals, but they are teachers first and foremost and surely their motivation is shared by teachers everywhere. As librarians, we have the opportunity to encourage and support these endeavors with the resources at our command: collections, equipment, facilities, appropriate materials—in a word, services—to help teachers attain their individual educational objectives.

NOTES

1. "A New Plan to Combine High School and College," *New York Times*, December 3, 1972.
2. *Liberty Partnerships Program*, Arthur Greenberg, Project Coordinator, LaGuardia Community College. Submitted to the University of the State of New York, State Education Department, April 3, 1989, p. 5.
3. Ibid., p. 6.
4. *Beyond High School Graduation Requirements: What Do Students Need to Learn at the International High School?* Marcia Slater, ed. New York: LaGuardia Community College, 1987/88, p. 55.
5. *After Three Years: A Status Report on the International High School at LaGuardia Community College.* Janet Leiberman et al. New York: LaGuardia Community College, 1988, pp. 18–19.
6. Statement of educational philosophy, International High School.

8
Readability Factors and Methods for Determining Reading Levels

Patsy H. Perritt

Even though readability formulas are being used more widely than ever before in schools, libraries, business, newspapers, and government, there are critics who argue for their disuse.[1]

This chapter will discuss the factors that determine the reading difficulty level of prose and the applications of evaluative methods for making such determinations for classroom and library settings. Current use of readability formulas will be surveyed.

NEED FOR DETERMINING READING DIFFICULTY LEVELS

Reluctant and disabled readers have very little motivation to read. This is a regrettable, yet understandable, situation. Anyone who finds any activity difficult, frustrating, and not pleasurable is unlikely to voluntarily participate in that activity on a regular basis. As a rule, we pursue those activities that give us a feeling of accomplishment and enjoyment, rather than those that are hard and bear little reward.

Teachers and librarians know the practical benefits and numerous pleasures derived from reading, but there are many who show little interest in developing or practicing such a necessary skill. Because reading is a survival skill for life in modern society, we continue to search for ways to break the deadlock against the development of reading skills. Common sense tells us to start at the beginning. As in all learning situations, initial experiences should be simplified to ensure success until the ability or motivation of the learner improves. This principle underlies the need to determine readability—low motivation calls for materials on a low level of difficulty.[2] On the other hand, high motivation can overcome high levels of difficulty, as illustrated by the virtually nonreading teen who pores over a driver training manual in order to pass the test for a license. One reading researcher has suggested that two years is the approximate jump in reading level that a highly motivated reader can make.[3]

FACTORS INFLUENCING READING DIFFICULTY

"This book is too hard" (and numerous variations on the same theme) are familiar words to teachers and librarians. The teenager who makes such a pronouncement has made an estimate of the book's readability and has passed judgment on his or her own ability related to the difficulty of the materials. A number of factors influence the degree of difficulty for the individual reader. Some of these are inherent in the language: vocabulary and levels of meaning, sentence length, sentence structure, complexity of concepts and levels of abstraction, and variations in format and organization. Other factors are unique to the reader: interest, motivation, language competence, and experiential background.

METHODS FOR DETERMINING READING LEVELS

For many years reading specialists have sought ways of summarizing and objectively reporting on the difficulty of written material. One of the most common approaches has been, and continues to be, the use of readability formulas. These calculations typically rely on word length, word frequency, and sentence length because researchers have determined that these are important quantitative measures in predicting readability. The scores are usually based on sample passages taken from various parts of the texts and they represent an estimate of the reading difficulty of the full text. The results of these formulas are expressed as grade levels, but the grade-level scores are not intended to be taken as precise indicators or absolutes. Some researchers recommend that a readability level be considered as a point within a range of plus or minus one full grade level.[4]

Two of the most frequently used formulas for the elementary levels are the Fry Formula for Estimating Readability (see pp. 96–97) and the Spache Readability Formula. Those appropriate for use beyond the elementary level are the Raygor Readability Estimate (third grade–professional),[5] the Dale-Chall formula (fourth grade–college),[6,7] the Flesch Reading Ease formula (fifth grade–college),[8] the Gunning "Fog Index" (secondary–adult),[9] and the SMOG Readability Formula (middle grades and up).[10] Although these different formulas can yield slightly different readability scores for a given written work, all have been tested successfully for validity and the results can be used as one factor in evaluating the approximate difficulty of materials.

Because of the length and complication of most readability formulas, librarians and teachers have traditionally left calculating to reading researchers and specialists. However, when Edward B. Fry introduced his relatively quick readability formula, which requires only a few simple mathematical calculations,[11] the use of a formula to determine reading difficulty became more attractive. The Fry formula received additional visibility for librarians and teachers when Fry published an article in *School Libraries* entitled "A Readability Graph for Librarians, Part I."[12] In the 1984 *Handbook of Reading Research* George Klare states: "In fact, it seems safe to say that it [the Fry] is one of the most, if not the most, widely used of all current methods."[13]

Use of the Fry formula is recommended because it is easy and fairly quick, even when calculated manually, and is suitable for lower level (grade one) materials through college levels. The directions for manual calculation of the Fry readability formula are included in this chapter. They are taken from "Fry's Readability Graph: Clarifications, Validity, and Extension to Level 17."[14] A handy sliding scale, which can be used instead of plotting the graph, is available from Jamestown Publishers.[15] Also available from Jamestown is an extensive article on clarifications, research, and new uses of the graph, along with references.[16] Of special interest is notification of the availability of a Spanish version of Fry, known as FRASE (Fry Readability and Spanish Equivalent).[17]

It should be noted that the Spache formula, which is lengthy, does provide more precise grade-level designations from grades 1 through 3 and is preferable when reading levels that are more exact than one whole grade designation are needed. For example, a reading teacher who is seeking materials on a lower third-grade level would apply the Spache formula to identify such materials. (Directions for the Spache formula are included in *Good Reading for Poor Readers*.[18]) For most purposes, however, the Fry formula establishes reading level designations as successfully as the longer formulas.

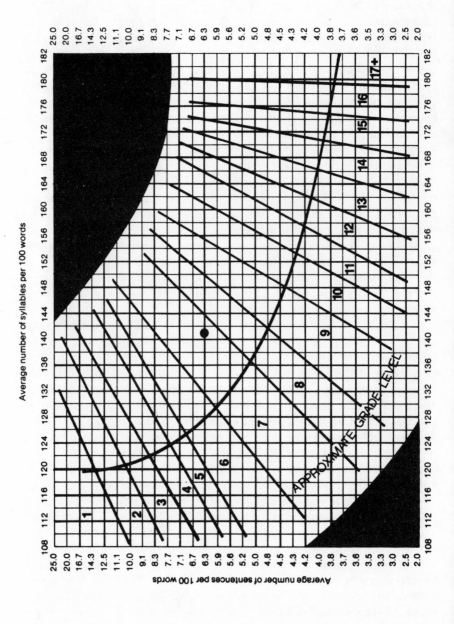

Average number of syllables per 100 words

Average number of sentences per 100 words

APPROXIMATE GRADE LEVEL

GRAPH FOR ESTIMATING READABILITY—EXTENDED
by Edward B. Fry, Rutgers University Reading Center, New Brunswick, NJ 08904

Expanded Directions for Working Readability Graph

1. Randomly select three (3) sample passages and count out exactly 100 words each, beginning with the beginning of a sentence. Do count proper nouns, initializations, and numerals.

2. Count the number of sentences in the hundred words, estimating length of the fraction of the last sentence to the nearest one-tenth.

3. Count the total number of syllables in the 100-word passage. If you don't have a hand counter available, an easy way is to simply put a mark above every syllable over one in each word, then when you get to the end of the passage, count the number of marks and add 100. Small calculators can also be used as counters by pushing numeral 1, then push the + sign for each word or syllable when counting.

4. Enter graph with *average* sentence length and *average* number of syllables; plot dot where the two lines intersect. Area where dot is plotted will give you the approximate grade level.

5. If a great deal of variability is found in syllable count or sentence count, putting more samples into the average is desirable.

6. A word is defined as a group of symbols with a space on either side; thus, *Joe, IRA, 1945,* and *&* are each one word.

7. A syllable is defined as a phonetic syllable. Generally, there are as many syllables as vowel sounds. For example, *stopped* is one syllable and *wanted* is two syllables. When counting syllables for numerals and initializations, count one syllable for each symbol. For example, *1945* is four syllables, *IRA* is three syllables, and *&* is one syllable.

Note: This "extended graph" does not outmode or render the earlier (1968) version inoperative or inaccurate; it is an extension.

(Reproduction permitted—No copyright.)

97

COMPUTER READABILITY DETERMINATIONS

Readability estimation programs are readily available for microcomputers, and it is possible to obtain difficulty levels of passages and/or entire books simply by typing or scanning text. There are programs that calculate readability based on only one method or on a number of methods simultaneously, such as *Readability Formulas** (2nd ed., 1989) for Apple II or IBM, which uses six formulas: Fog, SMOG, Flesch, Fry, Raygor, and Revised Spache. Almost every major formula has been computerized, and this allows use of a number of methods that have been previously utilized by only a few because of the complexity of the procedures.

Computers accomplish syllable, word, and sentence counts, as well as word matches and frequency, more quickly and less tediously than a person can count and compare, but users should note that passages of text must be typed in correctly or scanned or input from another text file, such as a document created on a word processing program, before calculations can be made. If a text file is not available, or scanning is not possible, the segment of the computer program that deals with text input should be scrutinized. Some programs lack convenient means for entering text samples and some lack an easy way to correct typing errors. These are important considerations in the evaluation of a computerized readability program.

LIMITATIONS OF READABILITY FORMULA APPLICATIONS

Perhaps the greatest inadequacy of all readability formulas, manual or computerized, lies in the fact that they only assess quantitative features of the written word. None includes the reader as part of the determination process. To date no formula has been developed that reflects the interaction between a reader and the reading material, nor has any formula been devised that includes some of the most powerful predictors of readability: interest, motivation, language competence, and experiential background.

Formulas produce only part of the information needed to successfully match a reader with appropriate material. What about the reading ability or skill of the reader? Unless a teacher or librarian has had a great deal of experience with graded materials and readers, it is practically impossible for him or her to determine a reader's functional reading level. Thus we must rely on various types of evaluation that indicate the

---

*Looking Glass Learning Products, Inc., 865 Busse Hwy., Park Ridge, IL 60068, 312-698-0292.

reader's level. If test scores or other evaluations are not available, this simple measure can be useful. Have the reader select a page at random in a book that has been graded by a readability formula and begin reading at the top of the page. Each time the reader encounters an unknown word, he or she puts a finger down. If all the fingers on one hand are down before the bottom of the page is read and if the reader is not able to recall main ideas from the page, the material is probably too hard for that reader and an easier selection should be made. This quick assessment is informally referred to as the "Greasy Hand Readability Test." It can be used by readers to help them locate materials at their level.

Matching readability levels of materials and reading achievement of students will not always result in comprehension or enjoyment. Often, the style in which a book is written makes it inappropriate for a disabled or reluctant reader. Flashbacks, metaphors, and inverted sentence construction are examples of unacceptable style.[19] The same may be said for choppy construction and hackneyed, inane, or just plain dull plots. Readability formulas cannot give the full picture of a written work.

Another word of caution. Formulas were not designed for specialized texts. Each field has its own unique and necessary terminology and an abundance of words like *aerodynamics* can render a formula useless. Also, frequent use of numbers, charts, and graphs makes the use of a formula impractical.

CRITICS OF READABILITY FORMULAS

In the mid-1980s the International Reading Association and the National Council of Teachers of English issued warnings about the use of readability formulas. They were particularly concerned about the application of formulas to reading and English texts.[20] Even the creators of the formulas acknowledge that calculations on limited variables cannot take into account such factors as writing quality and subject content or a reader's background knowledge. Edward Fry, who developed the Fry Readability Graph, issued a challenge to the critics in the *Journal of Reading* when he maintained: "Certainly readability formulas have limitations, but so has not using them."[21]

Although not intended as a direct criticism of the use of readability formulas, it should be noted that the review journal *Booklist* has discontinued Fry calculations on books reviewed for the "Easy Reading" reviews of children's books, a column that appears several times a year, and has discontinued the "High/Low" section on young adult books altogether. A look at the *Booklist* reviews of titles at the lower reading levels of third and fourth grades, which were selected for the 1989 "Recommended Books for the Reluctant Reader," reveals that only one of the titles was identified as appropriate for the reluctant reader and only one of the titles had a reading level notation. This lack of information in one of the major review journals for the library field will make it more difficult for librarians to identify low reading level materials.

TRADE PUBLISHERS AND READABILITY FORMULAS

An informal survey of publishers of titles that have appeared on the annual list of recommended titles for reluctant readers from the American Library Association yielded a variety of responses to questions about their company's use of formulas. Some indicated that they use the services of outside companies that apply a number of formulas, mostly by computer, several have employed outside consultants, and at least one said that they use the commercially available sliding scale of the Fry. These results show a wide variety of techniques used by publishers and should alert consumers to the generality of reading designations found in publishers' catalogs and/or in a few incidents on the verso of the title page.

Judith Druse, chair of the Recommended Books for the Reluctant Young Adult Reader Committee of the Young Adult Services Division of the American Library Association, suggests that each teacher or librarian use publishers' designations with caution and that a suitable method of readability estimation be employed consistently in the local setting. (Since its inception, this evaluation committee has used the Fry Readability Graph.)

RECOMMENDATIONS FOR USE OF READABILITY FORMULAS

Keeping in mind that readability levels determined by formulas are *estimates* and the shortcomings previously noted, the use of a readability formula is still recommended for teachers and librarians. Some indication of the difficulty of reading materials is necessary in order to avoid giving readers materials that will continue to frustrate them and reinforce their sense of failure.[22] The number of successful encounters with reading can be significantly increased if readability levels are known and appropriate materials are made available to the readers.

Greater use of readability formulas may also have the desirable side effect of increasing confidence and cooperation between teachers and librarians. Utilization of these professional tools could facilitate more sharing of resources and exchange of knowledge about readers and reading materials. This quotation from a textbook for reading teachers emphasizes the need for such cooperation:

> Periodically during the school year, classroom teachers should provide the media specialist with current information about the reading level of each student; the media specialist must also know the readability level of the materials in the library.[23]

Readability levels can be indicators of possible uses of materials. For example, a random sampling of picture books and easy-to-read books from the children's room of a major public library yielded reading ability levels from grades 1 to 7.[24] This wide range of reading levels indicates that not all of these books would be considered as independent reading for all the young children who typically frequent the picture book section of the library. Some of these books would be more appropriately recommended as books to be read aloud to children by adults. Likewise, teachers can benefit from knowledge of readability levels in determining the most appropriate uses of texts and supplementary reading material.

Readability formulas add an objective element to the analysis of readability, and as such, are among the most important criteria that should be applied in the evaluation of materials for disabled and reluctant readers.

NOTES

1. Edward B. Fry, "Reading Formulas—Maligned but Valid," *Journal of Reading* 32, no. 4 (January 1989): 292.
2. Edward B. Fry, "The Readability Principle," *Language Arts* 52, no. 6 (September 1975): 847–851.
3. Sidney W. Shnayer, "Relationships between Reading Interest and Reading Comprehension," in *Reading and Realism,* ed. J. Allen Figurel (Newark, DE: International Reading Association, 1969), pp. 698–702.
4. Joseph L. Vaughn, Jr., "Interpreting Readability Assessments," *Journal of Reading* 19, no. 8 (May 1976): 635–639.
5. Alton L. Raygor, "The Raygor Readability Estimate: A Quick and Easy Way to Determine Difficulty," in *Reading: Theory, Research and Practice,* ed. P. David Pearson, Twenty-sixth Yearbook of the National Reading Conference (Clemson, SC: National Reading Conference, 1977), pp. 259–263.
6. Edgar Dale and Jeanne Chall, "A Formula for Predicting Readability," *Educational Research Bulletin* 27, January 21, 1948, pp. 11–20.
7. Edgar Dale and Jeanne Chall, "A Formula for Predicting Readability: Instructions," *Educational Research Bulletin* 27, February 18, 1948, pp. 37–54.
8. Rudolf Flesch, *How to Test Readability* (New York: Harper & Row, 1951).

9. Robert Gunning, *The Technique of Clear Writing* (New York: McGraw-Hill, 1968), pp. 37–39.
10. G. McLaughlin, "SMOG Grading—A New Readability Formula," *Journal of Reading* 12, no. 8 (May 1969): 639–646.
11. Edward B. Fry, "A Readability Formula That Saves Time," *Journal of Reading* 11, no. 7 (April 1968): 513–516, 575–578.
12. Edward B. Fry, "A Readability Graph for Librarians, Part I," *School Libraries* 19, no. 1 (Fall 1969): 13–16.
13. P. David Pearson et al., eds. *Handbook of Reading Research* (New York: Longman, 1984), p. 691.
14. Edward B. Fry, "Fry's Readability Graph: Clarifications, Validity, and Extension to Level 17," *Journal of Reading* 21, no. 3 (December 1977): 242–251.
15. Edward B. Fry, *Fry Readability Scale (Extended)* (Jamestown Publishers, Box 9168, Providence, RI 02940. 1-800-USA-READ. $5.00).
16. Edward B. Fry, *Fry's Readability Graph: Clarifications, Research and New Uses* (Providence, RI: Jamestown Publishers, n.d.), 4 pp.
17. P. Vari-Cartier, "The Readability and Comprehensibility of Spanish Prose Materials as Determined by the FRASE Graph and the Cloze Procedure," unpublished dissertation, Rutgers University, New Brunswick, NJ, 1979.
18. George D. Spache, *Good Reading for Poor Readers* (Champaign, IL: Garrard, 1978), pp. 185–197.
19. [Stephanie Zvirin], "A High-Low Perspective," *Booklist*, September 15, 1979, pp. 111–112.
20. Bernice Cullinan and Sheila Fitzgerald, "IRA, NCTE Take Stand on Readability Formula," *Reading Today* 2, no. 3 (December 1984/January 1985): 1.
21. Fry, "Reading Formulas—Maligned but Valid," p. 295.
22. Judith Goldberger, "Some Changes and Clarifications," *Booklist*, April 15, 1979, p. 1301.
23. Martha Collins-Cheek and Earl H. Cheek, Jr., *Diagnostic-Prescriptive Reading Instruction: A Guide for Classroom Teachers*, 2nd ed. (Dubuque, IA: William C. Brown, 1984), p. 14.
24. Adrianne P. Hunt and Janet R. Reuter, "Readability and Children's Picture Books," *Reading Teacher* 32, no. 1 (October 1978): 23–27.

FURTHER REFERENCES

Blanchard, Jay S., and others. *Computer Applications in Reading*, 3rd ed. Newark, DE: International Reading Association, 1987.

Cheek, Earl H., Jr., and Martha Collins-Cheek. *Reading Instruction through Content Teaching*. Columbus, OH: Merrill, 1983, pp. 250–269.

Cheek, Earl H., Jr., and others. *Reading for Success in Elementary Schools*. Fort Worth, TX: Holt, Rinehart & Winston, 1989, pp. 486–490.

Fitzgerald, Gisela G. "Reliability of the Fry Sampling Procedure." *Reading Research Quarterly* 15, no. 4 (1980): 489–503.

Fry, Edward B. "The Readability Principle." *Language Arts* 52, no. 6 (September 1975): 847–851.

Gross, Philip, and Karen Sadowski. "Fog Index—A Readability Formula Program for Microcomputers." *Journal of Reading* 28, no. 7 (April 1985): 614–618.

Handy, Alice Evans. "The Quest for Quality High/Low Fiction." *The Book Report* 2, no. 2 (September/October 1983): 22–26.

Klare, George A. "Assessing Readability." *Reading Research Quarterly* 10, no. 1 (1974–75): 62–102.

Kretschmer, Joseph C. "Computerizing and Comparing the Rix Readability Index." *Journal of Reading* 27, no. 6 (March 1984): 490–499.

Munat, Florence Howe. "A Checklist for High/Low Books for Young Adults." *School Library Journal* 27, no. 8 (April 1981): 23–27. Discussion. *School Library Journal* 27, no. 10 (August 1981): 3.

Nelson, Joan. "Readability: Some Cautions for the Content Area Teacher." *Journal of Reading* 13, no. 3 (December 1969): 207–210.

Pauk, W. "A Practical Note on Readability Formulas." *Journal of Reading* 13, no. 3 (December 1969): 207–210.

Perritt, Patsy H. "High Interest/Low Reading Level Materials." In *Reaching Young People through Media* by Nancy Bach Pillon. Littleton, CO: Libraries Unlimited, 1983, pp. 60–68.

Readance, John E., and others. *Content Area Reading: An Integrated Approach.* Dubuque, IA: Kendal/Hunt, 1989.

Schuyler, Michael. "Computer Applications of Readability." *ACCESS: Microcomputers in Libraries* 2, no. 2 (April 1982): 12–19.

———. "Extending Schuyler's Program." *Journal of Reading* 26, no. 6 (March 1983): 550–552.

———. "A Readability Formula Program for Use on Microcomputers." *Journal of Reading* 35, no. 6 (March 1982): 572–589.

Zakaluk, Beverly L., and S. Jay Samuels. *Readability: Its Past, Present, and Future.* Newark, DE: International Reading Association, 1988.

ORGANIZATIONS

American Library Association. Recommended Books for the Reluctant Young Adult Reader Committee. Publication: annual list of recommended books appropriate for reluctant young adult readers. Contact: Young Adult Services Division, 50 E. Huron St., Chicago, IL 60611.

International Reading Association. Readability Special Interest Group. Membership $2 per year. Newsletter: *Emphasis Readability.* Contact: Annette Rabin, 1100 E. Lincoln Hwy., Coatsville, PA 19320.

———. Special Interest Group on Microcomputers & Reading. Contact: Kent Layton, Dept. of Elementary Education, P.O. Box 940, State University, AR 72467.

Part III
The Core Collection

9
High/Low Books for the Disabled Reader

Ellen V. LiBretto

This chapter's core collection of high interest–low reading level titles contains a recommended list of titles for the development of a high interest–low reading level resource library for any group serving the disabled adolescent reader. All titles are in print; in addition, many are especially useful as a component in English as a Second Language programs. Teenage disabled readers are those whose scores fall below the fourth-grade level on reading tests. This collection has been prepared as a selection tool and literature guide for those public and school librarians, teachers, tutors, and other youth workers who need to provide easy reading material for their clientele.

The following checklist of evaluation criteria illustrates the variety of questions that were considered in selecting material for this core collection and in preparing the annotations. Most titles reviewed were identified by their publisher as high interest–low reading level, although some were published for a general teenage audience and were included because they happen to be easy to read.

CHECKLIST OF EVALUATION CRITERIA

Is the appearance of the book suitable for teenagers?

Are there photographs or pictures of *teenagers*—or of children? Do they reflect the content of the book accurately?

Do photographs or illustrations contribute to the pace and texture of the narrative?

Are photographs or illustrations a substitute for characterization? If they were removed, could the book stand on its own?

Is the type overly large or set in wide margins to look like a reader? Or is the type set in regular sentence and paragraph arrangement?

Is the book awkward in shape (e.g., square) or unconventional in design (e.g., printed on glossy paper), setting it apart from other books geared to this age group?

Does the subject have teenage appeal? Is the topic current or of immediate interest to teenagers (e.g., roller skating, disco, popular sports)?

Can young people identify with the premise of the book?

If the subject is alien to teenage interest (e.g., historical or scientific), does the book have potential as adjunct reading for school courses or book reports?

Is the book a "first" book on a topic?

Does the book cover its subject with enough depth to stimulate interest for the disabled reader to want to read further?

Can the book serve as a bridge to more difficult material on the subject?

Does the book deliver what it promises?

Is the story censored?

If the book is a biography, are important facts about the figure's personal life omitted or brushed off? Is the portrait realistic?

If the book is fiction, does it compare favorably with other junior novels? Does it contain similar themes and characters?

Is the tone condescending or overly juvenile?

Is the publisher's reading level designation correct?

Are difficult words defined in the text?

If the book has a glossary or index, does this add significantly to the book's usefulness or does it make the book seem like a school text?

Most important, is the book *readable?*

These guidelines were originally developed in 1978 by the Committee of High Interest/Low Reading Level Materials Evaluation of the American Library Association's Young Adult Services Division. The guidelines are still in effect as the primary selection criteria for this third edition.

Central to all selection criteria is that the book be readable by its intended audience: the reading-disabled adolescent. The revised Fry Readability Formula has been applied to all titles here, and the reading level is included in the annotation as a guide to the user. In cases where the publisher's reading level indicator differed from the compiler's findings, the range of reading levels has been noted. (Titles with technical or scientific terms or acronyms tend to raise the reading level of certain passages of the text.) Books with Fry reading levels through the fifth-grade range have been included in this third edition of this core collection. The interest level designation indicates grade level interest for most teenagers; however, because there is such a wide range of maturity levels among adolescents, judgment is critical when recommending titles for individual teenagers.

In selecting fiction titles, emphasis has been placed on identifying books that reflect the American adolescent experience and that are of interest to an ethnically diverse population. In choosing nonfiction titles, I have listed many "just say no" and sports books, which are in preponderance in high/low literature; but there is also an abundance of titles written on a low reading level that express the powerful feelings of love, loss, and competition that identify the teenager. Such books are of tremendous concern because they offer an opportunity for reflection and conflict resolution for the reader. The editor was fortunate to locate titles that portray characters and themes of great passion: for example, *Push to the West* (Reiff), the journey of Norwegians to the West; *Better Off without Me* (Coret), a young mother's struggle with depression and alcoholism; and *Stallone* (Eichhorn), the biography of Sylvester Stallone and his struggle to express his creativity. And, indeed, there are titles of great compassion: In *Bride in Pink* (Bosley), Bonnie struggles with jealousy and a broken leg while trying to be a Children's Friend in a hospital; in *Speaking Out on Health* (Literacy Volunteers of New York City), literacy students write simply and earnestly about their health problems and how they have overcome them; and *My Name Is Rose* (Doiron) is the true story of a young woman's plight over an abusive father. These titles are not only easy reads but also serve as a springboard in the creation of a meaningful reading ladder for reluctant readers. They offer a way out for many at-risk teens, who are usually disabled readers. For many teenagers, living in isolation from the greater society, this first step in reading can also be a big step in personal growth.

I am particularly impressed by and thankful for some of the new and expanded output from many of the publishers included in this chapter. Among them, Literacy Volunteers of New York City, which has published small volumes (Writers' Voices Series) of easy-reading excerpts from such modern classics as *Love Medicine* (Erdrich), *Bless Me, Ultima* (Anaya), and *Fatherhood* (biography of Bill Cosby); New Readers Press, whose real lifelike fiction shows teenagers and adults dealing with real-life problems (depression, death, job loss, learning English); Fearon Press, whose broad range of easy-reading titles span the whole spectrum of literature, giving us science fiction, mysteries, and stories about the immigrant experience; and Turman Publishing, whose authors give the teenager an insider's look into the lives of sports heroes, rock stars, and other celebrities. Also, Scholastic Press is putting its Action series back in print in early 1990. These titles are models of easy-reading material, and their revised editions will be much used by their intended audience.

Since the publication of the first edition of *High/Low Handbook*, in 1981, many publishers have developed thematic series of a number of high/low titles—for instance, sports, biographies, love stories, and spy stories—and when this occurs, one title in the series is given an extensive summary and any other additional titles in the series that meet the checklist criteria are listed. Because series titles can be uneven, not all series titles may be cited.

Periodicals published for the disabled adolescent reader are of increasing importance. They are readily available for teenage purchase at drugstores, supermarkets, and bus terminals and are also forming an increasingly large part of the holdings of school and public library collections. A list of magazines to captivate the eyes of even the most recalcitrant teenager is in Chapter 6, "Periodicals Power: Magazines for Reluctant Readers."

Excluded from this chapter are books that are juvenile in design, format, or content; books with overly large or unattractive typefaces; and books that depict children rather than teenagers in illustrations or photographs. Workbooks and prepackaged kits geared for classroom use are also excluded. Many of the titles come with audiocassettes, reproducible worksheets for classroom use, and so on; such items have not been evaluated.

For each entry, the annotation serves a dual purpose: It is an aid to selection when purchasing, as well as a brief introduction to the scope of the book for use in booktalks or reader guidance. This chapter, greatly expanded for this third edition, represents a selected list of the best high interest–low reading level titles, most of which have been published between 1985 and 1990. These titles are recommended for use with low reading level teenagers in an independent reading situation. Although some of the titles are useful for the teenager just beginning to read, the major thrust in title selection has been to provide public and school librarians and teachers with a list of titles for teenagers with some reading skills. (Out-of-print titles listed in the first and second editions have been omitted.) A directory of the publishers of high/low titles that were used in this chapter appears in Appendix I: Core Collection Publishers.

1. **Abbot, Jennie.** *Good-Bye and Hello.* **Fearon, 1987. 64 pp. $3.00 paper (0-8224-2377-4). Fiction.**
   Subjects: New England; Romance
   Reading Level: Grades 4–5   Interest Level: Grades 7–12

Growing up in her beloved Nantucket, 22-year-old Mady, master carpenter, learned early on that living off an island economy was difficult. Dependent on the tourist season for work to carry the residents through the dreary winter months was the goal for all. Going "off island" for work was not appealing for Mady, although more and more of the young people went to Boston in search of steady employment. When Mady's boyfriend, Gary, proposes marriage and a life in Boston, Mady feels her world changing. But, as with many light teen romances, there is another man in the wings—an architect who promises not only love and marriage but an opportunity for Mady to use her expert carpentry skills to renovate one of the larger Nantucket houses. Other titles in the Double Fastback Romance series are *Chance of a Lifetime, Follow Your Dream, Kiss and Make Up, Love in Bloom, A Love to Share, Never Too Late, No Secrets, The Road to Love,* and *A Second Look.*

2. **Abels, Harriette Sheffer.** *The Mystery of Stonehenge.* **Crestwood House, 1987. 48 pp. $10.95 LB (0-89686-346-8). Nonfiction.**
   Subjects: Mysterious phenomena
   Reading Level: Grade 4   Interest Level: Grades 7–12

This is one of eight titles in The Mystery of . . . series that focuses on many of the puzzling phenomena of the ancient and modern worlds. The theories and myths that surround Bigfoot, the Pyramids, Killer Bees, the Loch Ness Monster, Stonehenge, UFOs, the Lost City of Atlantis, and the Bermuda Triangle are all explained using sketchy facts and often out-of-focus photographs to capture a mood and reinforce in true believers a feeling of witnessing the impossible. Teenagers love this genre, and indeed it is an area where fact is most probably fiction, so let teenagers read and come to their own conclusions. Black-and-white and color illustrations complement the text. Glossary and index.

3. *Adventure in Valdez.* Literacy Council of Alaska, 1985. 17 pp. $2.00. Fiction.

Subjects: Alaska

Reading Level: Grades 2–3   Interest Level: Grades 7–12

This is an innocent little tale of two young couples on a fishing trip to Valdez. The line drawings, although amateurish by corporate publishing standards, enhance the text that makes one yearn for the bliss of a weekend of fishing and the cookout that follows. Included is a recipe for halibut steaks: ½ cup butter, 2 tablespoons brown sugar, 1 tablespoon lemon juice, ½ teaspoon curry powder. Instructions: Melt butter. Add brown sugar, lemon juice, and curry powder. Brush sauce over halibut steaks. Baste halibut with sauce as the fish cooks on the grill. Cook approximately 10 minutes per side or until done. An idiom list accompanies the text. Some other titles in the series are *A Cabin in the North, Jake Comes Home, Elma Gets a Job, Friends in Fairbanks,* and *Toi's Story.*

4. Anaya, Rudolfo A. *Selected from Bless Me, Ultima.* Literacy Volunteers of New York City, 1989. 64 pp. $2.95 paper (0-929631-06-4). Fiction.

Subjects: Hispanic Americans; Southwest (U.S.)

Reading Level: Grades 4–5   Interest Level: Grades 7–12

Included here are selected passages from the novel *Bless Me, Ultima* by Rudolfo A. Anaya, who captures the flavor of life in a small New Mexican town and the impact magic has on the lives of its residents. Background information includes a brief history of the Chicano in the Southwest. The interplay of Spanish and English throughout the introduction and the excerpts impart the color of the Southwest and warm the soul. Thoughtful questions append the text. This is a title in the Writers' Voices series.

5. Andersen, T. J. *John Elway.* Crestwood House, 1988. 48 pp. $10.95 LB (0-89686-367-0). Nonfiction.

Subjects: Biographies – Sports; Sports, sports figures – Football

Reading Level: Grades 4–5   Interest Level: Grades 7–12

John Elway is a talented quarterback who became famous overnight when he refused to sign with the team that had chosen him in the NFL draft of college football players. After negotiating a solution to the stalemate, Elway became a member of the Denver Broncos and one of the most exciting players in the game. Besides his skill in football, this biography also shows the strong influence of Elway's family in his life and his support of the Denver community. Numerous black-and-white photographs accompany the text.

6. **Angelou, Maya.** *Selected from I Know Why the Caged Bird Sings and The Heart of a Woman.* **Literacy Volunteers of New York City, 1989. 64 pp. $2.95 paper (0-929631-04-8). Nonfiction.**

Subjects: Biographies – Writers; Black Americans; Women
Reading Level: Grades 4–5   Interest Level: Grades 7–12

Included here are selected excerpts from *I Know Why the Caged Bird Sings* and *The Heart of a Woman*. Maya Angelou's strengths as a woman and her enduring talent as a writer are heard in these excerpts that focus on her early childhood in Stamps, Arkansas, her parenting experiences, and her relationship with her mother. This multifaceted woman speaks about the universalities of life. The writings are preceded by a brief history of the civil rights movement. An appendix lists thoughtful questions to the reader. This is a title in the Writers' Voices series.

7. **Aylesworth, Thomas G.** *Movie Monsters.* **Harper & Row, 1975. 79 pp. $12.70 LB (0-397-31639-9). Nonfiction.**

Subjects: Monsters; Movies
Reading Level: Grades 2–3   Interest Level: Grades 7–9

Young people are fascinated by monster movies. This book devotes brief chapters to some of filmdom's most spectacular monsters, including King Kong, Godzilla, the Mummy, the Wolfman, and Frankenstein's Monster. Each chapter gives basic facts on the film's production and makes some mention of the special effects used. Black-and-white photographs throughout lend substance to a bare-bones text, which also provides brief biographical sketches of the actors who have portrayed monsters: Boris Karloff, Bela Lugosi, Lon Chaney, and John Barrymore, among others. The type is large, and sentence structure is largely simple. Filmography and index included.

8. **Ball, Jacqueline A.** *Everything You Need to Know about Drug Abuse.* **Rosen Group, 1988. 54 pp. $12.95 LB (0-8239-0811-9). Nonfiction.**

Subjects: Drug abuse
Reading Level: Grades 4–6   Interest Level: Grades 7–12

Using excellent quality black-and-white and color photographs, Ball traces the variety of drugs available, from heroin to cocaine to alcohol and caffeine, and examines their abuse and what can be done to prevent it. Tragic events such as the cocaine death of Len Bias are used in ways to demonstrate the dangers of drug abuse. Included are the special and dangerous effects of glue sniffing, smoking, Valium, and marijuana. From time to time the text lapses into a higher reading level, but the photographs are powerful enough to draw the reader in. A glossary appends the text.

9. **Banks, David.** *Sarah Ferguson: The Royal Redhead.* **Dillon, 1987. 63 pp. $9.95 LB (0-87518-369-7). Nonfiction.**
Subjects: Biographies – Royalty; Great Britain; Royalty
Reading Level: Grades 3–4   Interest Level: Grades 7–12

The marriage of Fergie and Andrew is a twentieth-century fairy tale. In this biography of the Duchess of York, teenagers get a close-up view of the everyday lives of royalty. Snapshots of Fergie's common life and her emergence as the partner to the man who is fourth in line to the British throne show us a way of life that most of us see only on film and television. Fergie emerges from these pages as a fun-loving and engaging personality. Color photographs.

10. **Barnett, Cynthia.** *Ben's Gift.* **New Readers, 1990. 62 pp. $3.50 paper (0-88336-210). Fiction.**
Subjects: Cerebral palsy; Disabilities; Physical disabilities
Reading Level: Grade 3   Interest Level: Grades 7–12

Although Ben has cerebral palsy, he is determined to lead a productive and independent life. Unfortunately, the owner of the boardinghouse in which Ben lives, Ben's brother, and the other lodgers only manage to make him feel helpless and alienated. When Ben learns that his brother is planning to take his wife to Hawaii on a second honeymoon, he decides to surprise them with a gift. His present gives them great joy and makes Ben realize that, in spite of the way others treat him, he is capable of doing things on his own. Line drawings.

11. **Baron, Connie.** *The Physically Disabled.* **Crestwood House, 1988. 48 pp. $10.95 LB (0-89686-417-0). Nonfiction.**
Subjects: Disabilities; Physical disabilities
Reading Level: Grades 4–6   Interest Level: Grades 7–12

The many kinds of disabilities that affect people are discussed using photos of disabled teens in sport and social situations. Baron discusses the various diseases and conditions that can cause physical disabilities, including arthritis, multiple sclerosis, muscular dystrophy, cerebral palsy, and visual and hearing impairments. Emphasis is placed on getting the most out of life regardless of the disability, using physicist Stephen W. Hawking as an example of a severely disabled individual who is living life to the fullest as a husband and a parent. Included is information on organizations about the physically disabled. A glossary/index is appended.

12. **Barrett, Norman.** *BMX Bikes.* **Watts, 1987. 32 pp. $10.90 LB (0-531-10272-6). Nonfiction.**
    Subjects: Bicycles; Sports, sports figures
    Reading Level: Grades 3–4   Interest Level: Grades 7–9

BMX Bikes is part of a series of full-page color photographs and beautifully illustrated sports and action titles that give kids the feeling that they are actually participating in the activity. Easy-reading text gives background, facts, and records, including a glossary of terms specific to the activity—for example, speed jump, endo, and whoops. Other titles are *Aircraft Carriers, Helicopters, Motorcycles, Submarines, Trucks, Airliners, Combat Aircraft, Military Helicopters, Racing Cars, Tanks,* and *Warships.*

13. **Bledsoe, Lucy Jane.** *Colony of Fear, Book I: 1692.* **Fearon, 1989. 72 pp. $3.90 paper (0-8224-4751-7). Fiction.**
    Subjects: American history; Historical fiction
    Reading Level: Grades 4–5   Interest Level: Grades 7–12

Colony of Fear is the first of eight volumes about eight generations (200 years) of the Roberts family. In Books I through IV, Bledsoe traces the Roberts family from Colonial times until 1850. S. D. Jones continues the family saga in Books V through VIII, covering the years 1853 to 1920. These slim volumes offer a snapshot view of American history as teenagers learn how the descendants of the Roberts family live through the various stages of our history.

In *Colony of Fear, Book I: 1692,* Samuel Roberts arrives in the new world, apprentices to a shoemaker, marries a minister's daughter, and becomes involved in the witchcraft trials. In *A Matter of Pride, Book II: 1733,* Frances Roberts, daughter of Samuel, marries a southerner. Then, moving to a rice plantation and discovering that she has married a pirate, she resolves to alone build a flourishing plantation. In *Two Kinds of Patriots, Book III: 1778,* the Roberts grandchildren are soldiers at Valley Forge during a harsh winter. They must overcome starvation and deal with traitors in their midst in order to survive. In *The Journey Home, Book IV: 1827,* the fourth generation of the Roberts family is involved in westward expansion. The family saga continues with 19-year-old Nicole Roberts, an orphan, searching for her family roots after her marriage to Wilson Wilder.

14. **Borisoff, Norman.** *The Dropout.* **Scholastic, 1975. 95 pp. $3.93 paper (0-590-02998-3). Fiction.**
    Subjects: Family problems; Jobs, job hunting; School dropouts
    Reading Level: Grades 3–4   Interest Level: Grades 9–12

When Chris's father suffers a heart attack, Chris's life turns upside down and he must accept adult responsibilities overnight. He completely pushes aside thoughts of his girlfriend and an upcoming scholarship and quits school so that he can help support his family. He does what he feels is necessary, but the overwhelming pressure takes its toll on his social and family relationships. Chris learns about himself and some of the realities of the work world when a dreamed-about promotion is given to someone else and an unscrupulous delivery man offers him a tempting but illegal way to make some much-needed extra money. At the end of the book we learn the good news that Chris's father will be coming home from the hospital, will receive half-pay while he's recuperating, and has an office job waiting for him when he's able to return to work. The worry and pressure lifted from his shoulders, Chris can now return to school, accept his scholarship, and start thinking about his own future again. Photographs throughout.

15. **Borisoff, Norman.** *Easy Money.* **Scholastic, 1981. 128 pp. $3.93 paper (0-590-30555-7). Fiction.**
    Subjects: Crime; Jobs, job hunting
    Reading Level: Grade 4   Interest Level: Grades 7–12

For Danny, a recent parolee, finding a job is not easy. When he is accepted with no questions asked as a messenger for a small print shop, he is very happy. But he soon notices that some of the jobs in the shop are illegal. Knowing full well that he is in violation of his parole if he continues to work at the firm, he learns that when there is easy money, there are frequently complicated and illegal activities. His perseverance to get to the source of the firm's difficulties is admirable. Photographs.

16. **Bosley, Judith A.** *Bride in Pink.* **New Readers, 1989. 89 pp. $3.50 paper (0-88336-761-0). Fiction.**
    Subjects: Child abuse; Nursing; Romance
    Reading Level: Grades 2–3   Interest Level: Grades 7–12

In this book we learn that Bonnie's dream has come true: She has the position of "Children's Friend" at Pacific Hospital. And a good friend she is to the many abused, neglected, and accident victim children who come to stay at the hospital. Bonnie's love and attention to these children often contribute to their healing, but her steadfastness and dedication also create feelings of jealousy among the nurses. Bonnie must proceed with caution so as not to fall into ugly traps set up by a mean-spirited coworker who is determined to create conflicts for Bonnie. Bonnie wins out overall because of her unselfish character and in the end wins the hearts of the hospital staff. In this book, not only does Bonnie become a grandmother but she falls in love with male nurse Ken, a man of equal compassion. Illustrated with line drawings.

17. **Bosley, Judith A.** *Don't Sell Me Short.* **New Readers, 1988. 80 pp. $3.50 paper (0-88336-758-0). Fiction.**

Subjects: Jobs, job hunting; Mental disabilities; Romance
Reading Level: Grade 4   Interest Level: Grades 7–12

Richard, a slow learner, graduates from high school after a struggle and enters the army only to be quickly discharged because of low test scores. Shortly after his discharge, his mother dies, his father remarries, and Richard begins to spend time with his grandfather. With his grandfather's encouragement, Richard uses his inheritance from his mother and buys an apartment. The sudden death of his grandfather leaves Richard without a mentor, and eventually he loses his property. He then takes some jobs caring for elderly housebound people and he finds the work both interesting and rewarding. Through the advice of a friend, Richard enrolls in a course to become a nurse's aide. He meets Mary in the same class and they study together. After completing their course they both work in a nursing home. The story ends as Richard and Mary celebrate their wedding with the residents of the nursing home. Charcoal drawings complement the text.

18. **Bosley, Judith A.** *Lady in Pink.* **New Readers, 1990. 64 pp. $3.50 paper (0-88336-212). Fiction.**

Subjects: Child care; Nursing
Reading Level: Grade 3   Interest Level: Grades 9–12

Although Bonnie loves being a housekeeper at Pacific Hospital, she wants to become closer to the children there. Bonnie, who has difficulty adjusting to the death of her husband, is particularly sensitive to the children's loneliness and need for affection. As she talks to each of the children and gets to know them better, they confide in her and look forward to her daily visits. Soon the staff is aware of the kind and loving care the children have been receiving and reward Bonnie by promoting her from housekeeper to "Children's Friend." Because of the bright, new uniform she is given, Bonnie is affectionately dubbed the Lady in Pink. Illustrated with drawings.

19. **Brisco, Pat.** *Campus Mystery.* **Scholastic, 1978. 127 pp. $3.93 paper (0-590-05228-4). Fiction.**

Subjects: Mysteries
Reading Level: Grades 3–4   Interest Level: Grades 9–12

When Clemmie Villalobos takes a job as a clerical assistant in the financial aid office of a junior college, she finds more challenge than she expected. Two young men immediately vie for her attentions. One is a campus policeman and the other is the campus radical. When a fire is set on the campus at night, the campus radical is suspected and arrested.

But who really set the fire? This photograph-filled mystery holds a surprise ending.

20. **Brisco, Pat.** *The Carnival Mystery.* Scholastic, 1974. 95 pp. $3.93 paper (0-590-03407-3). Fiction.

Subjects: Mysteries
Reading Level: Grade 2   Interest Level: Grades 7–9

Bad things have been happening lately to both the people and property of Sander's Carnival. The superstitious among them believe they've been jinxed. But Link, the young runaway who is the carnival's handyman, thinks it's a jinx of the two-legged variety. But who? And why? Link catches the "jinx" red-handed, but not before the reader is given a glimpse of some unusual characters: a midget couple, the fat lady and her husband, the fire-eater. The carnival oddities are portrayed as human beings with whom Link is close friends. Photographs throughout.

21. **Bromley, Dudley.** *Final Warning.* Fearon, 1981. 80 pp. $3.90 paper (0-8224-1932-7). Fiction.

Subjects: Atomic bomb; Science fiction
Reading Level: Grades 2–4   Interest Level: Grades 10–12

A nightmarish fantasy/science fiction about a strange couple that uses nuclear blackmail to extort precious materials. Arriving one night in the mythical Central American country of Santa Roca, Holly Lewis and her scar-faced brother Roman strike a deal with El Presidente to give him an A-bomb and half of their profits in return for sanctuary and his country's natural resources. Not only are the principal characters incinerated in a resulting thermonuclear holocaust but part of the United States is destroyed as well. A horrific prologue and postscript explain the ramifications of the self-styled anarchists' work. A former CIA agent recounts to a young man how he tried to find out what happened to Washington, D.C., as the pair travels East together.

Wildly imaginative; part of the Doomsday Journals series. Prophetically, the moral seems to be that building bigger bombs will never bring any nation closer to peace. Good fare for those who have an interest in Einstein's theory of relativity but need to understand it on a simple level. (A few pages explain the theory of how an atom bomb is constructed.) No illustrations.

Other titles in the Doomsday series by Dudley Bromley are *Fireball, The Seep, Bedford Fever, Lost Valley,* and *Comet.*

22. **Bundy, Kathryn.** *My Friend Ana.* **Kern Adult Literacy Council, nd. 8 pp. $.75. Fiction.**

Subjects: English as a Second Language; Hispanic Americans
Reading Level: Grades 2–3   Interest Level: Grades 7–12

A warm story with a homemade look that will delight many new readers to English as well as young people in tutoring programs. Ana, from Mexico, is learning English the real way. Her friend is teaching her to read by helping her to recognize signs: "Bus Stop," "Exit," "Watch Yourself," "No Smoking." Ana becomes motivated to learn English and to master the printed word when she becomes coated with paint after sitting on a bench with a sign she could not read that said: "Wet Paint!" There are many other simple titles in the Kern Adult Literacy series.

23. **Bunting, Eve.** *Blacksmith at Blueridge.* **Scholastic, 1977. 125 pp. $3.93 paper (0-590-05223-3). Fiction.**

Subjects: Jobs, job hunting; Women
Reading Level: Grades 3–4   Interest Level: Grades 7–10

"You can't keep running away. If you don't face things they grow up like weeds and choke you." That's Mel talking, but what she is saying is as much for her own benefit as her listener's. Mel has been running and hiding ever since a car accident left her with a now almost invisible scar near her left eye. Mel is the new blacksmith at Blueridge Stables, an unusual trade for a woman. The one consolation of her accident was that the insurance money enabled her to attend blacksmith school, buy her own van and tools, and get a job she loves.

There is initial resentment from Paddy, the young, handsome blacksmith already at Blueridge who now shoes almost all 30 horses there and doesn't want an assistant. There is also kind, elderly Benjamin, who has worked at this stable more than 30 years and now can only work on one or two horses a day. And there is beautiful Dee-Dee, the daughter of a rich onetime Olympic jumper. Because of her background, Dee-Dee feels pressured to jump, but is frightened by the near fatal accident of a friend. One of Dee-Dee's desperate schemes to avoid jumping almost costs Mel her hard-earned and much-loved job. A good story about two young women who learn to face up to their different problems.

24. **Bunting, Eve.** *If I Asked You, Would You Stay?* **Harper & Row, 1984. 151 pp. $12.89 LB (0-397-32066-3); $2.75 paper (0-06-447023-7). Fiction.**

Subjects: Romance
Reading Level: Grade 4   Interest Level: Grades 7–10

Seventeen-year-old Crow, Charles Robert O'Neill, sees from his window in an abandoned loft building the flailing figure of a person drowning in the ocean. Summoning all his energies, he grabs a dinghy and heads out to sea to rescue the soggy figure, who turns out to be a young woman named Valentine. An engaging relationship develops between these two very alone and lonely teenagers. Bunting has written this title in a traditional junior novel format. This title, as well as three other Lippincott page-turners, is designed without photos or illustrations but with universal appeal to the general teenage audience as well as the high/low reader. The three others are *The Haunting of Safe-Keep, The Ghosts of Departure Point,* and *The Cloverdale Switch.*

25. **Bunting, Eve.** *Nobody Knows but Me.* **Fearon, 1984. 40 pp. $1.65 paper (0-8224-3531-4). Fiction.**

Subjects: Romance
Reading Level: Grades 4–5   Interest Level: Grades 7–12

This is one title of ten from the Fastback Romance Books series, all written by Eve Bunting. Each title tackles issues that teens experience in dating and romantic entanglements. In *Nobody Knows but Me,* Ellen learns that her fascination with the football jock, Leo, flattens her emotionally, and she takes a second look at George, who seems to understand her feelings. Other titles in the series that leave teens with the understanding that relations with the opposite sex can be a positive learning experience are *Fifteen, For Always, The Girl in the Painting, Just Like Everyone Else, Maggie the Freak, Oh, Rick!, A Part of the Dream, Survival Camp!,* and *Two Different Girls.* No photographs, except for a nice glossy cover of teens in emotional poses.

26. **Burnett, Carol.** *Selected from One More Time: A Memoir.* **Literacy Volunteers of New York City, 1989. 64 pp. $2.95 paper (0-929631-03-X). Nonfiction.**

Subjects: Alcoholism; Biographies – Entertainers; Family problems
Reading Level: Grades 4–5   Interest Level: Grades 7–12

Selected here are excerpts from the story of Carol Burnett's life, *One More Time: A Memoir.* In Carol's own words, the reader comes to feel the great unhappiness and instability that Carol endured as a child of alcoholic parents and eccentric grandparents. Originally conceived as a letter to her daughters, Carol writes with an offstage pen conveying to the reader a mood rarely seen in public. The writing excerpt is preceded by a summary from the original text. An appendix lists thoughtful questions to the reader. This is a title in the Writers' Voices series.

27. **Butterworth, W. E.** *The Air Freight Mystery.* **Scholastic, 1979. 128 pp. $3.93 paper (0-590-05561-5). Fiction.**

Subjects: Airplanes; Mysteries
Reading Level: Grades 3–4   Interest Level: Grades 7–10

The management of Globe Air Freight thinks smuggling is going on in their planes because the FBI has been looking around. Rather than let them find out first, they hire Ernie Porter to investigate. Ernie chooses young, honest Steve Davis, the new man in Maintenance and Freight, to help him. Ernie gradually figures out what is being stolen (it's not drugs as originally suspected), but it takes clever Steve to work out how. Because he has been so instrumental in breaking up the smuggling ring, Steve is offered the tuition to go back to school to learn mechanics so that he can move up into a high-paying job. And, if he doesn't like being an airplane mechanic, the security department will always be more than happy to take him. A good mystery with many illustrations.

28. **Butterworth, William.** *The Hotel Mystery.* **Scholastic, 1979. 128 pp. $3.93 paper (0-590-30589-1). Fiction.**

Subjects: Jobs, job hunting; Mysteries
Reading Level: Grades 3–3.4   Interest Level: Grades 9–12

Chris Makros works as a maintenance man in a hotel. He is a conscientious employee who is called upon to fill in wherever and whenever he is needed—he's been chauffeur, busboy, and bellhop. A new chain has taken over the Parkhurst Hotel, and the new officers of the hotel suspect that someone on the staff is stealing supplies. As Chris is a trustworthy employee, he is put on the case with the new vice president in charge of operations. He helps uncover the thieves and expose their modus operandi. Chris is rewarded by being offered the job of bell captain and the promise of future advancement in the hotel management. He knows he has a real future in a job he loves. This is an exciting mystery with insights into interesting career possibilities for young people. Photographs throughout.

29. **Butterworth, William.** *Wrecker Driver.* **Scholastic, 1979. 93 pp. $2.95 paper (0-590-35554-6). Fiction.**

Subjects: Automobiles; Mysteries
Reading Level: Grades 3–4   Interest Level: Grades 9–12

Art works as a tow truck driver after school and on Saturdays, helping the highway patrol with accidents and disabled vehicles. Early one Saturday morning Art is called out to tow a Cadillac that has been in an accident. The car has a sticker indicating that it just came across the Mexican border, but the driver has no luggage! The highway patrol becomes suspicious. Further suspicions arise when a strange man, claiming to be the brother of the injured man, comes to the junkyard for the spare tire and wheel from the Cadillac. Art alerts the police, and with his help they catch the brother in what they believe is a drug-smuggling ring from Mexico. Photographs throughout.

30. **Carlson, Dale.** *The Frog People.* **Dutton, 1982. 75 pp. $8.95 (0-525-45107-2). Fiction.**

Subjects: Science fiction
Reading Level: Grades 1–2.5   Interest Level: Grades 7–12

Proud Point is a sleepy little town where Ann and Dan, two teachers at the high school, jog on the beach every day. One morning they find something that causes them to suspect that their resident scientist has really gone mad. Lying face down on the sand is a frog person, surrounded by many small, cut-up frogs. Sneaking into his lab they discover that Dr. Storm has developed a formula that will turn people into frogs. Why does he want to do this? He's convinced that the seas will once again rise up to cover the continents and he wants people to be prepared. Frog people can survive on land or in salt water.

He infects the water supply; and one by one, most of the inhabitants of Proud Point turn into frogs with pop-eyes, slit mouths, sticky tongues, green skin, and webbed hands and feet. They spend their days hopping around town in their jeans and congregating by the pond to catch flies. Suddenly, one day Dr. Storm, who inadvertently became a frog person, leads all the other frog people into the ocean to an unknown fate.

People begin turning into frogs around the world. Only those who jog, and therefore have a sufficiently altered metabolism, are immune. Finally an antidote is found. Illustrated throughout.

31. **Carlson, Dale.** *The Plant People.* **Photographs by Chuck Freedman. Dell, 1979. 96 pp. $1.25 paper (0-440-96959-X). Fiction.**

Subjects: Science fiction
Reading Level: Grades 1–2   Interest Level: Grades 7–12

An introduction to science fiction for teenagers who are just learning how to read. The story, simply told and involving few characters, centers around a strange fog that sweeps through a small southwestern town, leaving death and mystery behind. It is up to the teenaged hero, Mike Ward, to solve the mystery of the fog and to determine the cause of the strange cactus disease that attacks the town. Photographs depicting the events as they unfold accompany the sparse text.

32. Cavanna, Betty. *Romance on Trial.* Westminster John Knox, 1984. 95 pp. $10.95 (0-664-32715-X). Fiction.

Subjects: Romance; Teenage problems
Reading Level: Grade 4   Interest Level: Grades 11–12

Just when librarians think young teens are no longer reading this once-prolific author, here she comes with an up-to-date story of a high school senior, Valerie, the oldest child of a busy surgeon. Her mother works as dad's secretary, and daughter has to take over as surrogate cook and baby-sitter to younger siblings. When her strict parents stand by the rigidities of the 1950s—they ground Val a week after she stays out on a date with Ben past midnight—Valerie rebels and moves out. Ben's divorced mother takes Val in, and she sleeps on a cot in their sewing room. Fiercely independent, she finds two part-time jobs right away— one as a baby-sitter and one as a secretary to a YA novelist who needs someone to answer her fan mail.

Ben and Val's relationship is rather innocent and refreshing in these days of promiscuity in YA novels. Val's mother is direct in asking her daughter if she has slept with her boyfriend, and Val is equally as direct in responding that it's none of her mother's business. Even Ben's mother asks her if she will remain chaste while living under the same roof.

Val's 13-year-old sister's birthday party takes her home, especially after the younger sibling expresses how much she misses her sister. A letter to the YA author asking what a girl can do in a similar situation precipitates Val's decision to return home. The novelist's wise response, "Nobody wins," makes our protagonist realize that there are no pat answers on the path to adulthood. She goes home and wins respect and privacy from her family. For nonurban collections, a surefire hit for girls who may be considering moving out and need to know the harsh realities of the real world. No illustrations.

33. Cavanna, Betty. *Storm in Her Heart.* Westminster John Knox, 1983. 93 pp. $9.95 (0-664-32700-1). Fiction.

Subjects: Family problems; Teenage problems
Reading Level: Grades 4–5   Interest Level: Grades 7–12

Eighteen-year-old Anne Dalton is caught between her allegiance to her grandmother, a recovered alcoholic, and her recently divorced mother, now sharing her New York apartment with a new man. Spending the summer in Florida with her grandmother, Anne falls for Swifty, but he soon leaves to enter college in California. She decides to spend the school year in Florida, her decision prompted by meeting 24-year-old

Chris (Kit), who runs the local Audubon Society. (Grandma is very active in volunteer groups, among them the animal humane group.)

Anne doesn't mix well with her new classmates, until she and her grandmother nab a would-be robber in their home. Mom returns to ask Anne to live with her. (Her boyfriend has moved out.) A Florida hurricane keeps them all busy helping stranded victims. Walking along the beach after the tempest has subsided, Anne discovers a dead Haitian "boat infant" whose body has floated ashore. This plot contrivance could have been stronger; Cavanna barely allows Anne to touch on her feelings. Her mother implores her to return to New York, and Anne, at last, is catapulted into believing that she is needed. Good fare for young sheltered teen girls. No illustrations.

34. **Cebulash, Mel.** *The Face That Stopped Time.* **Fearon, 1984. 32 pp. $1.65 paper (0-8224-3465-2). Fiction.**
   Subjects: Mysteries
   Reading Level: Grade 4+   Interest Level: Grades 7–12

High school teacher Lorraine Smith is killed while entering the home of George Hawkins. It is difficult for the police to understand why Hawkins would shoot this young woman. In the course of unraveling the mystery, Detective Paul Suriano discovers that Hawkins's son committed suicide while in high school. Linking the son's suicide and the mysterious shooting of the teacher, Suriano uncovers the ill-fated rationale that Hawkins uses to get revenge. This is one of 12 titles in the Fastback Mystery series; the others by other authors are *Bill Waite's Will, Cardiac Arrest, Dawson's City, The Diary, A Game for Fools, The Good Luck Smiling Cat, The Intruder, Janie, Mad Enough to Kill, No Witnesses,* and *Shootout at Joe's.*

35. **Cervantes, Esther DeMichael, and Alex Cervantes.** *Barrio Ghosts.* **New Readers, 1988. 80 pp. $4.50 paper (0-88336-315-1). Fiction.**
   Subjects: Ghost stories; Hispanic Americans
   Reading Level: Grade 4   Interest Level: Grades 7–12

This is a collection of five short stories that center around teenagers who live in Latino neighborhoods in Los Angeles. Here are two examples of stories from the collection: "The Haunting of Lake La Luna" tells of a place that is haunted by the ghost of a woman who searches for her lost children. "I Was a Teenage Cat" is a fantasy about a teenage boy who changes bodies with his cat for a short time. Preceding each story is a "Words to Know" section that gives definitions of the Spanish words used in the story and sample sentences. The text is complemented with charcoal drawings.

36. Charuhas, Mary. *Stages in Adult Life.* Scott, Foresman, Lifelong Learning Division, 1982. 64 pp. $3.45 paper (0-673-24140). Nonfiction.
Subjects: Decision making; Life stages
Reading Level: Grades 4–5   Interest Level: Grades 9–12

An interesting book on the predictable "passages" we all go through on our way from young adulthood to old age. The book shows the reader how the difficult and usually frightening decisions we have to make (or refuse to make) at different life stages can affect the rest of our lives and ultimately determine our happiness. It emphasizes how important it is to make well-thought-out decisions, even if they are painful. If we are too afraid to risk, we will never grow. The chapters explore each of the life stages through concrete examples of the situations in which different individuals and couples find themselves. Then we are shown these same people five years later, and we can see how the decisions they made, or didn't make, have affected their lives.

A very well-written book that should cause teens to think about their own lives and may help them to better understand the older adults in their lives who are perhaps going through their own life stages.

37. Chirinian, Alain. *Motorcycles.* Messner, 1989. 64 pp. $9.98 LB (0-671-68029-3); $4.95 paper (0-671-68034-X). Nonfiction.
Subjects: Motorcycles; Sports, sports figures
Reading Level: Grade 3   Interest Level: Grades 7–12

The next time you are awakened by the roar of a motorcycle, just consider that its 60 miles per hour speed may have been reached in 2 to 5 seconds. An astounding statistic to ponder as Chirinian takes us on a tour of 14 outstanding two-wheel champion bikes, most notable among them the many varieties of Harley Davidson's Honda's and Yamaha bikes. Black-and-white photographs enhance an abbreviated text that enchants even the most taciturn teenage reader. Includes a glossary of car terms. A title in the Tough Wheels series. Index.

38. Chirinian, Alain. *Muscle Cars.* Messner, 1989. 64 pp. $9.98 LB (0-671-68028-5); $4.95 paper (0-671-68033-1). Nonfiction.
Subjects: Automobiles; Sports, sports figures
Reading Level: Grade 3   Interest Level: Grades 7–12

The 1967 Chevy Corvette launched the production of the American muscle car. Reaching a maximum speed of 150 miles per hour, this fiberglass body with fins and curves conveys a tremendous feeling of automotive power. Chirinian includes 13 other muscle car classics, among them the 1969 Pontiac GTO, the 1968 Shelby Mustang GT500, and the 1970 Dodge Challenger R/T—all speed demons—built by American automotive companies with options to "soup up" the engines to muscle car status. Black-and-white photographs of all cars enhance the sparse text replete with statistics. Includes a glossary of car terms. A title in the Tough Wheels series. Index.

39. **Chirinian, Alain.** *Race Cars.* **Messner, 1989. 64 pp. $9.98 LB (0-671-68030-7); $4.95 paper (0-671-68035-8). Nonfiction.**
    Subjects: Automobiles; Sports, sports figures
    Reading Level: Grade 3　　　　Interest Level: Grades 7–12

A survey of the fastest cars on earth. From the 260 plus miles per hour Oldsmobile Aerotech driven by champion race car driver A. J. Foyt to the most expensive car (over $1 million), the Formula One with speeds of 190 miles per hour. Among the 14 cars included is the popular NASCAR and Funny cars. Chirinian, using black-and-white photographs in simple and clear language, excites and pleases the reader, citing statistics that demonstrate the uniqueness of each model. Includes a glossary of car terms. A title in the Tough Wheels series. Index.

40. **Chirinian, Alain.** *Weird Wheels.* **Messner, 1989. 63 pp. $9.98 LB (0-671-68031-5); $4.95 paper (0-671-68036-6). Nonfiction.**
    Subjects: Automobiles; Sports, sports figures
    Reading Level: Grade 3　　　　Interest Level: Grades 7–12

Cars to delight the imagination of young people who dream of driving a car with an unusual shape on a difficult terrain. There are brief descriptions and photographs of 14 cars of unusual design and some with gull-wing doors: Fireaero GT, with monster trunks with 66X43X25-inch wheels; spacecrafts on wheels that travel at 110 miles per hour; swamp buggies that are part boat and part race car; and so on. Glossary of car terms. A title in the Tough Wheels series. Index.

41. **Christian, Mary Blount.** *Bigfoot.* **Crestwood House, 1987. 48 pp. $10.95 LB (0-89686-341-7). Nonfiction.**
    Subjects: Folklore; Mysteries
    Reading Level: Grade 4　　　　Interest Level: Grades 7–12

On almost every continent in the world, a strange, manlike hairy beast has been sighted and has become a part of legend and folklore. People in Russia, Asia, and the American Northwest have all reported encounters, and yet there is no concrete evidence of the Yeti's existence. To American Indians, he is called Sasquatch. Could a creature this size live among us undetected? This title explores existing evidence of Bigfoot encounters and engages the reader in determining the truth or fantasy of Bigfoot. Well documented with photographs and illustrations.

42. **Christian, Mary Blount.** *Just Once.* **New Readers, 1990. 48 pp. $3.50 paper (0-88336-208). Fiction.**

Subjects: Women – Battered
Reading Level: Grade 3   Interest Level: Grades 9–12

A victim of wife beating, Cora fears for her own life and the safety of her baby. Although her husband does not want her to work, Cora accepts a part-time job in a flower shop to make ends meet. When her husband finds out about her job, he brutally attacks her. Unwilling to press charges, Cora decides to take her baby and move out of the apartment. Seeking refuge in a bus terminal, she sees a sign for WIFEAID and contacts the group. Cora is grateful for the moral support and the new home she receives. Illustrated.

43. **Christian, Mary Blount.** *UFOs.* **Crestwood House, 1987. 48 pp. $10.95 LB (0-89686-347-6). Nonfiction.**

Subjects: Africa; UFOs
Reading Level: Grade 4   Interest Level: Grades 7–12

The Dogon tribe of Mali in West Africa claims that they are descendants of ancient astronauts who came from a planet orbiting the star Sirius. It is one of the great unsolved mysteries that these tribesmen know facts about planets and astronomy that they could have observed only through sophisticated scientific equipment, which they do not possess. Across the globe, people have sighted strange objects, for example, "saucers" in the skies. Some have documented the sightings with physical evidence as well. Could it all be imagination? Could each encounter with a UFO have a rational, natural explanation? This title, of enormous interest to all teenagers, especially for the high/low reader, discusses the theories and entices the reader to examine the evidence. Illustrated with photographs. Glossary and index included.

44. **Clark, Maria.** *Runaway Home.* **Janesville Literacy Council, 1989. 10 pp. $.50. Fiction.**

Subjects: Runaways; Teenage problems
Reading Level: Grade 3   Interest Level: Grades 7–12

An easy-to-read title on contemporary issues. Child adoption, teen pregnancy, runaway teens, jail term service, and the feelings related to loss due to death and guilt are all handled in this title and other titles, such as *Mary Comes Home, The Drop-Out, For the Love of Kim, The Picnic,* and *A Hard Lesson.* In *Runaway Home,* a teenager realizes that life on the street and in shelters is a harrowing experience. Spotting a sign that promises free bus transport on Greyhound, the teenager decides to turn himself into the police as a runaway and accepts the police's help in the return home to his mother. Line drawings break up the text. This collection from Janesville is uneven in content and quality. However, the renderings come from the heart and teenagers will respond to the characters and the situations.

45. **Clark, Steve.** *Wade Boggs: Baseball's Star Hitter.* **Dillon, 1988. 59 pp. $9.95 LB (0-87518-377-8). Nonfiction.**

    Subjects: Biographies – Sports; Sports, sports figures – Baseball
    Reading Level: Grades 3–4   Interest Level: Grades 7–12

    A biography chronicling the career of one of the most popular superstars in the major leagues. From his youthful beginnings on the sandlots in Georgia, Wade Boggs always knew that he would be an athlete. However, just being a talented hitter was not enough. He had to spend six hard years training in the minors, perfecting his playing skills, before he would be given a chance with the Boston Red Sox. Throughout this time, Boggs received a great deal of help and support from his coaches, his wife, and his family. Boggs's apparent modesty and dedication make this an appealing biography of a champion. Photographs throughout.

46. **Clarke, Thomas J.** *People and Their Religions.* **Parts I and II. Cambridge, 1983. Approx. 40 pp. ea. $2.25 ea. paper (0-8428-9609-0; 0-8428-9610-4). Nonfiction.**

    Subjects: Religion
    Reading Level: Grades 4–5   Interest Level: Grades 7–12

    The world's five major religions—Judaism, Christianity, Islam, Hinduism, and Buddhism—are discussed in chapter format. Quotations from the great books of each are incorporated into the text for greater understanding of the beliefs.

47. **Claypool, Jane.** *A Love for Violet.* **Westminster John Knox, 1982. 76 pp. $8.95 (0-664-32697-8). Fiction.**

    Subjects: Family problems; Romance
    Reading Level: Grades 2–4   Interest Level: Grades 7–10

    Violet feels like an outsider; her classmates always tease her, "Why are your sneakers so old?" So what if she comes from a close-knit but poor family with five siblings? When her mother is hospitalized for a benign tumor, Vi has to take off from school to take care of the baby and young twins. Violet kids herself that she is Cinderella, but Dad finally agrees to allow a friend to take over and give the burdened teen a few hours off.

    Vi has a crush on Tony, a popular, well-to-do boy. He calls to find out why she is out of school, but Vi's cynical response is misinterpreted by the young man to be a rejection. This is the furthest thing that Vi could wish, but she stoically accepts her situation. When the family's finances become desperate, Vi digs into her savings to buy groceries. Then she is left with nothing to spend for a prom dress. Her mother finds a used, antique dress the same color as Violet's name. Not wanting to insult her ailing mother, she wears it to the dance. It doesn't stop Tony from wanting to dance with and date her.

For today's teens, this is a bit old-fashioned and distant. The boy-asks-girl-to-dance segment is handled nicely and is emotionally honest. Quick fare for a special reader. No illustrations except for a floral decor that introduces each chapter.

48. **Cohen, Daniel.** *Monsters You Never Heard Of.* **Archway, 1986. 112 pp. $2.50 paper (0-671-44484-0). Nonfiction.**

Subjects: Monsters
Reading Level: Grade 4   Interest Level: Grades 7–10

The emphasis on monster lore here is on lesser-known creatures. Reported accounts are "told as true," but solid evidence of these monsters' existence is sorely lacking. Tall tales about the Jersey Devil from the New Jersey Pine Barrens, Spring Heeled Jack from London, the Chicago Phantom Kangaroo, and a wide variety of huge snakes are presented in separate short chapters accompanied by detailed line drawings that reveal the monsters' many eerie characteristics. Indexed.

49. **Cohen, Daniel.** *Real Ghosts.* **Archway, 1984. 128 pp. $2.50 paper (0-671-62670-1). Nonfiction.**

Subjects: Ghost stories
Reading Level: Grade 4   Interest Level: Grades 7–12

This is a collection of the best and most well-documented ghost sightings, mostly from England, drawn from parapsychological research. Included here is the famous tale of RAF pilot Lieutenant David McConnell's haunting flight to Tadcaster. Although this was an ill-fated flight for McConnell, who met his death in a plane crash at 3:25, his roommate at the air base, Larkin, claimed to have engaged him in conversation in their room at precisely that time.

Following each account of a ghost sighting, Cohen examines the event and presents evidence that might prove or disprove the tale. Other sightings discussed include searching ghosts, ghosts on film (many of which are revealed to be overexposed prints), ghosts that talk, and ghosts that haunt historic buildings. Cohen's research is interesting in that it gives the disabled reader a perspective on history not usually found in high/low books, which tend to have themes emphasizing modern trends. Includes photographs and illustrations. Indexed.

50. **Cohen, Daniel.** *Real Magic.* **Putnam, 1982. 109 pp. $8.95 (0-396-08095-2). Nonfiction.**

   Subjects: Magic; Supernatural events
   Reading Level: Grade 4   Interest Level: Grade 7

As the title indicates, this book explores the strange world of the occult and not the hand-is-quicker-than-the-eye magic of the stage. Using a historical perspective, Cohen introduces the reader to ten supernatural topics, including alchemy, incantations, water dowsing, voodoo, and fortune-telling. He even includes a chapter on how to cast a spell.

In many of the chapters Cohen relates a magical event from history, expresses the doubts that some people have, and leaves it up to the reader to decide if it really could have happened. In other cases he explains how some supposed magic actually has a rational explanation. He presents the power of suggestion as the real power in voodoo and carefully explains how a fortune-teller uses powers of observation and knowledge of human nature to figure out what a customer wants to hear. In general, he has a skeptical view of the whole business. Photos and line drawings throughout. Includes an index.

51. **Cohen, Daniel.** *Science Fiction's Greatest Monsters.* **Archway, 1980. 122 pp. $2.50 paper (0-671-44485-9). Nonfiction.**

   Subjects: Monsters; Science fiction
   Reading Level: Grade 3   Interest Level: Grades 7–12

Cohen has a reputation for capturing young people's interest in the weird and unusual, in the occult, and in the supernatural. This time he highlights the most famous monsters from science fiction books, movies, and television. Starting out with a simple overview of the science fiction writers H. G. Wells, André Maurois, William Tenn, and Eric Frank Russell, Cohen describes some common themes, plots, and characteristics of alien beings in the works of these writers. Cohen's reference to the sexist nature of early science fiction films is well documented by reference to the classic "girl-in-distress" image so prominent in the portrayal of women in monster and alien films. The people behind the monsters, the actors, are also discussed, with brief descriptions of the roles they play.

Because Cohen has used media of every kind as his background for exploring the use of monsters in science fiction, there is an added bonus for teachers and librarians. Constant reference to television favorites, such as "Star Trek" and "Battlestar Galactica," and film classics, such as *War of the Worlds* and *Invasion of the Body Snatchers*, provides a familiar context for most young people. Films, such as *Alien, Close Encounters of the Third Kind*, and *The Empire Strikes Back*, are included to keep the reader informed of the latest trends in the genre. Although this book tests out on the third-grade level according to the Fry Readability Graph, terminology is often difficult and not always defined. Many photographs follow the text. Indexed.

52. **Cohen, Daniel.** *The World's Most Famous Ghosts.* Simon & Schuster, 1989. 112 pp. $2.75 paper (0-671-69145-7). Nonfiction.

Subjects: Ghost stories
Reading Level: Grade 4   Interest Level: Grades 7–12

A lively account of well-known ghost appearances throughout history. Among those included are ghosts that haunt the White House, the Tower of London, West Point, and the Drury Lane Theatre in London. The brief chapter format, with attractive photographs of haunted residences, makes this particularly suitable for teenagers who cannot complete an entire book. Each interesting chapter is devoted to the story of a particular spirit.

53. **Cohen, Susan, and Daniel Cohen.** *What Kind of Dog Is That? Rare and Unusual Breeds of Dogs.* Dutton, 1989. 131 pp. $12.95 (0-525-65011-3). Nonfiction.

Subjects: Dogs; Pets
Reading Level: Grades 3–4   Interest Level: Grades 7–12

You don't have to love dogs to fall in love with the rare breeds photographed here. Each chapter focuses on one of the 25 breeds featured. Among them are the Akbash, known for guarding the flocks and herds of Turkish shepherds; the Argentine Dogo, known as the hunting dog; the Coonhound, which is the preeminent hunting dog; the Havanese, of Cuban origin, about the same size as the French poodle, and the Xoloitzcuintli (Xolo), the Mexican hairless that dates back to 1500 B.C. Included is a list of organizations on rare breeds.

54. **Collins, Tom.** *Steven Spielberg: Creator of E.T.* Dillon, 1983. 63 pp. $9.95 LB (0-87518-249-6). Nonfiction.

Subjects: Biographies – Moviemakers; Extraterrestrial people; Movies
Reading Level: Grades 3–4   Interest Level: Grades 7–12

When he was seven years old, Spielberg saw a movie about creatures from Mars attacking Earth. Hurrying home from the theater, he took a plastic model of the human head he had built and outfitted it with an air force cap and red lights. He then hid his monster in a long walk-in closet and proceeded to terrorize his three sisters. At age 12, Spielberg was making home movies of toy train crashes; at age 21, he directed his first television movie for Universal Pictures. The films that followed—*Jaws, Close Encounters of the Third Kind, Raiders of the Lost Ark, Poltergeist,* and *E.T.*—have been seen and enjoyed by millions of moviegoers.

Steven Spielberg has not forgotten the help he received as a young filmmaker. He is proud of all the talented young people he has hired to work on his pictures. This biography reveals the fascinating career of a very creative individual. Photographs throughout. Large print.

55. **Cone, Molly.** *Paul David Silverman Is a Father.* **Photographs by Harold Roth. Dutton, 1983. 55 pp. $8.95 (0-525-44050-X). Fiction.**

  Subjects: Marriage, teenage; Pregnancy and parenthood
  Reading Level: Grades 2–3   Interest Level: Grades 7–12

High school student Paul David Silverman and his girlfriend Cathy find she is pregnant and decide to marry. Both Paul and Cathy have career plans, which they realize will be interrupted by their early marriage and child-rearing responsibilities. Using the last of his Bar Mitzvah money to set up house, they solemnly agree to live up to the marriage contract both have shared in writing. These are two very mature teenagers who receive emotional and financial support from their parents. By the story's end, both teens and their families seem to have adjusted to the birth of the baby. Realistic photographs accompany the text.

56. **Cordaro, Scott.** *Ace Bradley.* **Fearon, 1987. 32 pp. $1.80 paper (0-8224-2921-7). Fiction.**

  Subjects: Historical fiction; War, war stories
  Reading Level: Grades 4–5   Interest Level: Grades 7–12

Ace Bradley is part of The War Flashbacks series that takes actual events in wars and fleshes them out by using heroic deeds to place the character and incident in historic perspective. Jim Bradley is working his family farm in Kansas, in 1918, when his father appears with a letter and a telegram. The letter is from Ben, his older brother who is a fighter pilot in France; the telegram is a brief note informing the family that Ben was shot down in Toul, France, in battle between the 94th Squadron and a German air patrol headed by Manfred von Richthofen. Jim vows to avenge his brother's death. Although underage, he enrolls in Jackson Air School, his goal to shoot down "The Red Baron." An epilogue summarizes "The Facts" surrounding the episode. Using the theme of war and the role that young people play in war, the series introduces actual events in history through situations that will expand the global views of American teenagers. Other titles in the series are *Attack on Pearl Harbor, A Brave Act, The British Are Coming, Gettysburg Messenger* (Civil War), *Guns for the General* (American Revolution), *In a Combat Zone, The Lost Battalion, U.S.S. Indianapolis,* and *Victory at Inchon* (Korean War, 1950).

57. **Cordaro, Scott.** *The Gold Jump.* **Fearon, 1987. 32 pp. $1.80 paper (0-8224-2938-1). Fiction.**

Subjects: Biographies – Sports; Black Americans; Sports, sports figures
Reading Level: Grades 4–5   Interest Level: Grades 7–12

Although *The Gold Jump* is about Jesse Owens's record-breaking broad jump at the 1936 Olympics held in Berlin, there is more here than a chronicling of one athlete's performance under the stress of racial prejudice, Hitler's presence, and the pressure to excel. Part of the series called Flashbacks Sports, Cordaro takes the reader to the actual event, re-creating a fictional framework around the historic event so that the reader may gain more of an understanding of the times. Use of sports as a theme to introduce historic events is a brilliant idea that helps to round out the information needs of the disabled adolescent reader. An epilogue summarizes "The Facts" surrounding the actual event. Other titles in the series that help to flesh out events from other decades are *The Bet, The Boys of Winter, Double the Glory, The End of a Streak, A Hard-Driving Lady* (Janet Guthrie—Indy 500), *The One-Woman Team* (The Babe), *The Super Upset* (Joe Namath), *The Thriller in Manila* (Frazier/Ali), and *The Triple Crown Duel.*

58. **Coret, Harriette.** *Better Off without Me.* **New Readers, 1989. 80 pp. $3.50 paper (0-88336-762-9). Fiction.**

Subjects: Depression (mental); Drug abuse; Family problems
Reading Level: Grade 4   Interest Level: Mature teenagers

A young wife and mother, Elsa feels overwhelmed with the care of three young children and a husband who she feels does not understand her. Out of control, she begins to slip into a pattern of alcohol and drugs, thereby neglecting her children. A trip to Florida to see her mother results in a near disaster for Elsa and her children as her youngest child eats poison while Elsa overdoses during an attempted suicide. Coret takes us on the road to Elsa's recovery describing the therapy and medication that Elsa must adhere to until she is able to return to an understanding husband and the care of her three children. Teenagers who are themselves suffering from depression or who have friends and relatives who are victims of depression will find this a life-affirming title. Recommended for mature teenagers.

59. **Coret, Harriette.** *In and Out the Windows.* **New Readers, 1990. 64 pp. $3.50 paper (0-88336-201-5). Fiction.**
    Subjects: Disabilities; Mental disabilities; Schizophrenia
    Reading Level: Grade 3+   Interest Level: Grades 9–12

When 17-year-old Kit begins to hear voices and hallucinate, her parents accuse her of taking drugs. No one suspects that she suffers from schizophrenia until she attempts suicide and is hospitalized. Under psychiatric care and drug therapy, Kit slowly recovers. Because she gains weight and becomes lethargic, her boyfriend convinces her to stop taking the medicine the doctor prescribed. Kit's strange behavior returns and she is brought back to the hospital where she learns that only through medication can she lead a normal, happy life. Illustrations.

60. **Corman, Avery.** *Selected from Kramer vs. Kramer.* **Literacy Volunteers of New York City, 1989. 64 pp. $2.95 paper (0-929631-01-3). Fiction.**
    Subjects: Child custody; Divorce; Family problems
    Reading Level: Grades 4–5   Interest Level: Grades 7–12

Selected here are excerpts from the novel *Kramer vs. Kramer* by Avery Corman. Corman's voices are expressed eloquently as two parents haggle over the custody of their young son. Students who read these excerpts will have an opportunity to reflect on their own lives as they review the thoughtful questions in the appendix. This is a title in the Writers' Voices series.

61. **Cosby, Bill.** *Selected from Fatherhood & Time Flies.* **Literacy Volunteers of New York City, 1989. 64 pp. $2.95 paper (0-929631-00-5). Nonfiction.**
    Subjects: Biographies – Entertainers; Black Americans
    Reading Level: Grades 4–5   Interest Level: Grades 7–12

Selected here are the excerpts from Bill Cosby's books *Fatherhood* and *Time Flies.* In Cosby's own words, the reader comes to gain insight into how Cosby feels about aging. Humorous episodes from his life intermingled with the "Cosby/Huxtable" character we see on television paint a portrait of a multifaceted family man. The writings excerpted are preceded by biographical information about Cosby. An appendix lists thoughtful questions to the reader. This is a title in the Writers' Voices series.

62. **Cowsill, Virginia.** *Read to Me: Favorite Childhood Tales.* **New Readers, 1990. 32 pp. $7.95 (set of four) (0-88336-981-8). Fiction.**

Subjects: Nursery tales
Reading Level: Grades 2–3   Interest Level: Young children

Designed for parents as a read-aloud story for their children, this four-book set includes three traditional nursery tales—*Little Ugly Duck; The Duck, the Bird and the Little Red Hen;* and *The Gingerbread Boy*—and an original Christmas Story, *The Golden Webs.* Line illustrations on each page flesh out the text.

63. **Creighton, Susan.** *Greg Norman.* **Crestwood House, 1988. 48 pp. $10.95 LB (0-89686-371-9). Nonfiction.**

Subjects: Biographies – Sports; Sports, sports figures – Golf
Reading Level: Grades 4–5   Interest Level: Grades 7–12

Greg Norman grew up as an Australian beach boy and was never really interested in golf until, at the age of 16, he picked up his mother's clubs and decided to try hitting a few balls. From that time on Greg knew that he wanted to make his living playing golf and he immediately set out to accomplish his goal. After studying the game, and working to perfect his own skill, Greg began touring the European tournament circuit and eventually became one of the highest paid players in the U.S. professional golf world. Numerous black-and-white photographs accompany the text.

64. **Crone, Moira.** *The Life of Lucy Fern.* **Parts I and II. Cambridge, 1983. 48 pp. ea. $2.25 ea. paper (0-8428-9600-7; 0-8428-9601-5). Fiction.**

Subjects: Foster children; Native Americans
Reading Level: Grades 2–3   Interest Level: Grades 9–12

A 13-year-old Lumbee Indian girl, Ruth Fern, gives birth to a baby girl in the woods. Out of shame and fear, she abandons the baby, allowing it to become the foster child of an older childless Lumbee Indian couple. At age five, the child Lucy is again abandoned, this time by the death of her foster mother. In this saga of the life of Lucy Fern, Crone has drawn a very realistic portrait of a foster child who grows to adulthood, along the way getting to know her natural mother and discovering who her real father is. For the mature teen.

65. **Cunningham, Chet.** *Apprentice to a Rip-Off.* **Scholastic, 1979. 127 pp. $3.93 paper (0-590-05558-5). Fiction.**

Subjects: Crime; Jobs, job hunting
Reading Level: Grade 4+   Interest Level: Grades 8–12

Johnny is working as an apprentice carpenter but is restless and bored with his life. He wants to pack up, get on his Honda, and just keep going. But Johnny has responsibilities: a widowed mother, a younger sister and brother, and a girlfriend who wants to settle down. Johnny is approached at work by a carpenter who asks him to go in on a burglary of the company supply shed. At first the money sounds good, but Johnny cares too much for his boss and is too ethical to commit a crime. Instead, he tips off the police and helps to catch the thieves. Johnny realizes that carpentry is a good profession; and his boss respects him and promises him a future in the business. A fast-paced story with insights into the job of carpentry for young people. Photographs throughout.

66. **Cutting, Edith.** *A Quilt for Bermuda.* Scholastic, 1978. 95 pp. $2.95 paper (0-590-35560-0). Fiction.

Subjects: School
Reading Level: Grades 2–3   Interest Level: Grades 7–10

A senior class trip to Bermuda is a costly venture. Fund-raising efforts such as car washing are organized, but the students soon realize that more money is needed. Barb meets this challenge by organizing a quilting project. Several students will sew and help assemble the many pieces so that the finished quilt can be sold and the funds used to pay for the trip. But vandals break into the school and damage the lovely pieces of fabric needed to complete the project. A simple story that shows spirit, cooperation, and perseverance among teenagers. Photographs accompany the text.

67. **Darling, David J.** *Diana: The People's Princess.* Dillon, 1984. 62 pp. $9.95 LB (0-87518-282-8). Nonfiction.

Subjects: Biographies – Royalty; Royalty; Women
Reading Level: Grades 3–4   Interest Level: Grade 7–12

Diana Frances Spencer was just 20 years old when she married Prince Charles and became the Princess of Wales. Less than a year later she had not only won the hearts of the British people but she had also given them a male heir to the British throne.

Young Diana loved caring for small children. Her tastes were not for schoolwork but for watching television and reading romances. This brief biography emphasizes Charles's courtship of Diana and her life as Princess of Wales. Color photographs of the royal couple on tour complement the simple text. Glossary and index are included.

68. **Day, Nancy Raines.** *Help Yourself to Health.* **New Readers, 1980. 80 pp. $3.75 paper (0-88336-540-5). Nonfiction.**
Subjects: Health, health problems
Reading Level: Grade 4   Interest Level: Grades 7–12

This oversize paperback is similar in style to, but much easier to read than, the very popular *Our Bodies, Ourselves,* which is a favorite among many teenagers. Twenty-six short chapters cover all aspects of the care and maintenance of the body. A brief overview of diet and exercise is followed by a particularly significant chapter on coping with stress. There is a list of questions to ask the doctor during an examination, as well as a description of what to expect from a gynecological examination. This is an excellent sourcebook for family medical problems. Photographs throughout the book depict people of all ages. Clear diagrams and drawings illustrate important or difficult-to-understand terminology.

69. **Dee, M. M.** *Mystery on the Night Shift.* **Scholastic, 1978. 128 pp. $3.93 paper (0-590-08337-6). Fiction.**
Subjects: Crime; Mysteries
Reading Level: Grades 3–4   Interest Level: Grades 8–12

Bo Bennett needs a job fast if he wants to continue seeing Debbie. So when he is given a chance to start working at Circle Truck Painting Company, things begin to look up for their relationship. But it's not long before Bo discovers there's some funny business going on that involves new trucks being rushed in, repainted, and rushed out. When he discovers that the trucks' serial numbers are being changed, he knows for sure that they are stolen. He receives an ominous note in his locker and a threatening phone call. Someone knows that he is onto the game, and that someone wants him to stop nosing around. Bo immediately suspects that J. R. Perez, an ex-boyfriend of Debbie's, who also works on the night shift, is the insider involved. After nearly getting himself killed, Bo discovers that he's wrong. In the end, not only does he get the reward for exposing the thievery, and a promotion, but he gets the approval of Debbie's father and his permission to continue dating her. Photographs throughout.

70. **de la Garza, Phyllis.** *Chacho.* **New Readers, 1990. 96 pp. $3.75 (0-88336-763-7). Fiction.**
Subjects: Hispanic Americans; Mexico
Reading Level: Grade 4   Interest Level: Grades 7–12

Chacho Rios, 17, lives on a ranch in rural Mexico and dreams of a life away from his bossy sister, Esperanza, who has inherited the family's ranch from their parents. Tired of the dust and monotony of his everyday life, Chacho invents an elaborate scheme to match his sister up with attractive and successful neighboring rancher Agustin Cervantes, a prosperous bachelor. In his innocence, he dreams up a scheme that involves the theft of one of Cervantes' prize horses that he feels for sure will serve as the bait and the chance meeting between his sister and Cervantes. But his scheme backfires (although Esperanza and Agustin do eventually fall in love), and Chacho is forced to come to terms with his sister and accept life in rural contemporary Mexico. This title offers glimpses of people living in a culture caught between modern and traditional values. Spanish words are defined in the text, and a glossary is appended. Pencil drawings punctuate the text.

71. **Dick, Jean.** *Bomb Squads and SWAT Teams.* **Crestwood House, 1988. 47 pp. $10.95 LB (0-89686-401-4). Nonfiction.**
Subjects: Jobs, job hunting; Police work
Reading Level: Grades 4–6   Interest Level: Grades 6–10

A police officer's job is rarely easy, but members of two special groups take on extra risks everyday. These people work in bomb squads and SWAT teams across America. For someone on a bomb squad, each day brings more risks of accidents and advanced training to help them deal with the latest explosives technology. SWAT team members also face exceptional risks on a day-to-day basis. They are the men and women who deal with hostage situations, sniper attacks, assassination attempts, and, because they are trained negotiators, they are often sent to talk down potential suicide jumpers. Always on call, these people help protect us from life's most violent possibilities. Numerous color photographs and a glossary/index acompany the text.

72. **Dick, Jean.** *Mental and Emotional Disabilities.* **Crestwood House, 1988. 48 pp. $10.95 LB (0-89686-418-9). Nonfiction.**
Subjects: Disabilities; Emotional disabilities; Mental disabilities
Reading Level: Grades 4–6   Interest Level: Grades 7–12

Using color photographs with facial expressions of depression, mental retardation, and other grimaces that evidence other than normal teenage facades in school and athletic settings, Dick explains the various treatments that are available for adolescents who are victims of dyslexia, aphasia, visual and hearing impairments, hyperactivity (attention deficit disorders), various emotional disturbances, stuttering, and other abnormal conditions. Stressing that counseling and medication are helpful for all adolescents with these disturbances, Dick gives us hope for resolving many of these problems by the onset of adult life. A glossary/index appends the text.

73. **DiFranco, Anthony.** *Pope John Paul II: Bringing Love to a Troubled World.*
Dillon, 1983. 71 pp. $9.95 (0-87518-241-0). Nonfiction.

Subjects: Biographies – Religion; Religion
Reading Level: Grades 3–4   Interest Level: Grades 7–12

This is a serious and comprehensive account of the life of Carolus
Joseph Wojtyla, known to millions as Pope John Paul II. The first non-
Italian pope in hundreds of years, Pope John Paul has become one of the
greatest leaders of our times. He has traveled to many countries in an
effort to renew the forces of love, justice, and peace in our troubled
world. Photographs illustrate the personal life of this man, who once
aspired to be an actor. The horrors of World War II and the invasion of
his native Poland led Wojtyla to study for the priesthood. A very readable biography of a fascinating public figure.

74. **Doiron, Rose.** *My Name Is Rose.* East End Literacy, 1987. 67 pp. $5.95 paper
(0-921-01307-4). Nonfiction.

Subjects: Child abuse; Family problems; Romance
Reading Level: Grade 1   Interest Level: Mature teenagers

Rose is a student at a nonprofit reading center in downtown Toronto. This is her story, in her own words, written while learning to read
and write at the center. Rose is a victim of an abusive and alcoholic father
who beats her and uses her to shop, clean, and cook for him. Her
mother, ill, is unable to care for her, so Rose spends her childhood and
adolescence in a series of foster and group homes. Finally, at the age of
16, she breaks away from her father, only to find herself in an abusive
relationship with a man. Eventually she finds a job, enters into a loving
relationship with Paul, and learns to read and write at the community
center. Photographs re-creating the joys and sorrows of Rose's life complement the text. Other titles in The East End Literacy series are *Raised
Up Down South, New Years 1960, Working Together, Getting Along, I Call It
the Curse, Let's Get Together, I've Come a Long Way, Eleventh Child,* and
Lonely Child. Teenagers will appreciate the biographical nature of these
beginning-level stories because they are filled with the hope for a better
life.

75. **Dolan, Edward F.** *Famous Firsts in Space.* Dutton, 1989. 144 pp. $13.95 (0-
525-65007-5). Nonfiction.

Subjects: Space exploration
Reading Level: Grades 4–5   Interest Level: Grades 7–12

An easy-to-read historic overview of the space program from the
launching in 1957 of *Sputnik* to the successful orbiting of the manned
craft *Discovery* in 1988. Moonwalks, dogs in space, and the *Challenger*

disaster are all discussed while pinpointing each as a vital and linked scientific discovery over the last 33 years. Sharp black-and-white photographs complement the text.

76. Duden, Jane. *Shirley Muldowney.* Crestwood House, 1988. 48 pp. $10.95 LB (0-89686-369-7). Nonfiction.

Subjects: Automobiles; Biographies – Sports; Women
Reading Level: Grades 4–5   Interest Level: Grades: 7–12

Shirley Muldowney has always loved going fast, from her earliest memories of her father putting her on his lap to "help him steer" his speeding car to her dominance of the racing world as one of its most remarkable drivers. Muldowney worked her way up from street racing to legitimate stock-car racing. After a fiery crash in 1973 she could have quit, but she persevered and became a national champion in top-fuel racing. A near-fatal crash in 1984 left Muldowney more banged up than she had ever been before, but it failed to stop her determination to keep on winning. Numerous black-and-white photographs accompany the text.

77. Durham, John. *New Life for Sarita.* Scholastic, 1971. 92 pp. $3.95 paper (0-590-35573-2). Fiction.

Subjects: Hispanic Americans; Romance
Reading Level: Grades 2–3   Interest Level: Grades 8–12

The only thing that dates this classic story are the miniskirts worn by Sarita. Sarita is a young woman caught between two cultures. Her father, a Mexican-American, does not understand how important it is for her to date Johnny Seguin. Although Sarita will soon be 18, her father does not want to let her go. It is fortunate for her that Johnny's mother helps Sarita's father to understand that Sarita must learn to make decisions herself. This is a favorite among many teenage girls. Photographs complement the text.

78. Eichhorn, Dennis. *Bon Jovi.* Turman Publishing, 1987. 76 pp. $2.95 paper (0-89872-213-6). Nonfiction.

Subjects: Biographies – Entertainers; Music – Rock stars
Reading Level: Grade 4   Interest Level: Grades 7–12

Jon Bon Jovi, born on March 2, 1962, in Perth Amboy, New Jersey, feels that as a kid he had a tough battle to fight to gain prominence as one of the top performers in the rock music world. At 14, he picked up guitar lessons from a neighbor, and by the time he was 16, he was playing in clubs with his group that he named the Atlantic City Expressway. Leaving school at 16, Jon went to work at The Power Station, a recording studio in New York, and it was here that he came into contact with the rock world and his taste in rock music became more refined. This young star has much to look forward to in the video and recording industry, together with his band, one of the most asked for on MTV. Filled with photographs.

79. **Eichhorn, Dennis.** *Cosby.* **Turman Publishing, 1986. 76 pp. $2.95 paper (0-89872-200-4). Nonfiction.**

Subjects: **Biographies – Entertainers; Black Americans**
Reading Level: **Grade 4**   Interest Level: **Grades 7–12**

Bill Cosby, star of stage, screen, and print, comes across as the lovable and naturally funny man that he is in this slim biography. Early photographs of the hit television show "The Cosby Show," as well as shots from his earlier film rolls and his real-life family, complement the easy-to-read text. To update this biography and allow low-level readers to a richer reading experience see also Cosby, *Selected from Fatherhood & Time Flies,* in this chapter.

80. **Eichhorn, Dennis.** *Cruise.* **Turman Publishing, 1987. 75 pp. $2.95 paper (0-89872-207-1). Nonfiction.**

Subjects: **Biographies – Entertainers; Disabilities; Movies**
Reading Level: **Grade 4**   Interest Level: **Grades 7–12**

Born Thomas Cruise Mapother IV in Syracuse, New York, on July 3, 1962, this young actor has transformed himself from a suburban teenager into a very talented actor. Falling into acting in high school after being sidelined by an athletic injury turned out to be a stroke of good luck for this naturally skilled actor. But, as Eichhorn recounts the young life of Tom Cruise, we see that he has much in common with many teenagers. For years, Cruise was unable to read because of undiagnosed dyslexia, so he developed an extraordinary ability to memorize, a trait that placed him in good stead while developing his acting talents. Cruise is also revealed as a mover and a thinker, always watchful of parts that will elevate his stature as an actor. After his break in *Godspell,* at a local dinner theater, Tom knew that the feeling he got from acting was more satisfying than anything he had ever experienced, so he moved to New York City and decided to give acting a ten-year try. His appearance in *Endless Love* led to a part in *Taps.* His desire to perform in films directed by the "greats" lead him to Francis Ford Coppola's *The Outsiders.* In this film version of what was once his favorite book, Cruise played a teenager working in a service station. Performing in *Risky Business* and *The Color of Money* with film giant

Paul Newman gave him the power to chart his own path. A most positive portrait of a young person with strong inner direction. Photographs throughout. A glossary appends each chapter.

81. **Eichhorn, Dennis.** *Fox.* **Turman Publishing, 1987. 76 pp. $2.95 paper (0-89872-210-1). Nonfiction.**
   Subjects: Biographies – Movies and television; Movies
   Reading Level: Grade 4   Interest Level: Grades 7–12

   It is hard to believe that this *Back to the Future* star still plays teenage parts on television and film. Almost 30, the Canadian-born Michael J. Fox seems to have located the fountain of youth. At 5 feet and 120 pounds, the "Family Ties" star seems content to grow with the cast, but in real life we see a maturing individual whose marriage seems secure and teenagers can expect to see Fox on screen for many years to come. Black-and-white photographs punctuate a fast-moving text. A glossary appends each chapter.

82. **Eichhorn, Dennis.** *Johnson.* **Turman Publishing, 1987. 74 pp. $2.95 paper (0-89872-206-3). Nonfiction.**
   Subjects: Biographies – Movies and television; Television personalities
   Reading Level: Grade 4   Interest Level: Grades 7–12

   Don Johnson, known to millions of teenagers as the man who made the partially shaved beard an instant status symbol, appears as a clean-shaven teenager in this slim biography that chronicles his birth to teen parents, his adolescence in juvenile detention, his early attempts at stage acting, and his movie breakthrough in 1969 as Stanley in *The Magic Garden of Stanley Sweetheart.* Achieving the fame of his dreams with the television show "Miami Vice," Johnson attributes his drug-free life-style to his relationship with Patti D'Arbanville, his very special person. Adding his record *Heartbeat* to his repertoire, Johnson is very confident that his multitalented media productions will enable him to choose any performance path. Photographs complement the short chapters, and a glossary appends each chapter.

83. **Eichhorn, Dennis.** *Jordan.* **Turman Publishing, 1987. 76 pp. $2.95 paper (0-89872-208-X). Nonfiction.**
   Subjects: Biographies – Sports; Black Americans; Sports, sports figures – Basketball
   Reading Level: Grade 4   Interest Level: Grades 7–12

   In this photograph-filled biography, Michael Jordan tells how it is to try to be the greatest star in basketball every time he walks out on the court. A giant commercial success, Jordan knows that his $2.5 million contract with Nike sold a half-million pairs the first month. As other companies line up to use Jordan to promote their products, more and more billboards and scorecards are filled with this very talented young sports star.

84. **Eichhorn, Dennis.** *Macchio.* **Turman Publishing, 1987. 76 pp. $2.95 paper (0-89872-212-8). Nonfiction.**
   Subjects: Biographies – Movies and television; Movies
   Reading Level: Grade 4   Interest Level: Grades 7–12

Young actor Ralph George Macchio, Jr., born in Huntington, New York, on November 4, 1961, got his start in show business by making commercials as a child. Since then, he has become very much the star of many classic teenage films—*Karate Kid* series, *Crossroads, Three Wishes of Billy Grier*—and playing Johnny, the main character in the film version of *The Outsiders*, by S. E. Hinton. Although almost 30, Macchio still retains the teenage look that gives him the ability to play youthful roles but frustrates him in capturing mature parts. Macchio leads a quiet life, recently marrying his girlfriend of ten years, Phyllis Fierro. A very easy-to-read biography, with photographs fleshing out the high points of this young man's life.

85. **Eichhorn, Dennis.** *Murphy.* **Turman Publishing, 1987. 75 pp. $2.95 paper (0-89872-209-8). Nonfiction.**
   Subjects: Biographies – Movies and television; Black Americans; Movies
   Reading Level: Grade 4   Interest Level: Grades 7–12

"I always said I'd be famous by the time I was 19 and a millionaire by the time I was 22," says Eddie Murphy. "I've been lucky." Eddie Murphy grew up with the unique ability to imitate. By the age of eight, he could talk like the cartoon characters on television, Bugs Bunny, Bullwinkle, Sylvester the Cat, as well as comics like Jerry Lewis and Laurel and Hardy. His entry into comedy clubs started at age 15, at the Roosevelt Youth Center on Long Island, New York, where he did an impersonation of soul singer Al Green. Looking out at the audience, Murphy says, "I knew it would be show biz for the rest of my life." Starring in the hit NBC show "Saturday Night Live" and in the successful film *Beverly Hills Cop* sealed his success. Now Murphy looks forward to marriage and children. Photographs throughout; a glossary appends each chapter.

86. **Eichhorn, Dennis.** *Springsteen.* **Turman Publishing, 1986. 75 pp. $2.95 paper (0-89872-204-7). Nonfiction.**
   Subjects: Biographies – Music; Music – Rock stars
   Reading Level: Grade 4   Interest Level: Grades 7–12

New Jersey–born rock star Bruce Springsteen is revealed as a man whose inner life comes across in the lyrics and music that he creates for a broad segment of the population. Teenagers who perform in bands or solo will appreciate Springsteen's early struggle to form a relationship with a band, an agent, and a woman. In his own words, music became his "purpose" for life, and indeed it is through his music that he is able to communicate his feelings and philosophy. The biography concludes with Springsteen's marriage to Julianne Phillips. Springsteen is a humanitarian with a vision. Photographs complement the short chapters. A glossary appends each chapter.

87. **Eichhorn, Dennis.** *Stallone.* **Turman Publishing, 1986. 76 pp. $2.95 paper (0-89872-205-5). Nonfiction.**

Subjects: Biographies – Movies and television; Movies
Reading Level: Grade 4   Interest Level: Grades 7–12

All the world knows about the extraordinary experience that Stallone has had while creating the monumental epics that *Rocky* and *Rambo* have come to be. But very few people know about the early and humble beginnings of Sylvester Gardenzio Stallone, born July 6, 1946, in New York's Hell's Kitchen. Eichhorn also tells the story of Stallone's son's autism and the demise of his marriage. A sensitive, energetic, and brilliant writer and actor, Stallone has become a twentieth-century philosopher. Full of black-and-white photographs of Stallone at work and at play.

88. **Eichhorn, Dennis.** *Tyson.* **Turman Publishing, 1987. 75 pp. $2.95 paper (0-89872-214-4). Nonfiction.**

Subjects: Biographies – Sports; Black Americans; Sports, sports figures – Boxing
Reading Level: Grade 4   Interest Level: Grades 7–12

A breezy biography of the early troubled life and career of the world heavyweight champion. Tyson, born June 30, 1966, in Brooklyn's tough Brownsville section, learned early on that fighting was essential for his survival. But, for Tyson, his constant fighting and petty thievery lead him to an arrest, and, at the age of 13 at 5 feet 8 inches and 200 pounds, he was sent to the Tryon School for boys. At Tryon, "he fought a lot and got put in lock-up sessions." But, for Tyson, Tryon offered a way out of the fruitless fighting that he had pursued. At Tryon he met Bobby Stewart, a former boxer who recognized talent in the untrained young Tyson. It was through Stewart that he met the famous Cus D'Amato, legendary boxing coach. Moving into the home of D'Amato and his wife Camille, Tyson flourished not only as a fighter but also learned to read. With Cus and

Camille living in Catskill, New York, Tyson found the home and parents he never had. Under the keen and nurturing management of D'Amato, Tyson's amateur status lasted a brief three years. Preparing for the pros, he watched boxing films and became a student of boxing history. Boxing as a professional meant money and fame for the 17-year-old, who entered the ring in 1985 to win his first bout with Hector Mercedes in 1 minute 47 seconds of the first round by a knockout. His next win was with Trent Singleton, also in the first round. Tyson is sincere in his gratitude to the late D'Amato when he says that without him he would have ended up dead or in jail. Winning is indeed this 20-year-old's style and this brief biography is fodder for dreams of fame and fortune for many teenagers who see sports as a way out of poverty. Photographs included. A glossary appends each chapter.

89. **Eichhorn, Dennis** *Whitney.* **Turman Publishing, 1987. 76 pp. $2.95 paper (0-89872-211-X). Nonfiction.**

Subjects: Biographies – Music; Black Americans; Music – Rock stars
Reading Level: Grade 4   Interest Level: Grades 7–12

From her first album, called appropriately enough *Whitney Houston,* this young woman never fails to succeed in her musical endeavors. Born in Newark, New Jersey, on August 9, 1963, the Houston home was filled with the sound of gospel and soul. Blessed with a positive outlook and wanting to grow musically, Houston refuses to let success spoil her. Her love of life and her belief in herself as just a regular person make Houston a good role model for many young women.

90. **Eisenberg, Lisa.** *Fast-Food King.* **Fearon, 1980. 64 pp. $3.90 paper (0-8224-1082-6). Fiction.**

Subjects: Mysteries; Women – Stories
Reading Level: Grade 3   Interest Level: Grades 7–12

The heroine, Laura Brewster, is an insurance investigator and assistant to the chief investigator at Atco Insurance whose investigations take her all over the world. There are six titles in the Laura Brewster series, all of which work to reinforce the image that Laura, although Nancy Drew-like in character, is a twentieth-century woman, competent and confident of her ability to carry out her job. The fast-food king of this title is Reginald Bumpo, creator of Bumpo Burger's secret hamburger sauce. When Bumpo is mysteriously poisoned by a dose of his concoction, Laura is flown to Australia to investigate the details for Atco Insurance. A fast-paced adventure with plenty of action. Small pen-and-ink drawings appear throughout the text. Other titles in the series, which take

Laura all over the world, are *House of Laughs, Killer Music, Tiger Rose, Falling Star,* and *Golden Idol.*

91. **Eisenberg, Lisa.** *On the Run.* **Fearon, 1984. 80 pp. $3.90 paper (0-8224-6265-6). Fiction.**
   Subjects: Crime stories; Women – Stories
   Reading Level: Grades 3–4   Interest Level: Grades 9–12

Amy Cougan is a nurse "on the run" for three years after having been wrongfully accused of murdering an elderly woman patient. She returns to take care of her 80-year-old mother, who is living alone, saddled with a broken hip. Just when the police arrive to inform Amy that she is cleared of the charges because the elderly woman's nephew admitted the crime, Amy flees.

In the interim, the two police officers—Eddy, a young widower, and Kate—try to provide some humor and love interest. Kate goes to a health food restaurant to sample a celery burger and finds Amy there as a waitress. When Amy sees her police file on the counter, she panics and pulls out her gun. She really goes beserk, even holding her good Indian friend as a hostage. In the middle of all this, the cook, Struthers, fakes a heart attack and Amy puts down her gun to give him his nitroglycerin pills! Contrived plot elements a la Hollywood sit-coms may be all right for unsophisticated teen readers, but some may not "buy" the pat ending. Still, the terror of the woman on the run is realistically portrayed.

Other titles in the South City Cop series by Lisa Eisenberg are *Hit Man, Break-In, Kidnap,* and *Murder behind the Wheel;* three copies of each title sell for $51.

92. **Eliot, Chip.** *Ivan Lendl.* **Crestwood House, 1988. 48 pp. $10.95 LB (0-89686-380-8). Nonfiction.**
   Subjects: Biographies – Sports; Sports, sports figures – Tennis
   Reading Level: Grades 4–5   Interest Level: Grades 7–12

Ivan Lendl began playing tennis at the age of four in his homeland of Czechoslovakia. Slowly he worked his way up through the ranks until he was ranked as the number one junior tennis player in the world. Lendl always had a reputation for being very quiet, almost rude at times, and his professional career did very little to dispel that image, until the world learned that he was still insecure in his use of the English language and a little unsure of Western customs. Eventually his tennis skill won him the admiration of the fans and a spot as one of the best tennis players in recent decades. Numerous black-and-white photographs accompany the text.

93. **Erdrich, Louise.** *Selected from Love Medicine.* **Literacy Volunteers of New York City, 1989. 64 pp. $2.95 paper (0-929631-02-1). Fiction.**

Subjects: Native Americans; Vietnam War
Reading Level: Grades 4–5   Interest Level: Grades 7–12

Selected here is the story "The Red Convertible" from the novel *Love Medicine.* Preceding the selection is background information about American Indians, the Vietnam War, and Erdrich herself. The excerpt concerns two brothers who travel together in a red convertible until the Vietnam War changes their relationship. Thoughtful questions append the text. This is a title in the Writers' Voices series.

94. *Feelings Illustrated.* **New Readers, 1977. 32 pp. ea. $9.50 (set of four) paper (0-88336-475-E). Nonfiction.**

Subjects: Feelings
Reading Level: Grades 1–3   Interest Level: Grades 7–12

This set of four slim books on loving, working, playing, and laughing is designed, for the most part, with attractive photographs and compact captions (often of a humorous nature) to depict the emotions the photographs convey. Excellent for the teenager who is just beginning to read, both as a browsing item and as an icebreaker in tutor/student pairs.

95. **Fischler, Stanley I.** *Montreal Canadiens.* **Creative Education, 1986. 32 pp. $12.50 LB (0-88682-092-8). Nonfiction.**

Subjects: Canada; Sports, sports figures – Hockey
Reading Level: Grade 4   Interest Level: Grades 7–12

Stanley Fischler captures the excitement of the Canadian national pastime sport with all the vigor that the players give their game. The text uses black-and-white photographs that document the Montreal Canadiens. Founded in 1909, the team predates the National Hockey League by eight years. Indeed, early on, the Montreal Canadiens were characterized by their exceptional speed and spirit. Fischler follows such great careers as that of Howie Morenz and Frank Selke, Sr. The team won five consecutive Stanley Cups from 1956 to 1960. Other titles in the NHL Today series include *Edmonton Oilers, New York Islanders,* and *The Toronto Maple Leaves.*

96. **Franz, Marion J.** *Fast Food Facts: Nutritive and Exchange Values for Fast-Food Restaurants,* **2nd ed. Diabetes Center, 1987. 54 pp. $3.95 paper (0-937721-21-2). Nonfiction.**

Subjects: Health, health problems; Nutrition
Reading Level: Grades 3–4   Interest Level: Grades 7–12

Fast Food Facts is an ingeniously written manual that charts the ingredients, such as fats, carbohydrates, protein, and sodium, and the calories for such American staple foods as the Big Mac (570 calories), Egg McMuffin (340), and one Roy Rogers biscuit (231). Since these are just snacks for most teenagers the caloric count and other vital food statistics noted for each product can educate "sloppy eaters" and lead the way to better selection of fast food while on the road or in a hurry. Published by the International Diabetes Center as part of its Wellness and Nutrition Library, this is a fine addition to the survival skill sections of high/low collections.

97. **French, Dorothy K.** *I Don't Belong Here.* **Westminster John Knox, 1980. 102 pp. $8.95 (0-664-32664-1). Fiction.**
   Subjects: Aging; Family problems; Health, health problems – Senility
   Reading Level: Grade 2   Interest Level: Grades 7–10

Sixteen-year-old Mary is sent by her parents to spend her senior year with her grandmother in the small town of Lost Valley, California. When Mary arrives in Lost Valley, she finds that her once vital grandmother has aged significantly and is unable to manage herself or her home. This is Mary's first exposure to senility. Emerging here, through the character of the grandmother, is an excellent portrait of an elderly person going through the stages of senility. Mary, who is in full adolescent bloom and coping with all the insecurities of that age, must quickly adjust to her grandmother's changing personality. The problems of the age difference between Mary and her grandmother will be immediately recognizable to young people, many of whom may be puzzled by the strange behavior of elder relatives. A small cast that includes a doctor, the cleaning woman, and the boy next door forms a support system for Mary. Although there are no photographs or illustrations, the clear and simple writing moves the story along.

98. **French, Dorothy K.** *Out of the Rough.* **New Readers, 1990. 64 pp. $3.50 paper (0-88336-213). Fiction.**
   Subjects: Sports, sports figures – Golf; Women – Stories
   Reading Level: Grade 3+   Interest Level: Grades 9–12

Sixteen-year-old Greta is thrilled to learn that Coach Savage has allowed her to join the boys' golf team. Bitterly resented for being the only girl on the team, Greta is determined to become the best golfer at Fields High. Although she experiences great disappointment when one of her teammates cheats and is eventually disqualified, Greta manages to bring her team to victory in the state tournament. Her triumph at winning is all the more rewarding because she has earned the respect and admiration of her peers. Drawings.

99. Frommer, Sara Hoskinson. *Kaleidoscope: A Collection of Stories.* New Readers, 1990. 32 pp. ea. $10.95 (set of eight) (0-88336-175-2). Fiction.

Subjects: Short stories

Reading Level: Grades 1–2   Interest Level: Grades 7–12

A set of eight very easy-to-read individually bound volumes that will hold the interest and stimulate the older reader. Each title tackles a situation in adult life and concludes the episode in a pleasing manner. Titles include *I'll Be Rich,* which deals with Marnee Wells, who has just received a chain letter and is struggling with a decision about what to do about it. *Dear Mary Ellen* is about a second wife who discovers a strange occurrence in the death of her husband's first wife. *Stop That Woman* concerns the identity of the robber of an armed bank truck. *No More Cats* tells about what happens when a beloved cat dies and a new kitten enters the household. Other titles in the series are *No Hunting; Hush, Little Baby; I Didn't Do It;* and *What Are Friends For?* Line drawings complement the text.

100. Gaines, M. C., ed. *Picture Stories from the Bible: The Old Testament in Full-Color Comic-Strip Form.* Illus. by Don Cameron. Scarf, 1979. 222 pp. $9.95 (0-934386-01-3). Nonfiction.

Subjects: Bible stories; Religion

Reading Level: Grade 4   Interest Level: Grades 7–12

Although the vocabulary used in the balloons that accompany the very attractive, brightly colored, comic-styled drawings in both this book and *Picture Stories from the Bible: The New Testament . . .* (1980) is not always as simple as one would like, these two titles cover the major stories of both the Old and New Testament and present them in a clear and readable format. These two abridged versions of Bible stories was originally published in 1943. (For the purposes of style, Gaines has revised the text of the 1943 edition.) Bible stories are constantly requested by young people. This set is very popular with those teenagers and adults who, because of a reading disability, are unable to read the legitimate text.

101. Galan, Fernando Javier. *A Long Road.* Cambridge, 1983. 30 pp. $1.95 paper (0-8428-9604-X). Fiction.

Subjects: Hispanic Americans; Immigration

Reading Level: Grades 2–3   Interest Level: Grades 10–12

Miguel must leave his wife and young family in San Luis, Mexico, and go to El Norte to seek work. Crossing the river at night, Miguel is able to hide from the border patrols and finds his way to Houston, Texas. Luckily, he is able to find work at a gas station, where in time he learns to become a mechanic. But he dreams each day of returning to his family. With help from friends in Houston, Miguel is able to begin the process of becoming a permanent resident, with great hope to bring his family to the United States, too. A gem of a high/low for older teens.

102. Galan, Fernando Javier. *One Summer.* Cambridge, 1983. 27 pp. $1.95 paper (0-8428-9605-8). Fiction.
   Subjects: Drug abuse; Jobs, job hunting
   Reading Level: Grades 3–4   Interest Level: Grades 9–12

Twenty-year-old David Ramon's dream is to become a social worker. He's also anxious to leave the small Texas town where he has grown up to experience a big city like New York or Chicago. At the suggestion of his priest, he applies for a social work position for the summer in New York City. David's work takes him to a halfway house for drug addicts. There he counsels young men, almost his own age. It is a summer of tremendous emotional and professional growth for David. For mature teens.

103. Galicich, Anne. *Samantha Smith: A Journey for Peace.* Dillon, 1987. 68 pp. $9.95 LB (0-87518-367-0). Nonfiction.
   Subjects: Women – Teenage
   Reading Level: Grades 3–4   Interest Level: Grades 7–12

The whole world grieved when in 1985, this young ambassador for world peace lost her life in a plane crash. This well-designed and well-documented biography traces Samantha's journey to the Kremlin. Writing a letter to Yuri Andropov about his new job caught the attention of the Russian leader and Samantha was invited to visit the Soviet Union. She toured the Soviet Union and joined the Children's Symposium for the 21st Century. Her death in a plane crash at age 13 brought home to the world how important children can be as ambassadors. The Soviet Union created a stamp in her memory. Her mother, Jane, established The Samantha Smith Foundation, an exchange program to encourage international friendship among young people. Teenagers will be inspired by Samantha's vision and she will not be forgotten. Includes photographs.

104. Gersdorf, A. G. *Eden's Daughters.* Fearon, 1987. 32 pp. $1.65 paper (0-8224-6152-8). Fiction.
   Subjects: Science fiction
   Reading Level: Grades 4–5   Interest Level: Grades 7–12

Ann and Sara are kidnapped at age 12 from a school dance. Now they are 20 and live in almost total isolation. They are being held by

Bluey a small, rather unattractive space creature. Bluey speaks little English, communicating for the most part with hand signals. Ann and Sara become oral historians, thinking that they are the only remaining earthlings, recording all the things on Earth that are important: Bruce Springsteen, break dancing, and all the other vital facts about life on Earth. But Sara and Ann are maturing and ask Bluey to bring boys as companions. The real fun begins when the "boys" arrive and the space creatures find out that the young people that they have captured are all girls—they were simply masquerading as boys when kidnapped during the dance because they had attended an all-girls school! Other Fastback Science Fiction titles in this series include *The Champion*, *Dateline: I.P.S.*, *The Flavorist*, *Hennesy's Test*, *Just in Case*, *Sinking Ship*, *The Spotter*, *Tripping*, and *Vital Force*.

105. **Gillianti, Simone.** *Rick Springfield.* **Simon & Schuster, 1984. 64 pp. $8.29 LB (0-671-53103-4); $2.95 paper (0-671-53104-2). Nonfiction.**
   Subjects: Biographies – Television; Music – Rock stars
   Reading Level: Grade 4+   Interest Level: Grades 7–12
   Known to millions as the former Dr. Noah Drake on "General Hospital," Rick Springfield is revealed as the superstar he really is. Winner of a Grammy for "Jessie's Girl," the American Music Awards Favorite Male Rock Vocalist, and the star of the movie *Hard to Hold*, the Australian-born performer has had an exciting career. Childhood details of his life as an "army brat" are briefly mentioned, although the focus of this book is on Rick's adult life. Gillianti emphasizes the hard times of Rick's career; stardom has not come overnight. Photographs of Rick's private and public life make this book exciting and personal. A book for fans and soon-to-be fans. Includes a discography.

106. **Glassman, Bruce.** *Everything You Need to Know about Stepfamilies.* **Rosen Group, 1988. 64 pp. $12.95 (0-8239-0815-1). Nonfiction.**
   Subjects: Family problems; Stepfamilies
   Reading Level: Grades 4–6   Interest Level: Grades 7–12
   Using excellent quality black-and-white and color photographs, Glassman discusses the problems and adjustments involved in having only one parent as a result of death or divorce. Skillfully written anecdotes flavor the text to give it a sensitive picture of the changes experienced when a stepparent enters the family. Real issues like changing last names, the adoption process, stepbrothers and stepsisters, and a new baby are all introduced as a way to demonstrate to teenagers that these

are indeed stressful times and that there are ways of handling the complex emotions that they may experience. A glossary appends the text.

107. **Gloeckner, Carolyn.** *Fernando Valenzuela.* **Crestwood House, 1985. 48 pp. $10.95 LB (0-89686-256-9). Nonfiction.**

Subjects: Biographies – Sports; Hispanic Americans; Sports, sports figures – Baseball

Reading Level: Grades 4–5   Interest Level: Grades 7–12

Fernando Valenzuela is not only a great pitcher, he is also a symbol for the Mexican communities in the United States. One of 12 children, Valenzuela knew from an early age that his skill in baseball could serve him well. When his older brothers joined a local Little League team, it seemed natural for Valenzuela to join. Eventually he proved himself to be a very talented pitcher, and at the age of 15 he was asked to play with a Mexican minor league team in his area. It was during this time that the scouts from the Los Angeles Dodgers saw him play and decided to talk him into moving to the United States. His success in the Dodger organization has made him a symbol for hard work and determination. Numerous black-and-white photographs accompany the text.

108. **Godfrey, Martyn.** *The Last War.* **Macmillan, 1989. 91 pp. $2.95 paper (0-02-041791-8). Fiction.**

Subjects: Nuclear warfare; War, war stories

Reading Level: Grade 4   Interest Level: Grades 7–12

Brad has survived a nuclear bomb attack and is hopeful that everything will be the same as it was before the attack. He hangs on to his hopes until he meets Angela, who shows him the futility of being a survivor. Brad and Angela face the horrors of a hunting wild dog pack, hordes of hungry, scavenging rats, and humans who have become hunters in their search for food. After Angela dies of radiation sickness, Brad faces the reality that there are no winners or losers in a nuclear war. Certainly not a hopeful picture of the future for teenagers, but many teenagers thrive on the maudlin. Charcoal drawings.

109. **Goodman, Michael E.** *Lawrence Taylor.* **Crestwood House, 1988. 48 pp. $10.95 LB (0-89686-365-4). Nonfiction.**

Subjects: Biographies – Sports; Drug abuse; Sports, sports figures – Football

Reading Level: Grades 4–5   Interest Level: Grades 7–12

Lawrence Taylor is one of football's most talented linebackers. His career began when, at 15, he joined a Jaycee football team just to be able to take a team trip to Pittsburgh. This led to a great career with the New

York Giants and to a battle with drugs. After breaking free of his drug addiction, "L.T." led the Giants to a Super Bowl championship and made a permanent name for himself in football. Having regained control of his life, Taylor plans to play for several more years and to stay away from drugs. Numerous black-and-white photographs accompany the text.

110. **Goodman, Michael E.** *Magic Johnson.* **Crestwood House, 1988. 48 pp. $10.95 LB (0-89686-382-4). Nonfiction.**

Subjects: Biographies – Sports; Black Americans; Sports, sports figures – Basketball

Reading Level: Grades 4–5   Interest Level: Grades 7–12

Earvin "Magic" Johnson, Jr., has been one of the most consistently great basketball players in recent history. Nicknamed "Magic" because of incredible moves on the court, he helped lead his college team to an NCAA championship and the Los Angeles Lakers to five NBA championships. A leader on and off the court, Magic is another spokesperson in the fight against drugs and donates much of his free time to helping charitable causes. Numerous black-and-white photographs accompany the text.

111. **Green, Carl R., and William R. Sanford.** *The Black Cat.* **Crestwood House, 1987. 48 pp. $9.95 LB (0-89686-310-7). Fiction.**

Subjects: Crime stories; Mysteries

Reading Level: Grade 4   Interest Level: Grades 7–12

Based on the Edgar Allan Poe short story of the same name (this title is based on the 1941 remake of the film *The Black Cat*). The story revolves around a rich old woman who lives in a house full of cats and is surrounded by greedy relatives eager to cash in on their future inheritance. The eccentric Henrietta Winchester is expected to die. Her money-hungry family has assembled at the house waiting for their inheritances. When she does not oblige them quickly enough, she is murdered. Teenagers will enjoy the antics as they read how the cats solve the crime. Black-and-white frames from the film throughout. Other titles in the Movie Monster series include *The House of Seven Gables* and *House of Fear.*

112. **Green, Carl R., and William R. Sanford.** *The Mole People.* **Crestwood House, 1985. 48 pp. $9.95 LB (0-89686-262-3). Nonfiction.**

Subjects: Archaeology; Movies

Reading Level: Grades 3–5   Interest Level: Grades 7–12

Green and Sanford have taken "B" movies and in narrative style have attempted to turn them into high/low stories. *The Mole People,* just one title in this series of eight, is about an archaeological expedition to Sumer in search of a 5,000-year-old civilization. Dr. Roger Bentley, chief archaeologist, discovers by accident a city of strange Albino people who hold the Mole people in bondage. In the process of unraveling the mystery of the molemen, Bentley falls in love with Adad, a non-Mole and non-Albino, an original throwback to the old Sumerian culture. All's well that ends well—and the junior high and up television generation will enjoy following this and the other titles in the Movie Monster series: *Black Friday, Bride of Frankenstein, Dracula's Daughter, Ghost of Frankenstein, The Raven, Tarantula,* and *Werewolf of London.*

113. **Green, Carl R., and William R. Sanford.** *The Revenge of the Creature.* **Crestwood House, 1987. 48 pp. $9.95 LB (0-89686-313-1). Fiction.**

Subjects: Monsters; Science fiction
Reading Level: Grades 4–5   Interest Level: Grades 7–12

Written as a sequel to the film *Creature from the Black Lagoon* (1954), scientists have now returned to the Amazon's Black Lagoon to capture the Gill Man for a research project. They soon become aware that this half-man half-fish creature has human feelings and problem-solving abilities. But when the Gill Man manages to escape from his laboratory pool, he not only terrorizes and kills anyone in his way, but he kidnaps Helen, a young research scientist, and the monster hunt begins. Finally, Helen is rescued but the Gill Man escapes to the sea so that Hollywood can use him in a future monster film. Photographs throughout.

114. **Green, Iris.** *Anything for a Friend.* **Scholastic, 1979. 127 pp. $2.95 paper (0-590-30590-5). Fiction.**

Subjects: Jobs, job hunting; Women – Stories
Reading Level: Grades 3–3.4   Interest Level: Grades 8–10

With the help of her friend, Margo, June gets a job as a beautician. She is happy doing the work she enjoys, earning money, and meeting new people, especially Tom, a beauty supply salesman. Trouble begins when June sees Margo stealing from the shop, and realizes that she is also stealing the shop's customers by having them come to her house for their haircuts. June does not want to tell the boss about Margo because Margo is her friend and helped her get the job in the first place. Finally, Carl, the owner, confronts the entire staff. June, however, stands up for herself, and Margo learns a harsh lesson. June wins the respect of her fellow workers and Tom's heart, too. An interesting, fast-paced story that gives insight into possible careers for today's young people. Photographs throughout.

115. **Greenya, Suzanne, and John Greenya.** *Lane Four.* **Scholastic, 1974. 95 pp. $2.95 paper (0-590-03459-6). Fiction.**

Subjects: Sports, sports figures – Swimming; Women – Stories
Reading Level: Grade 2   Interest Level: Grades 7–10

Mary Cutter is used to competing in lane four, the lane given to the swimmer with the best time. She has been winning races since she was ten, but now her coach asks her to compete in the butterfly, the one stroke she hates. Will she ever be able to win at this? Mary's hard-driving coach makes her put in much time and effort on this stroke and Mary begins to wonder if it is all worthwhile. Of course it is when she sets a new national record for the butterfly at the next big meet and ties the record in two other strokes. This is a well-written account of a hardworking athlete. Photographs throughout.

116. **Gunning, Thomas G.** *Amazing Escapes.* **Putnam, 1984. 108 pp. $8.95 (0-396-08324-2). Nonfiction.**

Subjects: Adventure
Reading Level: Grades 3–4   Interest Level: Grades 7–12

It took luck and courage for individuals and families to carry out these nine true escapes. Two East German families built a hot air balloon that lifted eight family members over the Berlin Wall to freedom. Teens can empathize with a 17-year-old escaping from Cuba who nearly froze while inside the wheel case of a commercial airplane. And they may shiver when reading how six men broke out of prison in Siberia and walked 4,000 miles through China and the Gobi Desert to freedom in India; four survived. Photographs and newsclips throughout.

117. **Gutman, Bill.** *Rookie Summer.* **Turman Publishing, 1988. 80 pp. $2.95 LB (0-89872-300-0). Fiction.**

Subjects: Sports, sports figures – Baseball
Reading Level: Grade 4   Interest Level: Grades 7–12

Bobby Blaine is 17 years old and lives in Iowa. His extraordinary baseball skills are seen by a major league scout. To Bobby's amazement, the scout wants him to play for the San Francisco Giants that summer. Bobby's parents reluctantly agree that he should have the chance to play in the big leagues. During the first two months as a Giant, Bobby's batting average was outstanding and he was receiving national press coverage. The club was starting an important series to determine first place when Bobby's streak of errors begins. The team loses, and Bobby has to face the fact that he has failed on the baseball field for the first time in his life. The most important thing that Bobby learns is that everyone has to learn how to fail and that he won't always be perfect. He returns home to his family and starts high school again with his friends—all with the knowledge that he still has time to pursue his dream as a baseball player.

118. Gutman, Bill. *Smitty.* **Turman Publishing, 1988. 78 pp. $2.95 LB (0-89872-301-9). Fiction.**

Subjects: Sports, sports figures – Basketball; Women – Stories
Reading Level: Grade 4   Interest Level: Grades 7–12

Valerie, a high school basketball star, has a bright future ahead of her when she is being recruited by colleges in her senior year. Her father takes a new job and the family moves to a small town. When she enrolls at her new school, Valerie finds that it does not have a girls' basketball team. The obvious solution to her dilemma is to play on the boys' team. Overcoming the hostility of the coach and team members, Valerie has a good season. As the story develops, the reader is made aware that Valerie is obsessed with basketball because of a deathbed promise she made to her brother to become the best player possible. Valerie does come to the conclusion that she cannot live her life for someone else and that there are more important things in life than just basketball.

119. Hallman, Ruth. *Gimme Something, Mister!* **Westminster John Knox, 1978. 103 pp. $8.95 (0-664-32638-2). Fiction.**

Subjects: Mysteries; Women – Stories
Reading Level: Grades 2–3   Interest Level: Grades 7–9

Fourteen-year-old Jackie visits her three spinster great-aunts in their old Victorian-style house in New Orleans. While there, she desperately wants to attend the Parade of Rex. Against the wishes of her aunts, but with the approval of the charwoman, Bertha, Jackie sneaks out to the celebration in the costume of a painter. A valuable necklace is thrown into the crowd and she catches it. Clutching the necklace and believing it to be a cheap trinket, she walks away from the crowd with her prize, only to be puzzled by the furious struggle and chase she is suddenly caught up in. Is the necklace only a fake, or could it be of real value?

There is a lot of humor to this slight mystery. Although all the characters are stereotyped in both locale and situation, the dialogue is spontaneous, and Jackie has the kind of spunk that carries the reader along to a rather unpredictable conclusion. Large type; no illustrations or photographs.

120. Hansel, Mark V. *What Is a Crime?* Cambridge, 1983. 26 pp. $1.95 paper (0-8428-9612-0). Nonfiction.

Subjects: Crime; Police work
Reading Level: Grades 3–4   Interest Level: Grades 7–12

Older teens who have trouble understanding what a crime is and how the criminal justice system works will find this slim volume informative. Youthful offenders involved with drugs and minor scuffles come to understand the role of Legal Aid, plea bargaining, and the functions of police, prosecutors, lawyers, judges, and the court.

121. Harralson, David M. *Jesus of Nazareth.* Cambridge, 1983. 40 pp. $1.95 paper (0-8428-9608-2). Nonfiction.

Subjects: Bible stories; Biographies – Religion; Religion
Reading Level: Grades 3–4   Interest Level: Grades 7–12

A short biography of Jesus told from the historical point of view as recorded in the New Testament. The text is largely in conversational format. Classic miracles, such as the raising of Lazarus from the dead, are recounted simply. The book ends with the Resurrection. No illustrations.

122. Harralson, David M. *Stories from the Old Testament.* Cambridge, 1983. 39 pp. $1.95 paper (0-8428-9607-4). Nonfiction.

Subjects: Bible stories; Religion
Reading Level: Grades 3–4   Interest Level: Grades 7–12

From the 39 books of the Old Testament, brief chapters in narrative format capture the essence of some of the stories. The Book of Genesis, the Story of Ruth, David and Solomon, and others survive this easy-to-read retelling. No illustrations.

123. Howard, Don. *Moving Dirt.* Scholastic, 1978. 129 pp. $2.95 paper (0-590-08339-2). Fiction.

Subjects: Construction work; Jobs, job hunting
Reading Level: Grade 4+   Interest Level: Grades 9–12

After graduation from high school Mark Hawkins accepts a job as a heavy equipment operator, and his first assignment is on a very dangerous construction job. But Mark learns quickly, enjoys the work, and makes friends with the other construction workers. Since construction is a seasonal business, Mark has a lot of time off, and he makes good use of his time by dating Kathy Faraday. On his second job assignment, tragedy strikes, and Mark's good friend Ben is killed. The union steps in and tries to get Mark and his coworkers to lie about Ben's death and blame it on negligence by the construction company. But Mark must tell the truth: Ben was killed because he drove his bulldozer recklessly. Mark refuses to lie for the union and maintains his integrity. In spite of Ben's death and the disillusionment with the union, Mark decides that heavy equipment operating is the job for him. This is an interesting moral story, and a good introduction to a career possibility for today's young people. Drawings illustrate the text.

124. **Hudson, Wade, and Valerie Wilson Wesley.** *AFRO-BETS Book of Black Heroes from A–Z.* **Just Us Books, 1989. 64 pp. $7.95 paper (0-940975-02-5). Nonfiction.**
Subjects: Biographies – Black Americans; Black Americans
Reading Level: Grades 3–4   Interest Level: Grades 7–12

Contemporary and historic personalities are profiled in this collection of 49 black men and women of achievement. The entries are concise and the book is designed for both browsing and as an adjunct to school assignments. Black-and-white photographs enhance the text.

125. **Hughes, Tracy.** *Everything You Need to Know about Teen Pregnancy.* **Rosen Group, 1988. 64 pp. $12.95 LB (0-8239-0810-0). Nonfiction.**
Subjects: Birth control; Pregnancy and parenthood
Reading Level: Grades 4–6   Interest Level: Grades 7–12

Using excellent black-and-white and color photographs, Hughes discusses such aspects of teenage pregnancy as the causes and nature of pregnancy, the proper care for mother and baby, and alternative choices such as adoption and abortion. The text includes birth control information and describes abortion methods. At-risk teens, who frequently have poor reading skills, need to become educated about the responsibilities involved in teen parenting. A forum for discussion should help resolve some of the questions teenagers may have concerning early pregnancy. A glossary appends the text; a list of agencies that provides information for intelligent decision making is also included.

126. **Hull, Jessie Redding.** *The Other Side of Yellow.* **New Readers, 1980. 63 pp. $3.25 paper (0-88336-706-8). Fiction.**
Subjects: Crime stories
Reading Level: Grade 4   Interest Level: Grades 7–12

Twenty-three years old, married, and a father, Brad Jensen is on the second day of his third job in six weeks. As he rushes to his next assignment to fix a furnace, his boss tells him on the radio that he has 20 minutes to get to the next place or get fired. Trying to beat a light, Brad hits a child and kills him. Brad is arrested and tried, found guilty, and begins serving his sentence. While in prison, Brad is encouraged by the warden to develop his skills in another field. In the meantime, CBers report that they had heard Brad's boss telling him to hurry although the boss had denied saying it. The dead child's mother also tells the judge that she had not been truthful at the trial, as she had quarreled with her child and he was late for school that day. Because people lied at the trial, Brad is released until a new trial can be held. Illustrated with pen-and-ink drawings.

127. **Hull, Jessie Redding.** *Take Care of Millie.* **New Readers, 1990. 64 pp. $3.50 paper (0-88336-216). Fiction.**

Subjects: Aging; Family problems
Reading Level: Grade 3+   Interest Level: Grades 9–12

After the death of her husband, Millie feels independent for the first time in her life. Concerned about her mother's welfare, Jan, Millie's daughter, convinces Millie to move into her apartment and to consider selling the house in which Millie has lived for the past 35 years. When Jan begins to make decisions for her mother and interferes with her daily life, Millie realizes that her happiness is at stake. In a dramatic confrontation, Jan tearfully confesses that just before her father died, he asked her to take care of Millie. Millie reassures her daughter that she is perfectly capable of looking after herself and is actually looking forward to a life of her own. Drawings.

128. **Ibbitson, John.** *The Wimp and the Jock.* **Macmillan, 1989. 85 pp. $2.95 paper (0-02-041792-6). Fiction.**

Subjects: Sports, sports figures – Football
Reading Level: Grade 4   Interest Level: Grades 7–12

" 'Randy—it's a baseball, not a soccer ball.' Coach Bronstein covered his face with his hands. 'Soccer balls we kick—*baseballs we catch!* ' "

"I looked down and stared at my feet—even my eyeballs were blushing. I hadn't *meant* to kick the baseball. But when someone hit a grounder right at me, I panicked and kicked it away. It was a natural thing to do."

Thus begins the football career of Randy, the most inept athlete the coach has ever seen. A humorously written story about Randy who is conned into trying out for the football team and the misadventures that follow. Illustrated with pen-and-ink drawings.

129. **International Diabetes Center.** *Simplified Learning Series.* **Diabetes Center, 1988. $19.95 set (0-937721-48-4). Nonfiction.**

Subjects: Health, health problems – Diabetes
Reading Level: Grades 2–3.5   Interest Level: Grades 7–12

This is a collection of 16 Low Literacy Level pamphlets that are designed to teach diabetics concepts about diabetes so that they can learn how to manage the illness better. Although the pamphlets are designed for adults, with their colorful and often humorous drawings, they are most suitable for the teenaged diabetic. Titles include *What Is Diabetes Type I*, *What Is Diabetes Type II*, *Giving Insulin 1 Kind*, *Giving Insulin 2 Kinds*, *Healthy Eating*, *Diabetes and Exercise*, *Blood Sugar Testing with Glucostix*, *Diabetes and Alcohol*, *Diabetes and Your Feet*, and a number of other fact-filled pamphlets.

130. **Jackson, Anita.** *A Deadly Game.* **Fearon, 1979. 48 pp. $3.90 paper (0-8224-6434-9). Fiction.**

Subjects: Mysteries
Reading Level: Grade 3   Interest Level: Grades 9–12

An anonymous character, while on a visit to a thrift shop, discovers an old dust-covered chess set. The message on the lid of the set is peculiar—"This is a game of life or death." The new owner quickly discovers the meaning of the message. The loser in chess games played with the set meets sudden death. Armed with this secret weapon, the new owner engages his uncle, brother, wife, and friend in a game. As each loses, sudden death is his or her fate, and the anonymous narrator inherits the fortunes of his family and friend.

Now a wealthy man, he is able to travel and to dabble in business dealings with large stakes. As he travels, he uses his mysterious chess set to gain entry into a variety of situations. Why does he suddenly reveal the secret of his game? As he challenges an expert chess player, he finds himself the loser, facing death. He writes this story as he awaits his own death. There is a definite Edgar Allan Poe quality to this eerie tale of one man's greed and eventual punishment. No illustrations or photographs.

131. **Jackson, Bernard.** *Modern Fables.* **New Readers, 1987. 64 pp. $3.25 paper (0-88336-310-0). Fiction.**

Subjects: Fables; Short stories
Reading Level: Grade 4   Interest Level: Grades 7–12

Twenty of Aesop's fables are updated in this book. The fable with the moral that size does not always count has a short, skinny kid saving the big, mean football hero with the Heimlich maneuver. The fable with the moral that slow and steady wins the race is told with two brothers competing academically—Grant, although bright and a good student, parties, while Howard stays at home working on his studies. Of course, Howard wins the competition and the prize. Charcoal drawings throughout.

132. **James, Stuart.** *The Firefighter.* **Scholastic, 1979. 127 pp. $2.95 paper (0-590-35547-3). Fiction.**

Subjects: Firefighting; Jobs, job hunting
Reading Level: Grades 3–3.4   Interest Level: Grades 8–12

Frankie Cargo is a firefighter who loves his job and has wanted to be a firefighter ever since he was a little boy. Problems arise when a man is killed during a fire, and John Pearson, a friend of the dead man, blames Frankie and threatens to "get him." Frankie is scared, not only because of Pearson's threats, but also because whenever a firefighter dies, it is a reminder to all of how dangerous the job really is. During a multialarm fire, Frankie must put all his personal feelings aside and work side by side with Pearson. He is even called upon to save Pearson's life. Frankie becomes a hero and gets a departmental citation, a promotion, and the respect of Pearson. An exciting story that gives a picture of the life and work of city firefighters. Photographs throughout.

133. *The Job Box: Pacemaker Occupational Resource Module,* **2nd ed. Fearon, 1989. 56 booklets. $93.00 (0-8224-4037-7). Nonfiction.**

Subjects: Jobs, job hunting
Reading Level: Grades 2.5–3   Interest Level: Grades 7–12

In this completely revised and updated second edition of the popular *Job Box,* these 56 photograph-illustrated pamphlets describe many entry-level jobs that teenagers with low reading levels can aspire for while working to attain their general equivalency diploma. Each pamphlet is devoted to a specific job and helps students analyze the duties, requirements, and rewards of each position. Job information includes Automotive, Building and Construction, Food Services, Industrial and Retail, Office and Clerical, Ranching, Farming and Horticulture, and Trades and Services positions. Photographs.

134. **Johnson, Linda Carlson.** *Everything You Need to Know about Your Parent's Divorce.* **Rosen Group, 1989. $12.95 LB (0-8239-1012-1). Nonfiction.**

Subjects: Divorce; Family problems
Reading Level: Grades 4–6   Interest Level: Grades 7–12

Using excellent black-and-white and color photographs, Johnson has presented teenagers with a guide to view divorce as the beginning of a different kind of family life and to lend understanding about what happens to the lives of their parents. Johnson tries to get teenagers to understand that divorce will affect the feelings of everyone and covers all the issues involved as the family divides: loss of the parent who left, custody, parent dating, parent remarrying, guilt, and loneliness. A glossary appends the text.

135. Jones, S. D. *Fortune in Men's Eyes, Book V: 1853.* **Fearon, 1989. 72 pp. $3.90 paper (0-8224-4755-X). Fiction.**

Subjects: American history
Reading Level: Grades 4–5   Interest Level: Grades 7–12

S. D. Jones continues Volumes V to VIII of the Roberts family saga begun by Bledsoe (see Lucy Jane Bledsoe, *Colony of Fear, Book I: 1692*, in this chapter), starting in 1853. As America enters a period of great social change, the next four titles in the series focus on the lives of the family members and how they deal with the changes in the still young America.

In *Fortune in Men's Eyes, Book V: 1853*, Matthew Wilder and his companion, runaway slave Zeke Rutlidge, seek gold in the West and come into conflict with the government's plans to resettle Indian tribes in the Colorado territory. In *The Debt, Book VI: 1877*, bitter feelings persist during Reconstruction and the sixth generation of the Roberts family must now deal with family divisiveness, carpetbaggers, and the Ku Klux Klan in a struggle to maintain their economic stability. In *A Splendid Little War, Book VII: 1897*, the seventh generation of the Roberts family has Olive Dunford, a newspaper columnist, expressing outrage at the treatment of the Cubans by the Spanish. When Olive's young cousin joins the army, Olive learns firsthand about the horrors of war. In *A Test of Loyalty, Book VIII: 1920*, World War I has ended. Harry Drewes, Olive's son, is a grown man. The eighth generation of the Roberts family are a privileged class in America (having made their fortune in paper mills), but Harry wants to discover firsthand what life is like for the working class in America. The eighth volume of the saga ends with the awakening of social consciousness in Harry and the growth of unions in America.

136. Jones, S. D. *The Puppeteer.* **Fearon, 1987. 64 pp. $3.00 paper (0-8224-2410-X). Fiction.**

Subjects: Mysteries; Spy stories
Reading Level: Grade 4   Interest Level: Grades 7–12

CIA agent J. K. Porter is still struggling over his failure to identify and capture the double agent he was after on his last assignment. While on vacation in the Maine woods, he tries to distance himself from the case, but is surprised when Tyson, his boss, shows up at the cabin. His fishing and vacation is interrupted by Tyson's conversation that returns to the unsolved case. Revealing information not itemized in a secret report that Porter had turned into Tyson prior to his vacation indicates to Porter that Tyson is indeed a double agent. The complex tale of Tyson's life as a double agent unravels as the reader learns that the KGB agent involved is Tyson's daughter. A terrific tale for the reader who is making good progress in comprehension and is learning to integrate the details of a complex plot and character construction. This is one title in the Double Fastback Spy series. Other titles are *Against the Wall, The Black Gold Conspiracy, Claw the Cold, Cold Earth, A Dangerous Game, The Deadly Cuckoo, The Last Red Rose, Picture of Evil, The Silver Spy,* and *Till Death Do Us Part.*

137. **Kaye, Annene.** *Van Halen.* **Simon & Schuster, 1985. 64 pp. $8.79 LB (0-671-55032-2); $3.50 paper (0-671-55031-4). Nonfiction.**

Subjects: Biographies – Music; Music – Rock stars
Reading Level: Grade 4+   Interest Level: Grades 7–12

The four men who make up the Van Halen rock group all showed early musical talent. The brothers, drummer Alex and guitarist Eddie, learned much from their father, a professional musician. Dutch by descent, they were later joined by vocalist David Lee Roth and bass player Michael Anthony. They are not only creative as songwriters and musicians but also seem to display an unusual compassion for animals, nature, and the people around them. The book is filled with photographs, and the writing style is smooth. One comes away with a very positive view of rock musicians. An exceptional high/low biography.

138. **Kehret, Peg.** *The Winner.* **Turman Publishing, 1988. 83 pp. $2.95 LB (0-89872-302-7). Fiction.**

Subjects: Health, health problems – Paralysis; Mysteries
Reading Level: Grade 4   Interest Level: Grades 7–12

Bart Collins is a runner with ambitions to win the state meet and other competitions. While running one morning, he notices a white van in front of Lisa's house and two men loading things into it. Later on, Bart is concerned when he learns that Lisa has not been in school and is missing. That same day Bart goes to a friend's house where they party. Ignoring his coach's advice, Bart uses alcohol and marijuana. Going out for a pizza, Bart is hit by a car and the accident paralyzes him. Kandi, a nurse, tries to help Bart overcome his depression by telling him that there are still worthwhile things that he can do from a wheelchair. He begins by telling the police what he knows about the white van the day Lisa disappeared. This helps the police to locate where Lisa is being held, even though one of the burglars tries to take Bart hostage. Bart gets away and by doing this he is given the courage to plan for a productive life, despite his paralysis, that even includes racing in his wheelchair.

139. **Keller, Roseanne.** *Fitting in Series.* **New Readers, 1990. 32 pp. $14.25 set (0-88336-986-E). Fiction.**
     Subjects: English as a Second Language; Hispanic Americans; Immigration
     Reading Level: Grades 1–2   Interest Level: Grades 7–12

A set of eight titles, each dealing with a person who is struggling to learn English. The characters come from a variety of backgrounds and cultures, including Laos, Mexico, Poland, and China. "Woman's Work, Man's Work" is a story about a young couple and their three children who come to the United States from Mexico for a better life. And life is good—until Ernesto is laid off from his job because he does not speak English. Carmen is forced to leave the care of her three young children to Ernesto while she seeks employment in a sewing factory. The role switch for this young couple is devastating for each of them, especially the housework for Ernesto, and he feels that there is no way out because, in his own words, "Carmen, I need to find a job." Ernesto stops speaking. His eyes burn. He is trying to hold back the tears. "But my English is such a problem." But help is on the way because the factory where Carmen works is going to offer free English classes to all the workers and their families. Other titles in the series that will lend understanding to young people about the difficulties that one encounters when they move to the United States and need to learn English are *Fighting Back, Honorable Grandfather, The Magic Village, The Race, Talk Like a Cowboy, The Trip,* and *You Are Not My Father.* Line drawings complement the text.

140. **Keller, Roseanne.** *Five Dog Night and Other Tales.* **New Readers, 1979. 32 pp. $1.85 paper (0-88336-320-8). Fiction.**
     Subjects: Adventure; Humor; Short stories
     Reading Level: Grades 2–3   Interest Level: Grades 10–12

A slim collection of four humorous short stories, all with survival as a theme. Each is illustrated with rather casual black-and-white line drawings. In the story "Bear in the Sky," the Heimlich maneuver saves a life during a plane trip. "Five Dog Night" is about two flyers who survive a crash landing. In "See You in Valdez," a boy must learn to care for his family after his father's departure to work on the Alaska pipeline. The final story, "When I Think of You," is about missing someone you love. A glossary appends the text.

141. **Keller, Roseanne.** *Two for the Road.* **New Readers, 1979. 32 pp. $1.85 paper (0-88336-319-4). Fiction.**
     Subjects: Humor; Short stories; Women – Stories
     Reading Level: Grades 1–2   Interest Level: Grades 9–12

A slim little volume containing two very short stories. In the first,

"Ms. Trucker," Ann is the central character. With humor and skill, a most contemporary message of the women's movement is delivered in a very simple format reminiscent of a primary reader (one sentence per line). The saga of Ann, a trucker, and Tom, a mechanic, trying to break out of their traditional roles, is hilarious. Older teenagers will understand the role identification scenario. The other tale, "The Ups and Downs of a Pikes Peak Peanut Pusher" (two and one-half pages), is a comical look at a man who pushed a peanut up Pikes Peak.

This title, and others in the series, are recommended by the publisher as adult basic education material, but older teenagers will find the books meaningful to their experiences as well. A glossary is included.

142. **Keller, Roseanne.** *When a Baby Is New.* **New Readers, 1984. 48 pp. $2.45 paper (0-88336-517-0). Nonfiction.**

Subjects: Pregnancy and parenthood
Reading Level: Grades 1–2   Interest Level: Grades 7–12

A charming guide to the care of the baby for new or expectant parents. The illustrations are especially appropriate. The reader experiences the joys and frustrations of child care through Lil and Bob, who have just become parents of a baby girl. Patience and love are stressed as primary to the well-being of both child and parents. The care and handling of the baby during feeding, washing, playing, and so forth, are demonstrated with humorous line drawings and a brief but serious-toned text.

143. **Keller, Roseanne.** *Who Can You Trust?* **New Readers, 1988. 16 pp. $1.25 paper (0-88336-92D-3). Fiction.**

Subjects: Crime stories; Mysteries.
Reading Level: Grades 3–4   Interest Level: Grades 7–12

Helen runs every morning. One day while running she is approached by a bicyclist, flashing a badge, who tells her that he is a policeman on the lookout for possible thieves in the neighborhood. Now, every morning he joins Helen on her run. One day Helen invites him to her home for coffee, and he checks the locks on the door and quizzes Helen on valuables hidden in the home. Several days later, he is caught robbing the house. A tidy surprise ending greets the reader when Helen's husband, a detective, appears to arrest the bogus detective. This is but one of the ten mysteries in this series that has been adapted from the Ellery Queen and Alfred Hitchcock mystery magazines. Other titles in the series are *A Dash of Murder, The Problem of the Pink Post Office, Mini-Scam, The Crystal Set, New Orleans Getaway, The Stolen Romney, Toasted Onions, Line of Fire,* and *Mr. Strang Picks Up the Pieces.*

144. **Kelley, Leo.** *Vacation in Space.* **Fearon, 1979. 64 pp. $3.99 paper (0-8224-3203-X). Fiction.**

Subjects: Astronauts; Science fiction; Space exploration
Reading Level: Grades 3–4   Interest Level: Grades 7–12

This is Steve Estrada's first long assignment in space. A new astronaut aboard the *Voyager*, he has become a victim of space fever midway through his assignment. He and a small crew are responsible for transporting sleeping humans to Galaxy 5. The humans are to build an Earth Colony on Planet 1 of Star 84 in Galaxy 5. But Steve is exhausted and all he can think about is how he can get off the speeding *Voyager*. The crew recognizes Steve's exhaustion and it is suggested they all take a vacation in Space World, the vacation satellite, for some much needed rest and recreation. While vacationing, Steve meets beautiful Sybil, who casts a spell over him. He falls so in love with her that he walks right into her trap. Sybil is part of a clandestine space network whose mission is to kidnap the sleeping humans aboard the *Voyager* and send them to Planet Ming as slaves to work in the Ming Mines. Fortunately for Steve and the crew, Sybil's plan is foiled. An imaginative science fiction story, which is one of six in the Galaxy 5 series. Other titles in this series by Leo Kelley about Steve Estrada and the crew of the *Voyager* are *Goodbye to Earth, On the Red World, Dead Moon, Where No Sun Shines,* and *King of the Stars.* All contain several pen-and-ink sketches of Steve and the crew members.

145. **Kenna, Gail Wilson.** *Along the Gold Rush Trail.* **New Readers, 1982. 96 pp. $3.75 paper (0-88336-752-1). Fiction.**

Subjects: Frontier life (U.S.); West (U.S.)
Reading Level: Grade 3   Interest Level: Grades 9–12

Yearning for fortune and adventure, Eugene heads for California during the 1849 gold rush. Undaunted by the hardships of prairie life and the dangers of the Santa Fe Trail, he is determined to become a miner. Weary, hungry, and penniless, Eugene survives through the help of a doctor he befriends along the way. Together they make the journey west, crossing mountains and deserts in order to reach the California gold fields. At journey's end, Eugene has matured considerably, manifesting courage, humanity, and an indomitable spirit. Drawings.

146. **Keran, Shirley.** *Underwater Specialists.* **Crestwood House, 1988. 48 pp. $10.95 LB (0-89686-400-6). Nonfiction.**

Subjects: Diving, underwater; Jobs, job hunting
Reading Level: Grades 4–6   Interest Level: Grades 7–10

Most people consider diving to be a leisure activity, but there are some who make their living underwater. These divers work different areas, such as marine biology, archaeology, marine geology, offshore oil drilling, demolition, and rescue. All professional divers have one thing in common: they are highly trained and use elaborate safety measures to protect themselves. In order to be certified, divers must complete training courses that teach them how to use the various pieces of equipment and how to avoid problems while underwater. These courses are available in many areas, making diving a career that anyone can try. Numerous color photographs and a glossary/index accompany the text.

147. Kevles, Bettyann. *Listening In.* Scholastic, 1979-4. 95 pp. $2.95 paper (0-590-30579-4). Fiction.
Subjects: Deafness; Disabilities; Physical disabilities
Reading Level: Grades 3–4   Interest Level: Grades 7–11

A leak in a gas main has exploded, leaving Kate deaf and her parents dead. Kate, suddenly handicapped, is forced to learn sign language. This tragedy has caused a major disruption in her life, and adjustment to the change is coming slowly. The one thing that makes her feel happy and needed is the work she is doing with monkeys at the zoo. Kate has been working with several monkeys, teaching them sign language. She is making great progress and finds the job rewarding.

The reader assumes at this point that the author's theme is to show us how a young woman, recently handicapped, can make a comeback to society, in this case working in sign therapy with monkeys. Instead, the author has decided to use Kate's deafness as a transitional theme. A new monkey who enters the laboratory is a visitor from outer space and communicates with Kate via mind-speak. The monkey, Zee, has a mission to return to his planet with the history of earth. Although the story is a little farfetched, young people with a hearing disability will be comforted by knowing of Kate's feelings of inadequacy as a result of her hearing loss. Her struggle to overcome her handicap will give them confidence to persevere. Attractive photographs complement the text.

148. Keyishian, Elizabeth. *Everything You Need to Know about Smoking.* Rosen Group, 1989. 64 pp. $12.95 LB (0-8239-1017-2). Nonfiction.
Subjects: Health, health problems – Smoking; Smoking
Reading Level: Grades 4–6   Interest Level: Grades 7–12

Using excellent black-and-white and color photographs, Keyishian discusses the dangerous effects of smoking. The variety of health hazards that smoking presents, the addictive nature of nicotine, and the difficulties that one encounters when trying to quit are handled in a format that will enable high/low readers to gather enough information so that they can make intelligent decisions about smoking. A glossary appends the text.

149. **Koenig, Teresa.** *Bruce Springsteen.* **Crestwood House, 1986. 32 pp. $9.95 LB (0-89686-303-4). Nonfiction.**

Subjects: Biographies – Music; Music – Rock stars
Reading Level: Grades 4–5   Interest Level: Grades 7–12

Bruce Springsteen grew up in an era that felt the influence of Elvis Presley and the Beatles, and that atmosphere gave him the motivation to become the rock star he is today. Born in New Jersey, Springsteen spent much of his teenage life playing the guitar and composing songs. By 1972, he had played with many different bands and finally signed with a record company. Springsteen's music has met with both great critical acclaim and huge public popularity. Springsteen is the "rocker" of the common man, but he is certainly not a common talent. Numerous photographs accompany the text.

150. **Koenig, Teresa.** *Lionel Richie.* **Crestwood House, 1986. 32 pp. $9.95 LB (0-89686-302-6). Nonfiction.**

Subjects: Biographies – Music; Black Americans; Music – Rock stars
Reading Level: Grades 4–5   Interest Level: Grades 7–12

Growing up in Alabama, Lionel Richie learned about music from his grandmother. Her efforts began to pay off when Richie met the group that would become the Commodores. Brought in as a saxophone player, Richie soon became a lead singer for the group and the composer of many of their hit songs. After ten years with the band, he decided to go out on his own and has become one of the hottest recording stars of the last 20 years. Numerous photographs accompany the text.

151. **Kropp, Paul.** *Baby, Baby.* **EMC, 1984. 96 pp. $4.50 paper (0-88436-962-5). Fiction.**

Subjects: Adoption; Pregnancy and parenthood
Reading Level: Grades 4–5   Interest Level: Grades 9–12

Sixteen-year-old Lori has been seeing more of her high school beau despite her mother's protestations and friends' warnings against the possible consequences of a romantic involvement between two very young people. Lori allows herself to be swept away by her feelings for Dave, and this new passion makes her act irresponsibly. When Lori becomes pregnant, she is faced with some very hard choices. Each is given serious consideration, but the idea of abortion as the easiest, practical resolution is closed to her from the outset. In her decision to have the baby and give it up for adoption, Lori is not motivated by any formally moral or religious arguments, but by an overwhelming love and responsibility that she begins to feel for the child.

This sobering story of Lori's painful maturation is not marred by antiabortion sermonizing, but is in itself a simple testimony to a young girl's developing humanity.

152. **Kropp, Paul.** *Burn-Out.* **EMC, 1982. 96 pp. $4.50 paper (0-88436-815-7). Fiction.**

Subjects: Adventure; Crime stories
Reading Level: Grade 3   Interest Level: Grades 7–12

Chewie, Bob, and Cindy suspect that arson is responsible for the series of fires in their neighborhood—a suspicion confirmed when they are nearly suffocated by a sudden fire in the house they've chosen to investigate. Fleeing from the flames, they are spotted by approaching police cars and, consequently, believed to be the perpetrators of the crime. Rather than giving themselves up to the police, the group becomes increasingly determined to hunt out the real arsonists. Their innocent adventure turns out to be a desperate fight for survival. An exciting account of three amateur detectives learning about the implicit dangers of taking the law into one's own hands.

153. **Kropp, Paul.** *Dead On.* **EMC, 1982. 96 pp. $4.50 paper (0-88436-816-5). Fiction.**

Subjects: Canada; Ghost stories; Mysteries
Reading Level: Grade 4   Interest Level: Grades 7–9

When Larry and his family move from Montreal to their newly inherited house in Saskatoon, there is more than the rural nature of their new community for the family to adjust to. The vast, old Victorian house is costly to heat. Larry's father had intended to farm some acreage behind the house, but an early frost makes this impossible. Even sleeping is difficult; because of the eerie coldness that sweeps suddenly through the house, there is often a ringing sound coming from the basement and the attic.

A visit to the attic in search of the source of the ringing noise produces no clues. Instead, Larry finds a photograph of a young woman who bears a striking resemblance to his sister, Janet. An elderly neighbor identifies the photograph as that of Mary Telsky, Janet's great-great-aunt. The neighbor is also a medium who convinces Janet to communicate with the spirit, Mary. Ridding the house of the spirit and discovering a fortune in gold make a convincing ending to this very slight ghost story. Characters are believable and the plot is plausible.

The one drawback is the line drawings, which tend to detract from a very good story.

154. Kropp, Paul. *Death Ride.* **Macmillan, 1989. $2.95 paper (0-02-041793-4). Fiction.**

Subjects: Accidents; Drug abuse; Health, health problems – Paralysis
Reading Level: Grade 4   Interest Level: Grades 7–12

Tim, bored with school and life in general, starts hanging around with a group of kids who are into drinking and drugs. A car is demolished in a crash over a cliff during the first party that he attends with them. Tim even gets involved in a car theft, but it all seems exciting to him. One night Tim takes his father's new car and joins his new friends for a night of alcohol and drugs and gets into a race with another car of youngsters. Tim was driving and his car is struck by a train. Three of the kids in the car are killed, one of whom is his beloved cousin Lenny. Tim is so guilt-stricken over the deaths that he is paralyzed until a friend Jodie helps him to overcome his guilt and to begin walking again. The story ends as Tim picks up the pieces of his life and gives a speech at a school assembly telling his story to other young people in the hope that he can help someone else. Illustrated with charcoal drawings.

155. Kropp, Paul. *Dirt Bike.* **EMC, 1982. 96 pp. $4.50 paper (0-88436-817-3). Fiction.**

Subjects: Alcoholism; Friendship; Sports, sports figures – Bicycling
Reading Level: Grade 3.5   Interest Level: Grades 7–12

Randy, an aspirant to the Canadian dirt bike title, is a sure winner if he can only outmaneuver an equally strong contender, Bozo, at the All-Canada races in Banff. Randy has a loyal coterie of friends who provide him with moral support and his bike with free mechanical repairs. One of his mechanic friends, Dennis, is less fortunate than Randy. Dennis, unknown to himself, is a teenage alcoholic. When this tragic aspect of Dennis is finally revealed to his friends, they help him confront his drinking and give him an incentive to stay sober by training him for the coming races. His spirits revived, Dennis enters the competition. When Randy's chance of winning is frustrated by Bozo, Dennis demonstrates his true mettle by racing for his friend. A heartening story of the redeeming power of friendship.

156. Kropp, Paul. *Dope Deal.* **EMC, 1982. 96 pp. $4.50 paper (0-88436-818-1). Fiction.**

Subjects: Canada; Drug abuse
Reading Level: Grades 2–3   Interest Level: Grades 9–12

Brian, a young man in Vancouver, Canada, is living on his own and supporting himself by pushing marijuana. When Brian is arrested, he is forced to return to his father's house. There he discovers that his younger brother has taken up with a motorcycle gang that not only takes drugs but controls the local drug trade. This is a slightly moralistic tale that focuses on Brian's maneuvers to release his brother from the gang's influence. Line drawings tend to weaken the thrust of the plot, but teens of all ages will find much to discuss here.

157. Kropp, Paul. *Fair Play.* EMC, 1982. 96 pp. $4.50 paper (0-88436-819-X). Fiction.

Subjects: Racial prejudice
Reading Level: Grade 4.5   Interest Level: Grades 7–12

Carol Santelli encounters strong racist sentiment from her classmates when she accepts an invitation to a party from Andy Singh, a Pakistani from Uganda. While Carol stoically suffers the taunts of her classmates, her old boyfriend, Chris, rouses their racial prejudices to the extent that Andy becomes the object of malevolent pranks. What ensues is a dangerous confrontation between the young men with an outcome that shatters Chris's feelings of racial hatred. A taut dramatic account of the antagonism facing an interracial couple.

158. Kropp, Paul. *Gang War.* EMC, 1983. 96 pp. $4.50 paper (0-88436-963-3). Fiction.

Subjects: Gangs
Reading Level: Grade 3   Interest Level: Grades 7–12

Charlie and the Saints are local toughs who haunt the streets of Atlantic City. Unlike the big street gangs in New York City or the biker gangs out west, they are joined not by the thrill of violence but by a mutual need and loneliness. Each member of the Saints carries with him a history of childhood trauma. When the Saints' terrain is invaded by a real gang from New York City, the guys insist that Charlie lead them into war. Charlie hesitates; his friendship with streetwise Lisa makes him reconsider the necessity of violence for asserting one's position. However, peer pressure proves too strong for Charlie to refuse to fight in the rumble. The confrontation between the Punks and the Saints takes an unexpected turn that shatters illusions about switchblade heroism forever.

159. Kropp, Paul. *Hot Cars.* EMC, 1982. 96 pp. $4.50 paper (0-88436-820-3). Fiction.

Subjects: Canada; Physical disabilities; Mysteries
Reading Level: Grades 2–3   Interest Level: Grades 9–12

A Canadian setting is the backdrop for this slight mystery involving automobile theft. Robert and his father, Crazy Phil, own a junkyard.

Crazy Phil has been in the junkyard business since before Robert was born. Business is not all that good and they just about break even. Ever since a warehouse opened next to the junkyard, unexplained events have plagued Crazy Phil. Mud is forced into the gas tank of his truck and his watchdogs are poisoned. Strange men who work at the warehouse make an offer to Crazy Phil to purchase his property. Robert and his friend, Dave, already suspicious since the dogs' deaths, decide to investigate the warehouse, hoping to find clues that can help explain the mysterious chain of events.

A compact little mystery with a small cast. Of added interest here is the character of Robert, who is handicapped from birth. He is shown wearing leg braces, which for the most part do not inhibit his life-style. An objection to the format of the book is the use of line drawings, which are never as effective as photographs for use with older teenagers.

160. Kropp, Paul. *Jo's Search.* Macmillan, 1989. 96 pp. $2.95 paper (0-02-041794-2). Fiction.

Subjects: Adoption; Canada; Family problems
Reading Level: Grade 4   Interest Level: Grades 7–12

Jo, 15, gets into an argument with her parents about her readiness to date. She becomes very angry and runs off to her room, screaming, "You're not my real mother." With help from her friend Kate and Kate's mother, Jo begins the search for her real mother. Using baptismal records and telephone books, with some assistance from older residents in her hometown, Jo tracks down her mother in Calgary. Jo's adoptive parents understand her need to seek the truth about herself and give her the adoption papers for Christmas at about the same time that Jo's detective work about her past is completed. A visit at Christmastime in Calgary with her birth mother fills in the missing pieces of Jo's life and she comes to the realization that although Ruth and Jim are her adoptive parents they are actually her "real" parents.

161. Kropp, Paul. *No Way.* EMC, 1985. 96 pp. $4.50 paper (0-88436-821-1). Fiction.

Subjects: Crime stories; Shoplifting
Reading Level: Grades 2–3   Interest Level: Grades 7–9

Fourteen-year old Peter relies on his shoplifting skills to impress his friends with his bravery. But when he is caught trying to steal a lawn mower, his friends quickly abandon him, leaving him to accept full responsibility. He is arrested, brought to court, and placed on probation. Throughout the proceedings Peter is cynical, refusing to acknowledge the seriousness of his crime. Under a new program called service placement, Peter is able to work off the terms of his probation. His job will take him back to the very hardware store where he was arrested for shoplifting. Only now he will work behind the counter. His former friends continue to plague him, pressuring him to steal now that he is in this most advantageous employment situation. It is up to Peter to face up to his new commitment and to make real choices about right and wrong. A thoughtful story that will encourage discussion. Pen-and-ink drawings accompany the text.

162. **Kropp, Paul.** *Runaway.* **EMC, 1982. 96 pp. $4.50 paper (0-88436-822-X). Fiction.**
    Subjects: Alcoholism; Child abuse; Family problems
    Reading Level: Grades 2–3   Interest Level: Grades 7–10

Kathy finds that the only way to get away from her abusive father is to run away. After a brutal beating, Kathy packs her meager belongings and leaves home to live with her grandparents. She also quits school and takes a job as a waitress. Away from the pressures of home, Kathy still finds little peace. Her father and her boyfriend continue to make demands on her. However, leaving home was a wise move for Kathy; it gave her breathing space. After her grandfather convinces her to seek help at AA, Kathy decides to return home to an uncertain environment. A realistic story that many teenagers will identify as similar to their own, this will create a forum for thought and discussion. The line drawings should be ignored, unfortunately, as they tend to lessen the impact of an otherwise believable text.

163. **Kropp, Paul.** *Snow Ghost.* **EMC, 1983. 96 pp. $4.50 paper (0-88436-964-1). Fiction.**
    Subjects: Adventure; Canada; Drug abuse
    Reading Level: Grade 3   Interest Level: Grades 7–12

Martin, a predictable product of a socioeconomically depressed upbringing, suffers from a severe case of low self-esteem. Saddled with neglectful parents and indifferent teachers, Martin has found refuge in constructing a defense of hostile behavior and drugs. When a popular high school teacher invites Martin to accompany him on a survival adventure in the Canadian bush, Martin agrees to what will ultimately prove to be a trial of courage and resourcefulness. An affecting story of a troubled adolescent's self-discovery and healing.

164. **Kropp, Paul.** *Wild One.* **EMC, 1983. 96 pp. $4.50 paper (0-88436-965-X). Fiction.**
    Subjects: Horses; Sports, sports figures – Horse racing
    Reading Level: Grade 3.5   Interest Level: Grades 7–12

Kate, 13 years old, has learned everything there is to know about horses by helping out at the stables at Cherry Hill farm. When she sees a beautiful, high-spirited horse, Wild One, abused by its trainer, she takes decisive steps to rescue it from its torment. She succeeds in exposing the trainer's mistreatment of the horse to its owner, and, in reward, she is given Wild One to train for the coming races. In spite of her affection for the horse, Kate fears that it is indeed too "wild" to race. Her conviction that Wild One is a champion is put to the test in the climactic final episode. An inspirational story of a girl's determination to make a winner of a "dark horse."

165. **LaRocca, Charles.** *Burn Barrel.* **New Readers, 1988. 96 pp. $3.50 paper (0-88336-760-2). Fiction.**

Subjects: Crime stories; Disabilities; Mysteries
Reading Level: Grades 4–5   Interest Level: Grades 9–12

Harry spent his teen years in Vietnam. There, he learned to fight. But when the war was over, he still felt angry and used his fists to get his way. Violence caught up with him and he spent time in prison. Now he is out of prison and wants to start a new life—a life very different from the one he left behind. He starts out with a job as a cleaner in a plant, a job he got through the reference of his best friend. Things seem to be going well for Harry, but one evening while cleaning the men's room, he discovers what he thinks is a dead body. The killer appears and tells Harry that in order to clear himself he must perform certain tasks for the organization (the first task is to steal some confidential papers from a barrel before they are burned). Harry is unsure if his confrontation is reality or a hallucination. His emotions pile up and he needs to talk it out. Through a sympathetic and wise new girlfriend (who is blind), Harry finds out who his real friends are and is able to clear himself from a very ugly situation. This is a real spine tingler. Pen-and-ink drawings complement the text.

166. **Laubach, Frank C.** *The Story of Jesus.* **3 parts. New Readers, 1979. 62 pp. ea. $3.00 ea. paper; $7.95 set (0-88336-538-3). Nonfiction.**

Subjects: Bible stories; Biographies – Religion; Religion
Reading Level: Grades 1–2   Interest Level: Grades 7–adult

This three-part series covers the major events in the life of Jesus, from birth to his ascent. Part One, which deals with Jesus' birth and ministry, is written in a line-by-line format. Parts Two and Three are written in chapter format and focus on the parables of Jesus and his death and resurrection. Originally copyrighted 1946. Color drawings reminiscent of Sunday School text capture the spirit of each short chapter.

167. **Laymon, Richard.** *The Lonely One.* **Fearon, 1987. 32 pp. $1.65 paper (0-8224-3769-4). Fiction.**

Subjects: Horror stories
Reading Level: Grade 4+   Interest Level: Grades 7–12

All alone, Doreen sits on the carousel, when suddenly a young man begins to talk to her. But Doreen, more than a little cautious, resists his advances. However, Ron persists and even manages to kiss Doreen until her secret forces her to retreat from him and the world. Later on that evening, while in the process of a vicious assault on the beach, Doreen reveals her true self—she is a vampire! With no photographs or illustrations, Laymon is able to build a high level of suspense that will hold the interest of all readers. This title is part of the Fastback Horror series. Other titles in the series by Laymon and others are *Night Ride, Night Games, Live Bait, The Caller, Guts, The Disappearing Man, Mad Dog, The Masterpiece, Message for Murder, No Power on Earth,* and *Tomb of Horror.*

168. **Laymon, Richard.** *Marathon Man.* **Fearon, 1985. 32 pp. $1.65 paper (0-8224-6499-3). Fiction.**

Subjects: Sports, sports figures – Running
Reading Level: Grade 4+   Interest Level: Grades 7–12

For 17-year-old Rod Claymore, winning the marathon seems a most important thing. Now that he was competing in his seventh race, he understood the strategy of the 26-mile grueling run and planned to use skills learned in the last two marathons he had won. However, during the last leg of the journey, where his win is almost assured, he decides to reverse his direction to join Tex, an injured runner. Rod learns that although winning is important, it's equally important to compete; he tells Tex, "I'll beat you next time." This is one of eight titles in the Fastback Sports series.

169. **Laymon, Richard.** *Thin Air.* **Fearon, 1986. 64 pp. $3.00 paper (0-8224-6504-3). Fiction.**

Subjects: Mysteries
Reading Level: Grades 4–5   Interest Level: Grades 7–12

Peggy has disappeared into thin air without a trace. Dennis, while explaining his wife's disappearance to the police, is near hysteria. Doubting Dennis's story, the patrolman begins the search of the area where Peggy vanished and is almost sucked into the same abyss. The S.O.S. Squad (an update of the famous television show "Mod Squad") is called in to solve the puzzling disappearance. The reader can have a good time with this slim volume while watching the S.O.S. Squad use psychic and weird methods and risk their lives to rescue Peggy from the creatures from another universe. Other titles in the S.O.S. Double Fastback series are *The Return, The Night Creature,* and *The Beast.*

170. **Leder, Jane Mersky.** *Marcus Allen.* **Crestwood House, 1985. 48 pp. $10.95 LB (0-89686-251-8). Nonfiction.**

Subjects: Biographies – Sports; Sports, sports figures – Football
Reading Level: Grades 4–5   Interest Level: Grades 7–12

Marcus Allen has always been an amazing athlete. In high school he lettered in basketball, baseball, football, and track. When he went to the University of Southern California on a football scholarship, Allen took along lots of dreams. After playing fullback, Allen finally found his best spot as a tailback and won the Heisman Trophy in 1981 as the best college football player in the country. The Los Angeles Raiders knew potential when they saw it and by drafting Marcus Allen they gave a future superstar a new home. Numerous black-and-white photographs accompany the text.

171. **Leder, Jane Mersky.** *Martina Navratilova.* **Crestwood House, 1985. 48 pp. $10.95 LB (0-89686-252-6). Nonfiction.**

Subjects: Biographies – Sports; Sports, sports figures – Tennis; Women
Reading Level: Grades 4–5   Interest Level: Grades 7–12

Undoubtedly one of the greatest female tennis players of all time, this biography of Navratilova gives some unusual insight into the character of a superstar. After a brilliant career as a child tennis prodigy in Czechoslovakia, Navratilova sought political asylum in the United States and was finally able to enjoy the rewards of her skill. Unfortunately, this freedom almost led to the end of her career. Her efforts to overcome the excesses that tempted her are the basis of the second half of the book. Ultimately, Navratilova did overcome her problems, with the help of several close friends, to become the premier woman in tennis. Numerous photographs accompany the text.

172. **Leder, Jane Mersky.** *Wayne Gretzky.* **Crestwood House, 1985. 47 pp. $10.95 LB (0-89686-255-0). Nonfiction.**

Subjects: Biographies – Sports; Canada; Sports, sports figures – Hockey
Reading Level: Grades 4–6   Interest Level: Grades 7–12

Hockey star Wayne Gretzky has a special talent—he can see everything on the ice at once—it is as if he can see in slow motion. Born in Brantford, Ontario, on June 26, 1961, Wayne's father built him a skating rink when he was two and began the kind of coaching that clinched him a position on a professional team when he was still in high school. From Junior A hockey with the Sault Sainte Marie Greyhounds, he was nick-named "the Great Gretzky" and excited his fans while playing as an Oiler. The book ends before his move to the Los Angeles hockey team. Replete with black-and-white photographs that highlight plays from his most memorable games.

173. **Lee, Leslie.** *Day after Tomorrow.* **Scholastic, 1974. 93 pp. $3.95 paper (0-590-35557-0). Fiction.**
   Subjects: Family problems; Runaways; Stepfamilies
   Reading Level: Grades 3–4   Interest Level: Grades 7–10
   Bonnie is having a very hard time accepting her new stepfather, Ray. Her mother is upset because Bonnie is being difficult at home and in school. Bonnie's older brother, Clarence, who accepts the new family situation, tries his best to be understanding, and Ray is patient and loving, sure that Bonnie will one day accept him. Bonnie sees running away as her only answer and talks two friends into going with her. In flight, they are caught by the police, and Kevin, having been in trouble before, is arrested and threatened with reform school. Feeling responsi-ble, Bonnie turns to Ray for help. He stands by her and helps to get probation for Kevin. Bonnie finally realizes that she, her mother, her brother, and Ray are really a family because they can face their problems together. Photographs throughout.

174. **Liberatore, Karen.** *Coming Home.* **Fearon, 1987. 64 pp. $3.00 paper (0-8224-2328-6). Fiction.**
   Subjects: Horror stories; Mysteries
   Reading Level: Grades 4–5   Interest Level: Grades 7–12
   Sara Collins and her husband, Andrew, are driving furiously through the Ozark mountains in Missouri looking for Uncle John's farm, desperate to reach it before Uncle John dies. But when they arrive at the old decrepit and eerie farmhouse, they learn that Uncle John is already dead and buried. But the real trouble begins when Sara, who spent her childhood with Uncle John on the farm, inherits the farm and wants to stay on, leaving her California home. Andrew is more than a little suspicious of the isolated farmhouse and meets with a tragic end while trying to per-suade Sara to return to California with him. Andrew becomes insane by the circumstances that took place on the farm. This is an amazing tale that will shock and please young fans of horror films and stories. Other Dou-ble Fastback Horror titles in the series are *The Bird, Deadly Rose, The*

Dollhouse, The Experiment, Fast Forward, Fun House, Halloween Hunt, Mind Grabber, and *Weekend Vacation.*

175. **Lindsay, Joanne Warren.** *Do I Have a Daddy?* **Morning Glory Press, 1982. 45 pp. $3.95 paper (0-930934-17-2). Nonfiction.**
    Subjects: Pregnancy and parenthood; Single parents
    Reading Level: Grades 3–4   Interest Level: Grade 7+
    In simple yet logical terms, Lindsay offers a read-aloud story for single parents to use as a springboard for discussion when asked the often painful question "Do I have a daddy?" Also included is a thoughtful guide to young single mothers about how to handle the feelings she experiences when telling her child about the father. Attractive line drawings complement the read-aloud text.

176. **Lipner, Barbara Erdman, and Robert Fredericks.** *Leaders of the Old West, Book I.* **Book-Lab, 1983. 32 pp. $19.95 set (87594-202-4). Nonfiction.**
    Subjects: American history; Biographies – Western (U.S.) heroes; West (U.S.)
    Reading Level: Grades 3–5   Interest Level: Grades 7–12
    A collection of four brief biographies of heroes of the Old West. These books teach comprehension through the cloze experience, with the level of reading rising as the student progresses through the text. These are not casual reads; there is detail about the life of those covered, as well as historic coverage about the period. Although there is a textbook quality about the style of this collection, the subjects covered are not available in any other high/low material. Leaders of the Old West: Chief Joseph, Davy Crockett, Louis Jolliet, and Sacajawea. The three other slim paperbacks are: Outstanding Women: Coretta Scott King, Maggie Kuhn, Mother Jones, Susan B. Anthony; Sports Personalities: Pelé, Babe Didrikson Zaharias, Satchel Paige, Wilma Rudolph; and Show Business Greats: Annie Oakley, Louis Armstrong, Harry Houdini, Marian Anderson. The fill-in nature of these books might make them more appropriate for the classroom rather than for an independent reading situation. Photographs.

177. **Littke, Lael.** *Tell Me When I Can Go.* **Scholastic, 1979. 128 pp. $2.95 paper (0-590-35562-7). Fiction.**
    Subjects: Aging; Death; Health, health problems – Invalidism
    Reading Level: Grades 3–4   Interest Level: Grades 9–12
    Leaving home is never easy, but for 17-year-old Janet the decision to strike out on her own is made more difficult because of her commitment to care for her invalid mother. Because her mother is confined to bed

most of the time, Janet is also responsible for all the household tasks and for the care of her younger brother. When she graduates from high school, her friends leave home and move to jobs and the city. Unable to leave with them, Janet is left alone with no job prospects. Relying on her own resourcefulness to make a living on the family property, she makes a $175 investment in worms to develop a worm farm. The worm farm flourishes and Janet finds her business demanding and rewarding.

As the condition of her mother continues to deteriorate, Janet's relationship with her brother becomes more maternal, and indeed this painful period becomes one of great emotional growth for her. A thoughtful, sensitive treatment of death. Photographs throughout.

178. **Lorimer, Janet.** *The Glory Girl.* **Fearon, 1987. 64 pp. $3.00 paper (0-8224-2395-2). Fiction.**
    Subjects: Sports, sports figures – Fencing; Women – Stories
    Reading Level: Grades 4–5   Interest Level: Grades 7–12

Holly Kramer, a college student, is juggling school, tournament fencing, and part-time management of her college fencing club. All seems to be going well for Holly until a new student, Donna Hays, from back East joins the club. Donna is indeed a superior player, and it is clear to the coach and the other members of the team that Donna can share the secrets of her winning bouts with the weaker players. Donna tries to displace Holly in the club hierarchy and almost succeeds until Holly begins to notice her snide maneuvers both on and off the gym floor. The values of good sportsmanship come pounding home as Donna, nicknamed "the Glory Girl," demonstrates that she will risk anything to win, including creating unsafe conditions on the gym floor that will cause injury to her team members. Other titles in the Double Fastback Sports series are *The Big Time, Break Away, Casey's Claw, Dirt Rider, The Hitter, The Mudder, The Rivals, The Sixth Man,* and *Willie's Choice.*

179. **Lyman, Marilyn F.** *The Girl Who Knew Rule One.* **Scholastic, 1972. 95 pp. $2.95 paper (0-590-02716-6). Fiction.**
    Subjects: Child abuse; Crime stories; Women – Stories
    Reading Level: Grades 2–3   Interest Level: Grades 7–10

Carla hurts. Her parents recently died, the aunt and uncle she lives with don't love her, and the only friends she has made in her new town have set her up for a shoplifting charge. Sitting in the police station she makes Rule One: "I will never care about any person or any thing, ever. I will never let anything hurt me again." Instead of being sent to a detention home, Carla is allowed to carry out her sentence by working at the hospital. There she meets a good-looking but drug-addicted young man who tries unsuccessfully to intimidate her into giving him blank prescription forms, and a sad, large-eyed little girl who is battered by her troubled parents. Carla breaks Rule One and almost loses her hospital assignment when she intervenes on behalf of this child. An exciting, touching story with several interesting characters whom many teenagers will relate to. Many photographs.

180. McCune, Dan. *Michael Jordan.* **Crestwood House, 1988. 48 pp. $10.95 LB (0-89686-364-6). Nonfiction.**

Subjects: Biographies – Sports; Black Americans; Sports, sports figures – Basketball
Reading Level: Grades 4–5   Interest Level: Grades 7–12

When people think of Michael Jordan, they think of a young man who loves to play basketball. A high school, college, and Olympics star, Jordan is one of the generation of young players who have put the excitement back into professional basketball. After signing a five-year contract with the Chicago Bulls, Jordan became a team leader and motivator. One unusual thing that was included in Jordan's contract was the provision that he be allowed to play anytime he wanted, whether it was with the Bulls or in a pickup game on the street. This "love-of-the-game" clause is a perfect example of how Jordan feels about his sport—he is being paid for something he loves to do for free. Numerous photographs are included.

181. McFall, Karen. *Pat King's Family.* **New Readers, rev. 1982. 64 pp. $2.65 paper (0-88336-328-3). Fiction.**

Subjects: Family problems; Pregnancy and parenthood
Reading Level: Grades 2–6   Interest Level: Grades 7–12

Pat King, married at 18 and now the mother of two young children, is faced with providing for the children and herself after her husband leaves. Teen mothers who are raising their children alone will identify with the emotional and economic support that Pat King must seek out while resolving her marital and family difficulties. An excellent book written with compassion, accompanied by pencil drawings. Writing style is line by line with a word list in the back.

182. McGravie, Anne V. *All the Way Back, A Story of Courage.* **Scott, Foresman, Lifelong Learning Division, 1982. 64 pp. $3.45 paper (0-673-24134). Nonfiction.**

Subjects: Biographies – Disabled persons; Physical disabilities; Sports, sports figures – Horseback riding
Reading Level: Grade 4   Interest Level: Grades 7–12

This is the story of Jim Brunotte, left a triple amputee by the war in

Vietnam. It's the story of his determined triumph over his handicap, and how he went on to inspire and help other handicapped persons to do the same. Jim learned to walk again, drive a car with hand controls, ski, and ride a horse. In fact, he designed a special saddle with no legs for himself and others so that they could experience the tremendous feeling of freedom found on horseback. He discovered that the handicapped developed new self-images and self-confidence after learning to ride a horse, and he owned and operated a ranch for the purpose of teaching others. Over the years he has received many awards for being so involved and caring.

183. McGraw, Barbara. *Those Who Dared, Adventure Stories from the Bible.* Scott, Foresman, Lifelong Learning Division, 1982. 64 pp. $3.45 (0-673-24138). Nonfiction.
Subjects: Bible stories; Religion
Reading Level: Grades 4–5   Interest Level: Grades 7–12
The Bible is a difficult book for poor readers. The author has taken seven stories of conflict and war from the Bible and rewritten them, keeping the original flavor as much as possible. Each story begins with an introduction so that the reader will know the events that led up to the story that is to follow. Teens who have heard the stories before will enjoy being able to read them themselves. Those who are not familiar with the stories may have difficulty with the unusual names of people and places. The Bible stories retold are "Deborah: A Judge in Israel," "A Sword for the Lord and Gideon," "David in Hiding: The King Who Waited," "Absalom, My Son, My Son!" "The Death of King Ahab," and "Queen of the Medes and the Persians."

184. McKimmey, James. *Buckaroo.* Scholastic, 1979. 127 pp. $2.95 paper (0-590-30591-3). Fiction.
Subjects: Cowboy stories; Mysteries; West (U.S.)
Reading Level: Grades 3–3.4   Interest Level: Grades 7–12
Gary Thompsen's dream has always been to be a cowboy, a buckaroo. He travels from his native San Francisco to Nevada and the Diamond W Ranch to realize this dream. Jess Keach, the ranch foreman, takes an instant dislike to Gary and makes his job very difficult. At the same time, however, Gary is getting stronger everyday in body and spirit in spite of Jess's harshness; and Vic Miles, the owner of the Diamond W, comes to admire Gary for his hard work. Gary finds out that Jess and his assistant, Bud, are involved with a group of cattle rustlers plaguing Vic. He catches them red-handed one night, but they try to kill him because he has found out their secret. Gary manages to escape from the cave in which they had hid him and helps the sheriff catch the

rustlers. Gary is promoted to the job of assistant foreman, knowing for sure that he has finally realized his dream. Exciting adventure story. Photographs throughout.

185. Malin, Amita. *Carlotta's House.* **Scott, Foresman, Lifelong Learning Division, 1982. 64 pp. $3.45 paper (0-673-L24128). Fiction.**
Subjects: Disabilities; Mental disabilities
Reading Level: Grades 3–4　　　　Interest Level: Grades 7–12

Twenty-four-year-old Susan has inherited her Grandmother Carlotta's house. It's a big house in a very small town and it's full of pleasant childhood memories. We learn, little by little, that something is not right with Susan. She leaves her grandmother's house exactly as she found it, begins to wear her grandmother's clothes, and even talks to her grandmother as if she were still alive and standing next to her. Her contact with the other people in town is negligible. When one day she overhears some men talking about her as if she were crazy, she runs home and is afraid to go out. She doesn't sleep at night and doesn't go out during the day. Finally, a worried neighbor contacts the town's visiting nurse and Susan receives the help she desperately needs.

A well-written story about a young woman who recovers from mental illness through counseling and developing personal relationships with others.

186. Malin, Barbara. *Night Prowlers.* **Scott, Foresman, Lifelong Learning Division, 1982. 63 pp. $3.45 paper (0-673-L24141). Fiction.**
Subjects: Ghost stories; Mysteries
Reading Level: Grades 3–4　　　　Interest Level: Grades 7–12

At first, when the sane, solid Simmons family begins to hear pounding on the walls at night, they think there must be a logical explanation: children throwing rocks, the pressure in the water pipes, a problem with the foundation. But after careful investigation, no logical explanation can be found. There are no clues. When small items in the house begin moving across tables and crashing onto the floor all by themselves, the family flees the house and begins to consider the possibility of a ghost.

If it's a ghost, it's a most unusual one, since it follows them to the motel. After their story is inadvertently written up in the newspaper, they are contacted by an investigator from PSI (Psychic Special Investigators) and the mystery is soon understood, if not completely solved: 12-year-old Scott, the moody son, is unwittingly causing poltergeist activity around himself.

The story is told entirely in the first person, but from all the different characters' points of view. With every chapter our perspective changes, and this makes the story fascinating. Well-written fiction based on factual occurrences.

187. **Mann, Peggy.** *The Drop-In.* **Scholastic, 1979. 129 pp. $2.95 paper (0-590-35568-6). Fiction.**
Subjects: Marriage, teenage; School dropouts
Reading Level: Grade 4+   Interest Level: Grades 9–12

Charlene and Chuck, high school seniors, are bored with school. Chuck dreams of his own apartment, plushly decorated, a place for him and Charlene. He thinks about Charlene all the time; he guesses he must be in love with her. When Charlene announces that she is quitting school to work full time in the supermarket, he quickly follows her. After all, he tells himself, if Charlene leaves school and he stays, she will probably meet another man. Against the wishes of his mother, Chuck accepts a job at the supermarket. The work is monotonous and he finds himself always thinking of school. Charlene is attracted to the other men at work, and Chuck feels pressured to ask her to become engaged so that he can keep her interested in him. Marriage and a baby quickly follow. Chuck loses his job, and they are poor. It is only a matter of time before the pressures become too much for Charlene. One day, when Chuck returns home from job hunting, there is a note from Charlene saying that she has left him and the baby.

Teenagers will identify with Chuck and Charlene's boredom at school. The outcome of their once simple relationship will provoke thought and discussion. Chuck's role as a single father who returns to school as a "drop-in" to attain his high school diploma is a contemporary twist that will intrigue many teens. Photographs throughout.

188. **Mann, Peggy.** *Girl Alone.* **Scholastic, 1976. 95 pp. $2.95 paper (0-590-35558-9). Fiction.**
Subjects: Romance; Women – Stories
Reading Level: Grades 3–4   Interest Level: Grades 8–10

Dorothy Nell and her mother have moved up north to live with her aunt and cousins. She is very homesick and shy and has trouble making friends at her new school. Ace, a school troublemaker, befriends her. Since he is the only person who has paid attention to her, Dorothy Nell agrees to go out with him. However, Ace stands her up on their first date and she finds out that he has been arrested for car stealing. She is both sad and relieved that she did not get further involved with him. Feeling alone and rejected again, she agrees to cook a fancy southern dinner for her cousin, Linda, and a few of Linda's friends. This is how she meets Tom, who becomes Dorothy Nell's first true friend, and she finds he was worth waiting for. Photographs throughout.

189. **Mann, Peggy.** *Now Is Now.* **Scholastic, 1975. 94 pp. $3.95 paper (0-590-02991-6). Fiction.**

Subjects: Family problems; Women – Stories
Reading Level: Grades 2–3   Interest Level: Grades 7–10

Mindy, the oldest of four children, baby-sits every night for her brothers and sister because her mother must work to support the family. When Mindy is asked to a dance by Tom, the most popular boy in school, she lies to her mother and goes to the dance, leaving the little children with her nine-year-old cousin. While she is out, baby Seth has an accident and Mindy has to rush him to the hospital when she gets home. Seth proves to be all right, but the incident results in a confrontation between Mindy and her mother. They both come away with a deeper understanding of each other's lives and problems. Mindy realizes her mother is struggling to keep the family together, and her mother realizes that Mindy is a mature, sensitive 16-year-old who needs time for herself and her friends. A moving story of family problems with the glimmer of hope in the end. Photographs throughout.

190. **Maxwell, Jessica.** *Madonna.* **Turman Publishing, 1986. 76 pp. $2.95 paper (0-89872-201-2). Nonfiction.**

Subjects: Biographies – Music; Music – Rock stars; Women – Biographies
Reading Level: Grade 4   Interest Level: Grade 7+

From her earliest childhood in Bay City, Michigan, Madonna Louise Veronica Ciccone felt she had the inner strength to be whatever she wanted to be. After the tragic death of her mother from breast cancer, Madonna threw herself into dance. Dancing her way through high school and two years of college enabled Madonna to audition and be accepted by the Alvin Ailey Dance Theater of New York. But dancing was only the beginning for this talented and versatile young woman's career. She has also performed as a drummer, singer, and actress. Black-and-white photographs highlight the very original style of a young woman who typifies the pop culture movement of the 1980s. A glossary appends each chapter.

191. **Micklos, John, Jr.** *Leonard Nimoy: A Star's Trek.* **Dillon, 1988. 62 pp. $9.95 (0-87518-376-X). Nonfiction.**

Subjects: Biographies – Movies and television; Movies
Reading Level: Grades 3–4   Interest Level: Grades 7–12

Mr. Spock has become a household word as a result of the popularity of "Star Trek." His Vulcan role has made the show one of the most popular ever presented on television. But this memorable Vulcan has more than his half-alien status to keep him in the public eye. Leonard Nimoy is a talented stage actor (*Equus*), film director (*Three Men and a Baby*), writer (*Vincent, from a Drama about the Artist Van Gogh*), as well as a versatile television actor ("Mission Impossible"). Nimoy is also a professional photographer. This lively biography moves in and out of Nimoy's public and private lives, tracing his career from his immigrant Russian Jewish roots to his current adventures in the movie *Star Trek IV.* The biography focuses on the enormous amount of work Nimoy has done to perfect his craft. His star on Hollywood's Walk of Fame has been well earned. The text is well illustrated with photographs.

192. **Miklowitz, Gloria D.** *Paramedic Emergency.* **Scholastic, 1977. 127 pp. $3.95 paper (0-590-35549-X). Fiction.**
Subjects: Jobs, job hunting; Paramedics
Reading Level: Grades 3–4   Interest Level: Grades 8–12
Jim has been through training to be a paramedic. The courses were tough, but the internship will decide if he can do it. Jim isn't sure he has what it takes. Will he ever be aggressive enough? He knows what to do, but he hesitates and is filled with self-doubt. This book has interesting subplots. There is an assertive female paramedic in class with Jim. He initially resents her, but grows to respect her. And Jim's father, who has a low-paying, unskilled job, decides to go back to school because he is inspired by Jim's courage in tackling difficult course work. This story is sure to appeal to young adults; it also supplies some background information on how to become a paramedic for those who might be interested.

193. **Miner, Jane Claypool.** *Choices.* **Scholastic, 1979. 96 pp. $3.95 paper (0-590-35566-X). Fiction.**
Subjects: Decision making
Reading Level: Grades 3–4   Interest Level: Grades 8–11
Seventeen-year-old George has been sent from foster home to foster home after his Uncle Mike, who had taken care of him since his parents died, was sent to jail. He is placed on the farm of Lizzie and Harry, his last chance before being sent to juvenile hall. Lizzie and Harry want to help George. They give him a baby lamb to nurture and care for, encourage him to get involved in the local 4-H Club (where he meets his girlfriend Sue), and make him feel part of their family. All goes well for George until Uncle Mike shows up. He wants George to help him steal Lizzie and Harry's savings and then run away with him. Uncle Mike is George's only "real" family, but George must make a critical choice about the direction his life is to take. He helps to save Lizzie and Harry's

money, realizing that they, not Uncle Mike, represent what is good for him. This is a moving story of a young man's problems and growth. Photographs throughout.

194. **Monroe, Judy.** *Dave Winfield.* **Crestwood House, 1988. 48 pp. $10.95 LB (0-89686-370-0). Nonfiction.**
   Subjects: Biographies – Sports; Sports, sports figures – Baseball
   Reading Level: Grades 4–5   Interest Level: Grades 7–12

Dave Winfield was always a talented kid who excelled in several sports, but loved baseball the most. After a brush with the law, he graduated with a college degree and a desire to make the world a better place. He has accomplished this, in some ways, by becoming an excellent baseball player and role model, and as an outspoken fighter in the war against drugs. Winfield has also been a longtime supporter of a scholarship program in his hometown of St. Paul, Minnesota, and began the Dave Winfield Foundation in 1977, which helps needy children in New York. Through his efforts on the field and off, Winfield has become an inspiration to many. Numerous photographs are included.

195. **Monroe, Judy.** *Prescription Drugs.* **Crestwood House, 1988. 48 pp. $10.95 LB (0-89686-414-6). Nonfiction.**
   Subjects: Drugs, prescription; Steroids, anabolic
   Reading Level: Grades 4–6   Interest Level: Grades 7–12

An overview of the history, uses, and testing phases of prescription drugs, this book also includes laws that protect the consumer and FDA regulations. Monroe describes how antibodies and other prescription drugs work to heal the body and to make pain go away. Especially interesting for teenagers is the description of how anabolic steroids work on the body, using examples of teenagers who have suffered irreparable harm by taking large dosages with the mistaken notion that they will become more adept as athletes. A timely volume. Color photographs. A glossary/index appends the text.

196. **Monroe, Judy.** *Steffi Graf.* **Crestwood House, 1986. 48 pp. $10.95 LB (0-89686-368-9). Nonfiction.**
   Subjects: Biographies – Sports; Sports, sports figures – Tennis; Women – Biographies
   Reading Level: Grades 4–5   Interest Level: Grades 7–12

Before she was four years old, Steffi Graf was begging her parents to let her hit a tennis ball. She won her first tournament at the age of six and turned professional at 13. Since that time Graf has become a respected member of the tennis community and one of its top-ranked women players. Having won almost all of the major titles and tournaments in the sport, Graf still makes time for her family and for some relaxation, taking several months off each year to get away from the tennis world. Graf is clearly a star on the rise. Numerous black-and-white photographs accompany the text.

197. **Monroe, Judy.** *Stimulants and Hallucinogens.* **Crestwood House, 1988. 48 pp. $10.95 LB (0-89686-415-4). Nonfiction.**
   Subjects: Drug abuse
   Reading Level: Grades 4–6   Interest Level: Grades 7–12

Monroe discusses the origins and uses of and laws against stimulants and hallucinogens such as marijuana, cocaine, and crack. Monroe stresses the many problems that drug addiction can cause in carrying out the normal aspects of everyday life and indicates the serious behavioral and physical changes that drugs can make in the life of an adolescent. The text is enhanced by color photographs of crack vials, pills, and implements for smoking and needle injecting. A glossary/index is appended.

198. **Montgomery, Herb, and Mary Montgomery.** *On the Run.* **Scholastic, 1976. 95 pp. $3.95 paper (0-590-35571-6). Fiction.**
   Subjects: Crime stories; Family problems; Personal growth
   Reading Level: Grades 3–4   Interest Level: Grades 7–10

Duke thinks that living at home with his alcoholic stepfather and emotional mother is just too difficult, so he steals a car and plans to run away with his girlfriend. Caught with the car, he is sent to Highland Hills, an experimental residential school without bars, locks, or fences. Duke has been in reform school before, but this is completely different and a cinch to run away from—or so he thinks.

The young men at Highland Hills learn to be responsible for themselves and each other. Most importantly, they learn to want to change. At first Duke rejects those he sees as do-gooders, who stop him at the gate as he tries to escape his first night there, and who probe him with personal questions at the regular rap sessions. Gradually he accepts that they really do care about him and he learns to care about them, too. He risks his life to save another young man from a fire in their dorm. A touching story about a self-destructive young man learning to respect and love himself and others.

199. **Morgan, Michael.** *Magic.* **Turman Publishing, 1986. 76 pp. $2.95 paper (0-89872-202-0). Nonfiction.**

Subjects: Biographies – Sports; Black Americans; Sports, sports figures – Basketball
Reading Level: Grade 4   Interest Level: Grade 7+

Los Angeles Laker "Magic" Johnson worked his way from a back-yard basketball court in Lansing, Michigan, to super-sports stardom. Stressing Magic's strong family ties, this is the kind of nurturing environment that helps to create a good team player. At 26, he has a bright future for continued Most Valuable Player and play-off victories. Black-and-white photographs of this 6-foot-8-inch Laker complement his life on and off the court. A glossary appends each chapter.

200. **Morgan, Michael.** *Prince.* **Turman Publishing, 1986. 75 pp. $2.95 paper (0-89872-203-9). Nonfiction.**

Subjects: Biographies – Music; Black Americans; Music – Rock stars
Reading Level: Grade 4   Interest Level: Grade 7+

There is a strong element of sadness that one feels while reading this slim volume on the star of his autobiographical film and album, *Purple Rain.* Born in 1958 in Minneapolis, this self-taught musician has achieved fame and fortune, but his 20-hour days devoted to creating and performing his music do not seem to satisfy him. He has imposed a tough standard for himself by stressing that the most difficult thing in life for an artist to achieve is not to repeat himself. He is also a humanitarian, having made many charitable contributions to helping educationally and emotionally disadvantaged children. A straightforward biography of a young man obsessed with his craft. Black-and-white photographs follow his career. A glossary appends each chapter.

201. **Morgan, Mike.** *Cher.* **Turman Publishing, 1988. 76 pp. $2.95 paper (0-89872-242-X). Nonfiction.**

Subjects: Biographies – Movies and television; Movies; Women – Biographies
Reading Level: Grade 4   Interest Level: Grade 7+

Cherilyn Sarkisian, known to millions as "Cher," began her performing career with her first husband Sonny Bono. Wearing bell-bottom slacks with flowing flower-child hair, they sang their way into the hearts of Yippie America. Switching gears in the 1970s to capitalize on the appeal of television's comedy/song/dance programming, Cher's new image spirited sexy clothing and a level of acting ability that far exceeded the demands of this kind of television performance. Morgan also shows Cher as a complex woman whose separation from Sonny and eventual divorce set her on a career as a serious actress that earned her respect in *Mask* and an Academy Award in *Moonstruck*. Photographs throughout. A glossary appends each chapter.

202. **Morrison, Lillian, comp.** *Best Wishes, Amen.* Harper & Row, 1974. 195 pp. $4.50 paper (0-06-446089-4). Nonfiction.

Subjects: Poetry; Spanish language – Poetry
Reading Level: Grades 3–4   Interest Level: Grades 7–10

In these more than 300 verses to recite aloud, to write in autograph albums, or just to read silently are verses and quips, some modern and many of the "roses are red" variety. A small collection of verses in Spanish is also included. Poor readers and those with better skills have enjoyed this collection of humorous and touching verse.

203. **Newman, Matthew.** *Dwight Gooden.* Crestwood House, 1986. 48 pp. $10.95 LB (0-89686-317-4). Nonfiction.

Subjects: Biographies – Sports; Black Americans; Sports, sports figures – Baseball
Reading Level: Grades 4–5   Interest Level: Grades 7–12

Dwight Gooden is widely recognized as one of the best pitchers to come to baseball in many years. Having grown up in a baseball haven, Tampa, Florida, Gooden was able to compete at an early age with some of the best Little League players in the country. When the New York Mets drafted him straight out of high school, Gooden decided to move to the pros and prove himself against the best players in the world. Due to the publication date of this book, no mention is made of Gooden's drug problems and rehabilitation, which is an excellent reason for an updated version. Numerous black-and-white photographs accompany the text.

204. **Newman, Matthew.** *Larry Bird.* Crestwood House, 1986. 48 pp. $10.95 LB (0-89686-314-X). Nonfiction.

Subjects: Biographies – Sports; Sports, sports figures – Basketball
Reading Level: Grades 4–5   Interest Level: Grades 7–12

Although he had always dreamed of becoming a professional basketball player, Larry Bird's journey to the pros was not an easy one. Following a brilliant high school career, Bird was in demand at over 200 colleges. But it wasn't until he had dropped out of two schools, married, and then divorced that Bird finally went on to fame at Indiana State University and then a superstar for the Boston Celtics. One of the best players of all time, Larry Bird has become a symbol of the best in basketball. Numerous black-and-white photographs accompany the text.

205. **Newman, Matthew.** *Lynette Woodard.* **Crestwood House, 1986. 48 pp. $10.95 LB (0-89686-316-6). Nonfiction.**

Subjects: Biographies – Sports; Sports, sports figures – Basketball; Women – Biographies
Reading Level: Grades 4–5   Interest Level: Grades 7–12

Lynette Woodard always loved playing basketball, but she could never get the older girls to let her play with them. Luckily, the boys in her neighborhood were always looking for another player, and after a few games she became one of the first kids picked to play. When she finally became a member of her school team, it was obvious that Woodard had a great deal of talent, as well as a strong desire to play and improve her game. After playing for several years on the U.S. Women's National team, and being chosen to play on the 1980 and 1984 Olympic teams, Woodard was recognized as one of the best women basketball stars of all time. Following the 1984 gold-medal win by the women's team, the Harlem Globetrotters realized that Woodard could be a tremendous asset, making her the first woman to play with men in professional basketball. Numerous black-and-white photographs accompany the text.

206. **Newman, Matthew.** *Mary Decker Slaney.* **Crestwood House, 1986. 48 pp. $10.95 LB (0-89686-319-0). Nonfiction.**

Subjects: Biographies – Sports; Sports, sports figures – Running; Women – Biographies
Reading Level: Grades 4–5   Interest Level: Grades 7–12

Mary Decker Slaney entered her first track competition at the age of 11. That cross-country race was the beginning of Slaney's love affair with running. Already a world-class athlete at the age of 14, she was still too young to achieve her goal of winning a gold medal in the 1972 Olympics. Injured and unable to compete in the 1976 games and kept from competing in 1980 due to the U.S. boycott, she finally ran in the 1984 Olympics. After a collision with another runner ended her hopes of a medal, Slaney still found the courage and determination to continue to run competitively. Numerous photographs accompany the text.

207. **Newman, Matthew.** *Patrick Ewing.* **Crestwood House, 1986. 48 pp. $10.95 LB (0-89686-315-8). Nonfiction.**

Subjects: Biographies – Sports; Black Americans; Sports, sports figures – Basketball
Reading Level: Grades 4–5   Interest Level: Grades 7–12

Patrick Ewing is a man who knew nothing about basketball before he came to the United States at the age of 13. When he arrived from Kingston, Jamaica, he found a sport that he loved, but he had to struggle with a new culture and the high expectations of those around him. After adjusting to his new life, Ewing helped his college team get to the final round of the NCAA championships for four years in a row and was a main factor in their championship win in 1984. He was also a team leader on the gold-medal basketball team at the 1984 Olympics. Ewing has overcome all obstacles to be one of the brightest new stars for the New York Knicks and all of basketball. Numerous black-and-white photographs accompany the text.

208. Nielsen, Nancy J. *Eric Dickerson*. Crestwood House, 1988. 48 pp. $10.95 LB (0-89686-366-2). Nonfiction.

Subjects: Biographies – Sports; Sports, sports figures – Football
Reading Level: Grades 4–5   Interest Level: Grades 7–12

Football running back Eric Dickerson grew up in a home where love and discipline went hand-in-hand. When he became interested in sports, this discipline helped him become one of the bright new stars in the game. After a successful career in college, Dickerson was drafted by his favorite team, the Los Angeles Rams, and it was with this team that he set a record for the most yards rushed during one season: 2,105. He was traded to the Indianapolis Colts in 1987 after he became involved in a contract dispute with the Rams. A man of great skill and talent, Dickerson will be a player to watch closely for years to come. Numerous black-and-white photographs accompany the text.

209. Nielsen, Nancy J. *Helicopter Pilots*. Crestwood House, 1988. 48 pp. $10.95 LB (0-89686-399-9). Nonfiction.

Subjects: Helicopter pilots; Jobs, job hunting
Reading Level: Grades 4–6   Interest Level: Grades 7–10

Everyday, whether or not we realize it, we benefit from the work helicopter pilots perform. They do the traffic reports every morning and evening, aid the police in searching for drugs or criminals, and help with the construction of new skyscrapers. They fly air ambulances that take patients to hospitals by the quickest route and rescue missions to disaster areas or shipwrecks. They are employed by every branch of the military and a wide range of private industries. They help fight fires, plant crops, and are often used by exploration groups to get right to the heart of new territory. Helicopter pilots are a highly trained group of people who make an impact on many aspects of our lives. Numerous color photographs and a glossary/index accompany the text.

210. **Nussman, Alf.** *The Sleepers.* **Fearon, 1987. 64 pp. $3.00 paper (0-8224-2366-9). Fiction.**

Subjects: Crime stories; Mysteries
Reading Level: Grades 4–5   Interest Level: Grades 7–12

Billy Mason is a comedy writer who lives quietly alone in his Queens, New York, neighborhood. Returning home after a long day's work, he enters the house, pauses for coffee, and clicks on the television. The bark of a dog disturbs him, and from his window he sees the older couple next door being mugged. Quickly dialing 911, Billy feels he has done his civic duty. But when the police arrive they discover the bodies of two men. Where is the older couple that Billy thought he saw mugged? Thus begins a story of hide-and-seek leaving Billy to uncover the spy ring that will prove his initial observations to be true. A fast-paced mystery that will appeal to fans of all ages. Other titles in the Mystery Double Fastbacks series are *The Actress, Brannigan's Folly, Death at the Border, The Devlin Affair, Family Reunion, The Lost Train, The Night Marchers, Vanished,* and *Voices in the Night.*

211. **Ogren, Thomas.** *Birthday Boy.* **New Readers, 1988. 64 pp. $3.50 paper (0-88336-757-2). Fiction.**

Subjects: Romance; School dropouts; Sports, sports figures – Boxing
Reading Level: Grade 4   Interest Level: Grades 7–12

A newborn baby, left on a busstop bench in St. Paul, is named Jackson Oaks by the nurses who care for the abandoned child. After being in orphanages and foster homes, he is finally adopted by the Fernandez family. Jackson does not do well in school and drops out in the eighth grade to take a job in a turkey plant. In his job he develops muscles and size that he uses to advantage in street fighting. Discovered by a manager, Jackson begins training to fight professionally. He meets a nurse, Madeline, when he needs stitches after his first professional fight. Madeline and Jackson become friends and she encourages Jackson to read by using cookbooks as they fix meals together. As their relationship grows so does Jackson's career. Boxing takes Jackson to other cities and he becomes a contender for a boxing title. Despite his success, Jackson feels that something is missing in his life that boxing, money, fast cars, and women cannot provide. He returns to St. Paul and Madeline. The story has an upbeat ending as Jackson and Madeline marry and he opens up his own restaurant. Charcoal drawings complement the text.

212. **Paden, Betty Burns.** *Truth Is Stranger Than Fiction.* **Scott, Foresman, Life-long Learning Division, 1982. 64 pp. $3.45 (0-673-L24139). Nonfiction.**

Subjects: Odd occupations and pastimes
Reading Level: Grade 4   Interest Level: Grades 7–12

An eclectic hodgepodge of "believe it or not" stories, including numerous examples of people and events in the areas of UFOs, acupuncture, yoga, twins, dreams, parapsychology, world records, and strange jobs. In the chapter on strange jobs, the author tells about a man who collects cobra venom, a New York "garbologist," a medium who finds ghosts for those who would like to adopt one, an armadillo racer, and a man who's taught his German shepherds to do simple math, among others. Anywhere from a paragraph to two pages is devoted to each person. Other chapters follow a similar format.

Lots of interesting, out-of-the-ordinary factual information that teens may enjoy sharing with their friends. Includes a glossary of important words.

213. **Parnwell, E. C.** *The New Oxford Picture Dictionary.* **Oxford University Press, 1988. 124 pp. $8.95 paper (0-19-434199-2). Nonfiction.**

Subjects: Dictionaries
Reading Level: Dictionary format   Interest Level: Grades 7–12

The New Oxford Picture Dictionary presents over 2,400 words clearly depicted in full-color contextualized illustrations. Vocabulary is introduced within 82 topics such as the space program, occupations, and sports. An index includes all vocabulary words with a clear, easy-to-follow pronunciation guide. The dictionary is especially useful with English as a Second Language students, but can also be effective in reading programs.

214. **Peterson, Tom.** *New York Knicks.* **Creative Education, 1989. 32 pp. $11.95 LB (0-88682-211-4). Nonfiction.**

Subjects: Sports, sports figures – Basketball
Reading Level: Grade 4   Interest Level: Grades 7–12

Peterson traces the history of the legendary New York Knicks from its beginnings in 1946. The world-title holders have a proud past with such basketball greats as Walt Frazier, Willis Reed, and Bill Bradley. Indeed, the present players Patrick Ewing, Kenny Walker, and Mark Jackson have a lot to live up to as they face the court in the 1990s. The book is punctuated with color action shots of famous plays and players that have endeared this team to fans nationwide. This title is one in a 23-volume series that includes a title on all city and state teams in the NBA.

Teenagers who live in the home city of the team will enjoy this brief historic overview of their basketball heroes.

215. **Phillips, Betty Lou.** *Brush Up on Hair Care.* **Illus. by Lois Johnson. Messner, 1982. 80 pp. $9.29 LB (0-671-43852-2). Nonfiction.**
Subjects: Hair care; Personal grooming
Reading Level: Grades 3–4   Interest Level: Grades 7–12

In a peppy, no-nonsense way, this book presents the facts on caring for one's hair. While emphasizing the importance of a good diet, the author discusses the different types, textures, and colors of hair and offers good advice for maintaining a healthy head of hair. Find out how to beat the frizzies, how to protect one's hair from all kinds of weather, and how much to tip the hairdresser. Suggestions on choosing the right shampoo and conditioner are offered along with hairstyling ideas. Line drawings and diagrams complement this sensible text. Includes an index.

216. **Phillips, Louis.** *Willie Shoemaker.* **Crestwood House, 1988. 48 pp. $10.95 LB (0-89686-381-6). Nonfiction.**
Subjects: Biographies – sports; Sports, sports figures – Horse racing
Reading Level: Grades 4–5   Interest Level: Grades 7–12

Few athletes in any sport have dominated their field as totally as "The Shoe." Since he began working in a stable at the age of 16, Willie Shoemaker has wanted to be the best jockey in the world. According to most people he has reached that point and no others can compare to his achievements. Despite riding in over 37,000 races, winning 8,500 times, and placing second or third another 10,300 times, Shoemaker has always been a very down-to-earth person who is devoted to his family and friends. Numerous photographs and a chart of his milestones accompany the text.

217. **Piggin, Julia Remine.** *The Lost One.* **Fearon, 1986. 88 pp. $3.90 paper (0-8224-6405-5). Fiction.**
Subjects: Macabre stories; Single parents
Reading Level: Grades 3.5–5   Interest Level: Grades 7–12

Celia Harker, single mother, lives in her parents' house caring for her son Beaumont. One day, while waiting for the school bus, Beaumont disappears, leaving Celia despondent. After months of hoping that her son will return, Celia pulls herself together and gets a job in an animal shelter. One day a large and friendly red-haired cat appears and Celia comes to believe that the cat is Beaumont. This macabre and bizarre tale tells the story of how Celia adapts her body and voice into catlike behavior so that she can be mother to the son who she believes has been returned to her as a cat. Other equally chilling tales in the Super Specter series are *The Man Who Couldn't Come Clean, A Guest from the Grave, Sometimes Nightmares Are Real, Maze of Terror,* and *A Game of Revenge.*

218. Platt, Kin. *The Ape Inside Me.* **Lippincott, 1979. 117 pp. $11.89 LB (0-397-31863-4). Fiction.**

Subjects: Emotional problems
Reading Level: Grade 3   Interest Level: Grades 8–11

Fifteen-year-old Eddie is unable to control his temper. He is usually a concerned and sensitive young man, but when a situation arises that he can't control, he starts throwing punches. Eddie realizes that his rage is often misdirected and, although he tries to contain his anger, he finds more and more that it is out of control. And so, in his own way, he has tried to deal with it by making an effort to understand this outpouring of feeling. He has named his temper Kong, after the great ape. Because Eddie is basically warm and concerned, Kong appears only in times of great personal frustration, or when Eddie feels he must play a kind of superman role to defend himself, friends, or relatives against what he feels is an unjust situation. Eddie is a natural for sports competition, but when approached by the coach, he says he has no interest in organized sports. His boss at the body shop where he works part time suggests that he look into prizefighting and links him up with a gym for some exposure.

Eddie's problems with family, school, and career alternatives are real. There is no easy route to success for him. He sees that without a high school diploma, and hard work to exorcise the rage within him, life holds nothing. The reader sees Eddie thoughtfully combining and selecting from his options with an eye on the future. Not a high/low formula story. No photographs or illustrations.

Two other titles by Platt written in the same style as this title also recommended are *Crocker* and *Broggs Brain.*

219. Platt, Kin. *Dracula, Go Home.* **Illus. by Frank Mayo. Dell, 1981. 87 pp. $1.25 paper (0-440-92022-1). Fiction.**

Subjects: Mysteries
Reading Level: Grade 3   Interest Level: Grades 7–9

Larry Carter spends the summer with his Aunt Shirley to work at her hotel. What starts out as a summer of housekeeping drudgery suddenly changes when A. R. Claud from Belgrade, a Dracula look-alike, registers in Room 13. Larry is immediately drawn to the sinister character of this newly arrived guest. Although his aunt dismisses him as an actor with the local summer theater group, Larry can't wait to uncover the real secret. Punctuated by goreylike drawings, this humorous tale is a superior high/low book.

220. **Platt, Kin.** *Run for Your Life.* **Photographs by Chuck Freedman. Dell, 1979. 96 pp. $1.95 paper (0-440-97557-3). Fiction.**
Subjects: Crime stories
Reading Level: Grade 2+   Interest Level: Grades 7–9

Fifteen-year-old Lee works a paper route to earn extra money for himself and his family. He likes delivering papers because it gives him additional opportunities to run. Lee's goal is to be the fastest miler. Suddenly, Lee's job is in jeopardy. Someone is opening the newspaper delivery boxes on his route with a copy of Lee's key to steal the money and the papers. Worried about the potential loss of his job, Lee releases his anxieties by running. But the boxes continue to be robbed, and he is asked to stop working so that the newspaper company can investigate.

One day, while out walking, he sees the thief in the process of emptying the boxes. Lee is a clever young man and decides, after studying the situation, that it would be more meaningful to challenge the thief on the track in an important meet than to turn him in to the police. A very good high/low title, written in a breezy, slangy style.

221. **Podojil, Catherine.** *Images of Courage.* **Scott, Foresman, Lifelong Learning Division, 1982. 62 pp. $3.45 paper (0-673-L24135). Nonfiction.**
Subjects: Biographies – Music; Black Americans; War, war stories
Reading Level: Grade 4   Interest Level: Grades 7–12

I really enjoyed reading this book, which contains three short biographies, adapted from full-length books. The first courageous person is Daisy Bates, the black woman who played a prominent role in the school desegregation battle in Little Rock, Arkansas, in the 1950s. Even though she and her husband were continually threatened, they held fast to what they believed in. The second biography is about a less well-known couple, the Trocmes of Le Chambon, France. The Trocmes were firm believers in nonviolent resistance and helped many Jewish refugees during World War II, even though they were putting their own lives in danger. Johann Sebastian Bach's life makes up the final part of this book. Although Bach is not often thought of in courageous terms, the author points out that indeed he was. He had the courage to stick by his musical convictions even when many around him were trying to persuade him to change his style. Includes a glossary.

222. **Podojil, Catherine.** *Mother Teresa.* **Scott, Foresman, Lifelong Learning Division, 1982. 64 pp. $3.45 paper (0-673-L24133). Nonfiction.**

Subjects: Biographies – Religion; Nursing; Women – Biographies
Reading Level: Grade 4   Interest Level: Grades 7–12

A fascinating biography of an interesting woman who was recently honored by receiving the Nobel Peace Prize. It begins with her childhood in Yugoslavia, then goes on to tell about her 20 years as Sister Teresa, a teacher in a wealthy school in Calcutta. We learn of her increasing concern for the forgotten poor, how she leaves her position at the high school, studies nursing, and goes off to live among the poor. She eventually is given permission to create a new order of nuns and we learn of the important work they do for the poor around the world, including the founding of hospitals, schools, hospices, and colonies for lepers. Includes a glossary, ten pages of photos, and a bibliography.

223. **Pollock, Rollene.** *Flying Wheels.* **Scholastic, 1979. 128 pp. $2.95 paper (0-590-05557). Fiction.**

Subjects: Crime stories; Sports, sports figures – Motorcycles
Reading Level: Grade 4   Interest Level: Grades 7–12

For 19-year-old Kevin, motorcycle racing is not only a sport that he enjoys for thrills, it also represents a strong job possibility. Working evenings for Old Man Maxwell's auto body shop as a mechanic and assistant manager, Kevin has great hopes of owning his own motorcycle shop someday. Moving ahead to realize his dreams, Kevin switches from dirt track racing to road racing, but encounters great resistance from his mother and his girlfriend, Sandy. Both insist he give up racing because they feel it is too dangerous. Kevin unhappily complies with their wishes. But a robbery at the auto shop, which leaves Old Man Maxwell wounded, forces Kevin to take full responsibility for running the business. In assuming this position and in helping to track down the armed robbers, Kevin reevaluates his own career and personal goals. Photographs complement the text.

224. **Poole, A. B.** *Cargo.* **Scott, Foresman, Lifelong Learning Division, 1982. 64 pp. $3.45 paper (0-673-L24130). Fiction.**

Subjects: Crime stories; Mysteries
Reading Level: Grade 4   Interest Level: Grades 7–12

Dee suspects that her husband, Jack, a long-distance truck driver, was not killed in an accident as the official report states. Believing that he was murdered, she calls on her husband's cousin, Nick, to help her. Dee is suspicious because she's been getting annoying phone calls, was followed to and from the bank, and the inside of their home was torn up as she sat in the funeral parlor. Then the insurance investigators find $50,000 worth of marijuana in the truck. Was Jack involved in drug dealing? All who knew him can't believe it, and even the FBI thinks that someone could have been trying to frame Jack by planting the marijuana there, even though he's dead. Nick is aided in his personal investigation by an attractive FBI agent, Lisa, and together they solve the mystery. It isn't easy because there's a complicated story of bungled blackmail and the involvement of organized crime. Well-written action mystery.

225. **Raber, Tom.** *Joe Montana, Comeback Quarterback.* **Lerner, 1989. 62 pp. $8.95 (0-8225-0486-3). Nonfiction.**

Subjects: Biographies – Sports; Sports, sports figures – Football
Reading Level: Grades 3–4   Interest Level: Grades 7–9

This photograph-filled biography, focusing on the college (Notre Dame) and professional sports life of the San Francisco 49ers quarterback Joe Montana, is largely a play-by-play account of many of his famous rescue wins. Although Montana is married and the father of two children, the sports aspect of his life overshadows the text, and personal material in the narrative is slight. A chart of his professional statistics with the San Francisco 49ers from 1979 to 1988 appends the text.

226. **Reed, Fran.** *A Dream with Storms.* **New Readers, 1990. 64 pp. $3.50 (0-88336-207). Fiction.**

Subjects: Adult education; Hispanic Americans; Immigration
Reading Level: Grade 3   Interest Level: Grades 10–12

This is a fine novelette with a feminist theme. Juan and Rosa are migrant workers. Their lives are not as desperate as those of many migrant workers, although they live in sparse circumstances, because Juan is a crew leader. Rosa dreams of getting an education. Their three children already are coming home from school with questions 25-year-old Rosa cannot answer. She hears about a training program for teachers' aides and asks Juan for permission to go to the course. Initially he refuses, but finally agrees to allow her to go—as if it were a hobby. They experience growth personally and together as a result of Rosa's completion of the course. A most sensitive story with very likable characters. Attractive charcoal-like drawings.

227. **Reeves, Thetis Powers, and Lawrence F. Reeves.** *The Career Box: Occupational Resource Module.* **Fearon, 1985. 56 booklets. $93.00 (0-8224-4035-0). Nonfiction.**

Subjects: Jobs, job hunting
Reading Level: Grades 3.5–5   Interest Level: Grades 7–12

A companion to *The Job Box* (see this chapter, entry 133) featuring occupations that require reading skills at approximately grades 4 to 6. The 56 booklets focus on career information in the following areas: Transportation and Travel, Construction and Precision Production, General and Protective Services, Sales and Retail Services, Health Services, Mechanics and Repairers, and Administrative Support. The pamphlets provide the basic requirements needed for many entry-level jobs for employment-oriented teenagers at a reading level that most reluctant readers can handle. Photographs.

228. **Reiff, Tana.** *Boat People: Hopes and Dreams, the Vietnamese.* **Fearon, 1989. 76 pp. $3.90 paper (0-8224-3685-X). Fiction.**

Subjects: Immigration; Vietnamese Americans
Reading Level: Grades 2–3   Interest Level: Grades 7–12

After a treacherous journey that involved robbery aboard ship, sailing through storms, and several near sinkings because of damage to their small, shaky craft, the Nguyen family finally arrived in Malaysia, where for three months they lived safely while making repairs to their boat. Forced to leave Malaysia, the boat people made their way to Indonesia, where the youngest Nguyen boy dies. From Indonesia, they were flown to San Francisco for a new life. The Nguyens were told by the authorities that because they were fishermen they should go to the Gulf Coast of Texas where they could join other Vietnamese and American families who worked as fishermen. But life was not easy in Texas, as the two cultures collide over fishing grounds, and it takes much compromise on both sides for the Nguyen family to find peace once again.

229. **Reiff, Tana.** *Chicken by Che.* **Fearon, 1988. 64 pp. $3.75 paper (0-8224-4606-5). Fiction.**

Subjects: Jobs, job hunting; Restaurant business
Reading Level: Grades 2–3   Interest Level: Grades 7–12

All the difficulties and trials of starting a new business are covered in this story. Che Acosta is a French chef who wants to own his own restaurant in a poor part of town and bring jobs and affordable food to the neighborhood. Everything goes well at first as he gets a bank loan and builds his restaurant. Then his troubles begin when he does not have enough people to work for him in the restaurant and customers get angry at having to wait. Stoves break down, there is a robbery, employees quit, and someone who works in the restaurant is stealing from the receipts. Che sticks with it, despite all the trouble, and he comes up with a plan to bring people back to the restaurant. In the end, he appears to be on his way to success. Each chapter is followed by a "Thinking It Over" section that has questions appropriate to the text.

230. **Reiff, Tana.** *Climbing the Wall.* **Fearon, 1988. 64 pp. $3.75 paper (0-8224-4603-0). Fiction.**

Subjects: Hyperactivity
Reading Level: Grades 2–3   Interest Level: Grades 7–12

Jeff and Sue's six-year-old child, Kenny, never seems to sit still, and they wonder whether he is ready for school. Sue feels that Kenny is not ready for school, but Jeff believes that Kenny is just a normal, energetic child. Kenny goes to school and seems to become even wilder and more uncontrollable. He is unable to sit still or finish his work. His teacher suspects that Kenny is hyperactive, and after some tests her diagnosis is proven correct. Drugs are suggested as the first choice of treatment, but Kenny's father opposes their use. A special diet for Kenny is tried, but it does not work. After consultation with a doctor, Jeff and Sue agree to try the drug therapy. The change in Kenny's behavior for the better is extremely noticeable and the prognosis for him is good. The causes and treatment of hyperactivity are discussed. There is a "Thinking It Over" section after each chapter that has appropriate questions about the text.

231. **Reiff, Tana.** *A Different Home: Hopes and Dreams, the Cubans.* **Fearon, 1989. 80 pp. $3.90 paper (0-8224-3684-1). Fiction.**

Subjects: Ethnic stories; Hispanic Americans
Reading Level: Grades 2–3   Interest Level: Grades 7–12

A heartwarming story of Mario who came at the age of 23 to the United States from Cuba, leaving all his family behind. Requesting assistance for employment, on arrival in Florida, he is sent to Ohio to work in international banking utilizing his bilingual skills. As the years go by, he marries, has children, and progresses in his career, but he always misses his parents. When news of the problems in Cuba reaches the United States, he leases a boat and is able to bring his parents to Florida from Cuba. It is his dream to bring his parents to Ohio to live with his family, but he realizes that his parents may be happier in Florida with its rich Cuban culture.

232. **Reiff, Tana.** *The Door Is Open.* **Fearon, 1988. 64 pp. $3.75 paper (0-8224-4604-9). Fiction.**

Subjects: Adult education
Reading Level: Grades 2–3   Interest Level: Grades 7–12

Lina came to the United States from Italy to get married and raise a family. Her children are now grown and her husband's business is successful. Although Lina helps her husband by doing the bookkeeping for the business, she has a dream of going back to school and getting a diploma. Al, her husband, would rather have Lina stay at home and keep things as they are, but Lina persists by enrolling in adult classes. She is a good student and gets her diploma and then goes on to college to pursue her goal of becoming a teacher. Her husband even finds the value of school when he joins a class for businesspeople. There is a "Thinking It Over" section after each chapter that has appropriate questions about the text.

233. Reiff, Tana. *The Family from Vietnam.* Fearon, 1979. 64 pp. $3.75 paper (0-8224-4320-1). Fiction.

Subjects: Family life; Immigration; Vietnamese Americans
Reading Level: Grades 1–3   Interest Level: Grades 7–12

It starts in 1975, during Operation Babylift in South Vietnam. Mai and Set, having worked for the Americans during the occupation, now fear for their lives. They travel with their three children to Tan Son Nhut air base hoping to board a plane to the United States. In the crush of people rushing to the planes, the family is separated. Once on the plane, Mai realizes that Set and their son are left on the ground. The reader's interest is captured here. In a fast-paced style, Reiff has the reader on edge as the tragic events in Set's life unfold, including the death of his son. Eventually, Set is reunited with Mai and their children who escaped with her.

In this brief little story, the emotional appeal of the separated family's tragedy is great. The author is to be congratulated for her success in telling the tale on such a low reading level. The impact is powerful and is delivered using a very limited vocabulary, short sentences, and short chapters.

234. Reiff, Tana. *For Gold and Blood: Hopes and Dreams, the Chinese.* Fearon, 1989. 76 pp. $3.90 paper (0-8224-3679-5). Fiction.

Subjects: Chinese Americans; Immigration; West (U.S.)
Reading Level: Grades 2–3   Interest Level: Grades 7–12

Soo Lee and his brother Ping dreamed of gold when they planned to leave their native China in 1851. Thoughts of prospecting filled their heads and hearts with gold fever. First they traveled to Hong Kong, then after a two-month voyage by ship, they arrived in California. But working for a gold company was not easy. Many times they found gold dust, and, finally, when they hit a big strike the foreman threw them out of the camp to take the gold for himself. After their unhappy experience with gold digging, the brothers split up, Ping remained to pan for gold, but Soo left to work on the railroad. The two brothers led separate and lonely lives in their new world and many years later, after the San Francisco earthquake, they were reunited. A warm and heartbreaking tale of two immigrants who came to America for a better life.

235. **Reiff, Tana.** *Hungry No More: Hopes and Dreams, the Irish.* **Fearon, 1989. 80 pp. $3.90 paper (0-8224-3680-9). Fiction.**

Subjects: Ethnic stories; Immigration; Irish Americans
Reading Level: Grades 2–3   Interest Level: Grades 7–12

The McGees arrived in Boston after the great Irish potato famine in the 1850s, hoping for a better life. And a better life they found indeed, but there was incredible hardship to overcome in their new land. Although Mr. McGee found work as a ditchdigger before joining the police force, his career as a policeman was interrupted by his service in the Civil War. With a large family to support and often enduring prejudice against the Irish, Mary McGee kept her family afloat by working as a maid. Returning from the Civil War, Johnny McGee entered politics, but, although life in Boston was indeed better for this hearty family, life was hard due to the enormous physical labor expended for survival.

236. **Reiff, Tana.** *Juan and Lucy.* **Fearon, 1979. 64 pp. $3.75 paper (0-8224-4317-1). Fiction.**

Subjects: Family life; Romance
Reading Level: Grades 1–3   Interest Level: Grades 7–12

Older teenagers and adults enrolled in literacy programs have already chosen *Juan and Lucy* as their favorite in this Lifeline series. It is written at a very low reading level with no illustrations to amplify the simple line-by-line text, except for an attractive drawing of Juan and Lucy in their wedding outfits on the cover. The straightforward delivery of the text conveys a realistic portrait of a young couple's relationship from their first meeting to their eventual marriage and family life. Juan and Lucy travel a rocky road to marriage, having first lived together. Once married, they are unable to conceive a child. Their problems and the solutions they work out together make for an appealing contemporary drama that easily holds the interest of the reader. Thoughtful questions at the end of each short chapter will aid comprehension development for the seriously disabled reader.

237. **Reiff, Tana.** *Just for Today.* **Fearon, 1988. 64 pp. $3.75 paper (0-8224-4605-7). Fiction.**

Subjects: Alcoholism
Reading Level: Grades 2–3   Interest Level: Grades 7–12

Biff has a problem with alcohol and will not admit it. His wife Linda drinks with him until she realizes that their drinking is causing more problems. Biff is abusive to Linda and she contacts Alcoholics Anonymous for help. She goes to a meeting of Al-Anon and learns that she does have a problem with alcohol. Linda accepts this, but Biff angrily rejects the idea that he is an alcoholic. Biff loses his job because of absenteeism and poor performance and he finally admits that he has a drinking problem. He attends his first A.A. meeting and finds that there is support and help available. This story explores the various aspects of alcoholism, provides questions that point out the signs of the disease, and gives methods of overcoming alcoholism. The story ends on an upbeat note as Biff and Linda continue with A.A. and Biff pursues a new career in a different field. Following each chapter is a "Thinking It Over" section that has appropriate questions about the text.

238. Reiff, Tana. *Little Italy: Hopes and Dreams, the Italians*. Fearon, 1989. 76 pp. $3.90 paper (0-8224-3677-9). Fiction.
    Subjects: Ethnic stories; Immigration; Italian Americans
    Reading Level: Grades 2–3   Interest Level: Grades 7–12
    The Trella family came to the United States from Italy by ship, landing at Ellis Island in the 1920s. Dominick Trella soon found work in construction and the family lived quite nicely, although in crowded conditions, in New York's Lower East Side. As the children grew (as did the family; it swelled to nine) the parents continued to live in the small rooms in the congested tenement. New York offered a way out for the Trella children, but the parents remained at home in Little Italy.

239. Reiff, Tana. *The Magic Paper: Hopes and Dreams, the Mexicans*. Fearon, 1989. 76 pp. $3.90 paper (0-8224-3686-8). Fiction.
    Subjects: Hispanic Americans; Immigration
    Reading Level: Grades 2–3   Interest Level: Grades 7–12
    This title captures the feeling that illegal immigrants must live with on a daily basis as they struggle with basic survival and ponder life's other needs such as marriage, learning English, choosing a career, and so on. The book centers on Lupe Garcia, who wants to visit her aunt and uncle in Los Angeles. Lacking a visa for travel, she is corralled into purchasing a counterfeit one that is accepted at the Mexico/California border. While in California, she is attracted by the high wages offered in the dress factory. She works illegally and becomes ill and is unable to return home within the time frame of her visa. Lupe is soon caught up in the cycle of being an illegal immigrant. But life is both bitter and sweet for Lupe. Falling in love with Benito means travel to Mexico to see her family but she is filled with sadness when she discovers that her entire

family has been killed in the earthquake. With great difficulty Lupe and Benito return to California and work to establish their residency prior to 1982 in order to acquire the green cards that will give them legal status.

240. **Reiff, Tana.** *The Missing Piece.* **Fearon, 1988. 64 pp. $3.75 paper (0-8224-4608-1). Fiction.**
Subjects: Marriage, teenage
Reading Level: Grades 2–3   Interest Level: Grades 7–12

Julie has her heart set on getting married. When her musician boy-friend moves into her small apartment, she takes on additional work at night so that she can supply him and his band with beer. She cleans up after them and looks forward to the day they will be married. But Bill has little interest in marriage and disappears when Julie pressures him to set a date. But Julie is fortunate in having a friend, Phong, who has a much more serious agenda for her life than marriage. It is through her associa-tion with Phong that Julie comes to see that her own talents and ambi-tions can be realized without the presence of a man in her life. Julie finds the missing piece in her own accomplishments. A serious lesson for many young women.

241. **Reiff, Tana.** *Nobody Knows: Hopes and Dreams, the Africans.* **Fearon, 1989. 76 pp. $3.90 paper (0-8224-3683-3). Fiction.**
Subjects: Black Americans; Civil rights; Women – Stories
Reading Level: Grades 2–3   Interest Level: Grades 7–12

The year is 1902, and life for many young black people in the South is one of endless farmwork and housework. Mattie and Nate decide that a move to a big city will offer them a new and better life than that of their parents. But their migration to Chicago is not easy as Mattie and Nate fight segregation and the difficult working conditions offered to the pre-union meat-packing workers. Nate becomes an activist, joining the black union, and life is good for this growing family. But tragedy strikes when Nate cuts his hand while cutting the meat. Lacking sufficient medical care, Nate suffers an infection and dies. Mattie is left alone with five children to support and struggles through the Depression as a maid. This is an all-too-true story of how one woman worked to support her family. We rejoice when at the conclusion of the book, Mattie returns to the South to challenge segregation at a lunch counter.

242. **Reiff, Tana.** *O Little Town: Hopes and Dreams, the Germans.* **Fearon, 1989. 76 pp. $3.90 paper (0-8224-3681-7). Fiction.**
Subjects: Ethnic stories; German Americans; Immigration
Reading Level: Grades 2–3   Interest Level: Grades 7–12

The lives of a German family who came to the United States about

1852 come full circle in this brief family saga that spans three genera-tions. Karl Hermann came to Wisconsin from Germany when he was 23 years old. After many years of dreaming about having a large farm in the United States, Karl's dream comes true. Not only was he able to acquire a farm with rich soil, but in time he married and had a large family. As the years went by Karl often thought of Germany, staying close to many German traditions, and remaining a German citizen. But when World War I breaks out, Karl's grandson is sent to fight and is killed in battle in France. The death of his grandson, who died as an American soldier, represents a turning point for Karl, who finally realizes that he is no longer a German but an American. A powerful read that will encourage discussion about national origins.

243. **Reiff, Tana.** *Old Ways, New Ways: Hopes and Dreams, the Eastern European Jews.* **Fearon, 1989. 76 pp. $3.90 paper (0-8224-3682-5). Fiction.**
   Subjects: Ethnic stories; Immigration; Jewish Americans
   Reading Level: Grades 2–3   Interest Level: Grades 7–12

   It is 1914, and New York's Lower East Side is teeming with newly arrived immigrants, many of them Jews from Eastern Europe. For many of these people New York was the promised land. With hard work, it was possible to learn a trade, such as shoemaking, and watch this skill grow from a one-man operation to a factory. And that is what Solomon Gold and his sons were able to accomplish. But along the way, in spite of financial prosperity, Solomon Gold was unhappy. Unable to accept his daughter's decision to join the theater and regarding as rejection his son's decision to marry out of his faith caused him years of unhappiness. Finally he and his children resolved their differences shortly before his death.

244. **Reiff, Tana.** *A Place for Everyone.* **Fearon, 1979. 64 pp. $3.75 paper (0-8224-4318-X). Fiction.**
   Subjects: Adult education
   Reading Level: Grade 2+   Interest Level: Grades 7–12

   Dot, a mature woman of 40, is tired of working long hours at a sewing machine in a factory. She yearns to be able to open up her own business. She has already made money by sewing and altering garments for friends; but Dot knows that she cannot run her own business, no matter how well she sews, because she can't read. One night, while watching television, Dot sees an ad for adults who want to learn to read. At first she is afraid she will be laughed at, but her desire to learn is so strong that she registers. While at school she meets other adults, some of whom are beginning readers and others working toward a high school equivalency diploma.

There can hardly be a title more meaningful for a beginning teenage reader than this. For a young person to see an adult face up to a reading deficiency and to succeed is an inspiration. The format of this title is identical to others in the series. Short sentences are grouped in small paragraphs with wide margins. Brief annotations follow chapters. No photographs or illustrations.

245. **Reiff, Tana.** *Play Money.* **Fearon, 1988. 64 pp. $3.75 paper (0-8224-4607-3). Fiction.**

Subjects: Financial problems
Reading Level: Grades 2–3   Interest Level: Grades 7–12

The pitfalls of using credit cards without thought are thoroughly explored here. Connie's marriage has broken up and she is on her own for the first time. She gets her first credit card by establishing credit with a department store. Then she applies for a major bank credit card. Connie finds buying so easy with credit cards that she calls it play money. In the beginning she keeps up with her payments, but soon she gets even more credit cards that allow her to charge in greater amounts. Connie is so in debt that she cannot possibly pay her monthly payments to her creditors. One of the people at the bank refers Connie to a budget counselor, David. He is an attractive young man who helps Connie to start a budget that will allow her to pay off her bills and clear her credit record. In addition to solving her money problems, Connie starts to build a relationship with David. Appropriate questions to the text are featured in the "Thinking It Over" section after each chapter.

246. **Reiff, Tana.** *Push to the West: Hopes and Dreams, the Norwegians.* **Fearon, 1989. 76 pp. $3.90 paper (0-8224-3678-7). Fiction.**

Subjects: Ethnic stories; Immigration; Norwegian Americans
Reading Level: Grades 2–3   Interest Level: Grades 7–12

In a Norwegian farmhouse, Lars and Karin Olsen sit dreaming about the rich farmland pictured in a book about the United States. Their plan is to leave by ship across the seas in early spring so they can arrive in the United States in the summer. Staying first with relatives in Minnesota enables them to save money so they can move farther west to acquire a homestead. Although the earth is fertile, life is harsh—first come locusts and then severe and lonely winters. It is not until other Norwegian families settle near the Olsen farm that they are truly happy once again.

There is much here about the pioneering spirit of Americans that young people will find exciting.

247. **Reiff, Tana.** *The Shoplifting Game.* **Fearon, 1979. 64 pp. $3.75 paper (0-8224-4319-8). Fiction.**
    Subjects: Crime; Shoplifting
    Reading Level: Grades 1–3   Interest Level: Grades 7–12
    Beth has an ordinary office job that pays very little. She wants nice clothes and jewelry. With her friends, Pam and Marty, she finds she can have anything by stealing. Even after Marty is caught and arrested for the theft of hair rollers, Beth still seems unable to stop. She is not even aware of the seriousness of her problem until she sees a film about a woman who is a habitual shoplifter. Yet Beth continues to shoplift, rationalizing that because it is so easy, the items she steals are meant for her.
    When Beth is finally accused of stealing by a small shop owner and is arrested, she thinks it's unfair. An understanding lawyer and shopkeeper work out an excellent plan to save Beth from the embarrassment of a hearing. The solution is for Beth to work for a week at the store where she was caught shoplifting in order to repay the owner for his loss. It is hoped that Beth's new job will also teach her how serious shoplifting is both for individuals and the economy in general. A short list of questions follows the brief chapters. The questions can be helpful to many young people wishing to test their reading retention skills. No photographs or illustrations.

248. **Reiff, Tana.** *So Long, Snowman.* **Fearon, 1979. 64 pp. $3.75 paper (0-8224-4321-X). Fiction.**
    Subjects: Drug abuse; Poverty
    Reading Level: Grades 1–3   Interest Level: Grades 7–12
    Billy is the narrator of this brief work of fiction that often reads more like a biography. He is an 18-year-old who recounts in detail his failure to complete high school, his dependency on drugs, and his inability to care for his young family. School was peripheral to Billy's goals in life, his interests being confined to the streets. The one bright light at school for him was music; but at 15, he was forced to leave for brutally attacking a teacher. Out of school with no job prospects, Billy turns to robbery. When caught, he is sent to a detention home, Boys Hall, which offers no constructive reform for Billy. Back on the street, Snowman gets him hooked on drugs. Now his life revolves around his habit. Even though he has been told that he has musical talent, he lacks the discipline to

apply himself to his horn. He would rather while away the day in a stupor listening to music.

This moving portrait, reminiscent of so many lives in our society, is a searching effort. It attempts to demonstrate how very difficult it is for an individual to break out of the cycle of poverty and drug addiction. No photographs or illustrations.

249. Reiff, Tana. *Take Away Three.* **Fearon, 1988. 64 pp. $3.75 paper (0-8224-4602-2). Fiction.**

Subjects: Divorce; Family problems; Marriage

Reading Level: Grades 2–3   Interest Level: Grades 7–12

Rennie, a long-distance truck driver, comes home after a long road trip and learns that his wife, Carol, is seeing another man. Rennie leaves the house immediately for another trip and when he comes back a week later, Carol has taken the two children and moved out. When he receives a letter from Carol's lawyer stating that she is filing for a divorce, Rennie finds a small apartment, buys some furniture, and begins to take shorter trips in order to have a place and the time for his children to stay with him on visits. The book explores the things that can go wrong in a marriage and the solutions that are available. Rennie and Carol agree to see a marriage counselor and the reader is left with the feeling that the problems in this family and marriage will be resolved. The "Thinking It Over" section after each chapter has appropriate questions about the text.

250. Reiff, Tana. *A Time to Choose.* **Fearon, 1979. 64 pp. $3.75 paper (0-8224-4322-8). Fiction.**

Subjects: Family problems; Marriage

Reading Level: Grade 3   Interest Level: Grades 9–12

Bob and Jan have been married for quite some time and have two small children. Their marriage is traditional: Bob goes to work at a job he hates, while Jan stays home to care for the children. In his spare time Bob works on his racing car, dreaming of racing in the Fourth of July competition. He spends so much time preparing his car for the big race that he loses his job. Out of work, he plunges full time into racing, but fails to win enough money to support the family. Forced to find a job Jan not only finds one she enjoys and is successful at but also meets another man.

By using very simple language with a very spare text the author is able to tell a good story that will provoke discussion among the young people who read this book. These are adult characters caught up in the problems of a modern society. The family and career decisions that Jan and Bob face are provocative for many teenagers who will find themselves in similar situations as they grow older. No photographs or illustrations.

251. **Roberts, Lawrence.** *Alley Fever.* **Scholastic, 1979. 93 pp. $2.95 paper (0-590-30582-4). Fiction.**
    Subjects: Ethics; Sports, sports figures – Bowling
    Reading Level: Grades 3–4   Interest Level: Grades 7–10
    Phil's job at the local bowling alley is perfect. It enables him to work in an environment that he loves: bowling. He hopes someday to be a champion. But when he is fired by the manager for fraternizing with the customers, he is angry and despondent. To his surprise, the customer in question is the owner of the bowling alley who was testing out conditions at the lanes. It turns out that Nick, the owner, is also an old-time friend of Phil's father, once a champion bowler and now living on disability retirement because of severe arthritis. Nick is disgusted with the unfair treatment that the manager has shown toward the bowling alley staff. When the manager is fired, Nick asks Phil's father to replace him. In spite of his handicap, he agrees. Once again Phil returns to work at the bowling alley. Although Phil now has renewed enthusiasm to go for a win in the upcoming tournament, his joy is soon clouded by the revenge taken against him by the son of the former manager. Ample suggestion is presented for discussion about ethics in this photograph-filled contemporary high/low story.

252. **Roberts, Lawrence.** *Big Wheels.* **Scholastic, 1977. 127 pp. $2.95 paper (0-590-05224-1). Fiction.**
    Subjects: Trucks
    Reading Level: Grade 3   Interest Level: Grades 9–12
    Terry has been job hunting since he graduated from high school two weeks ago. Finally he lands a job as a temporary helper at a trucking and warehouse company. Unfortunately, Rocky Martin, an old football rival with a malicious chip on his shoulder, also works there. Frank Ramos, a friendly man whom Terry has been assigned to help, witnesses the beginning of a fight between Terry and Rocky that occurs within the first hour of Terry's being hired. By contradicting Rocky's version of what happened, Frank earns himself a dangerous enemy.

    Rocky wants revenge badly and arranges for Frank to be involved in an accident. He unscrews the air hoses from the brakes of Frank's rig. Terry, however, is the next one to drive the rig at an unscheduled driving lesson on Sunday morning. After some harrowing moments speeding down a steep hill, the rig is brought under control. Frank and Terry know it was sabotage. So does Rocky's father, another driver, who orders Rocky never to set foot near the warehouse again.

Rocky now plans revenge against his father. Circumstances foil his well-thought-out plan, but not before he knocks Frank unconscious. Terry, rushing him to the hospital in the truck, is stopped for speeding and suspected of attacking the truck driver and hijacking the truck. It all gets straightened out in the end, of course, and Terry is not only promised a full-time job but is also offered truck driver training on salary. A book with some exciting moments that will appeal to many teenagers. Photographs throughout.

253. **Robison, Nancy.** *Department Store Model.* **Scholastic, 1977. 122 pp. $2.95 paper (0-590-05220-9). Fiction.**

Subjects: Modeling; Mysteries
Reading Level: Grade 4   Interest Level: Grades 8–12

Beautiful Kelsey Malloy wants more than anything to join the exciting world of modeling. Posing as a mannequin on her time off from her job as a clerk in a department store gives her a taste of the excitement and glamor she longs for. She is lucky and is asked to model a futuristic jumpsuit before some buyers. An immediate sensation, she is snatched up by Ms. Kirkland, the supervisor of the models at Piedmont's Store. Then follow lessons in makeup application and a stint at distributing free cosmetics. Soon she is asked to model in the Back to School and Bridal shows. But modeling is no longer fun for Kelsey. Unknown to her she is caught up in a web of thievery and mystery. A fast-paced story with a no-fail contemporary theme. Photographs throughout.

254. **Robison, Nancy.** *Janet Jackson: In Control.* **Dillon, 1987. 51 pp. $9.95 LB (0-87518-368-9). Nonfiction.**

Subjects: Biographies – Music; Black Americans; Women – Biographies
Reading Level: Grades 3–4   Interest Level: Grades 7–12

The baby sister of the famous Jackson Five never really thought of herself as having a serious musical talent. She began her career more or less on the sidelines of her popular siblings. At age seven she created imitations of famous people and, in a show in Las Vegas, brought down the house with Mae West's, "Why don't you come up and see me sometime?" Eventually she was cast in acting roles on two popular television series, "Good Times" and "Diff'rent Strokes." Now she is an award-winning musician and recording star. This slim biography concentrates on Jackson's personal and professional growth and the strength she engenders from her large and supportive family. Photographs.

255. **Rosenthal, Nadine.** *When the Job Fits: Pacemaker Career Readers.* **Fearon, 1986. 64 pp. $1.50 paper (0-8224-1212-0). Fiction.**
   Subjects: Jobs, job hunting
   Reading Level: Grade 2   Interest Level: Grades 7–12
   When the Job Fits is one of ten photograph-illustrated stories. This title features a fictional character, Rosa Gomez, aged 19, uncertain and insecure about her first career move. Exploring a shopping mall with her mother gives her insight into possible employment, and with perseverance and a little luck she gets a job as a retail clerk in "junior sportswear" for the Christmas rush. Other titles in the series explore what it's like to be a nurse's aide, machinist, retail sales worker, local truck driver, plumber, beauty operator, security guard, carpenter, drafter, and assembler. Boxed set with read-along cassette available with teacher's guide.

256. **Roth, Arthur.** *Demolition Man.* **Scholastic, 1978. 127 pp. $2.95 paper (0-590-35567-8). Fiction.**
   Subjects: Jobs, job hunting; Peer pressure
   Reading Level: Grades 3–4   Interest Level: Grades 8–12
   Bruce graduated from high school nearly a year ago but still hasn't been able to find a steady job. He is suddenly motivated to find employment quickly when he gets the opportunity to see the inside of a camper and dreams about owning one himself. He convinces his uncle to let him help with demolition work and his uncle's offer of $5 an hour seems very good. But his street friends, threatened by his ambition and employment, repeatedly pressure Bruce to deal drugs instead. He's tempted by the $500 a week, but his girlfriend, Kathy, threatens to leave him if he takes it.
   Bruce's uncle offers him the chance to remove the valuable pieces from the buildings they demolish, and with Kathy's labor and encouragement, Bruce opens a small storefront to sell a mahogany staircase, a marble mantlepiece, and various other pieces. Just when it looks as if they will have to close the store because they don't have the rent money, a man offers them $200 for the staircase, and they also find $20 gold pieces hidden beneath a junk table, which are worth about $2,000. Aside from the unrealistic ending, this is an encouraging book about a young man who resists peer pressure and works hard toward realizing his dream.

257. Rothaus, James R. *Kansas City Royals.* Creative Education, 1987. 46 pp. **$11.95 LB (0-88682-138-X). Nonfiction.**

Subjects: Sports, sports figures – Baseball
Reading Level: Grade 4   Interest Level: Grades 7–12

Rothaus captures the Royals from their beginning in 1969 to the all-star game in 1986. Statistics round out the play-by-play re-creations of such Royal players as Frank White, George Brett, Orlando Cepeda, Big John Mayberry, Hal McRae, and Bo Jackson, who are shown at play. There are 26 titles on major league baseball teams in this series—from the Atlanta Braves to the Toronto Blue Jays. All the titles will be especially enjoyed by students of baseball. Includes black-and-white and color photographs.

258. Rothaus, James R. *The New York Giants.* Creative Education, 1986. 47 pp. **$14.95 LB (0-88682-041-3). Nonfiction.**

Subjects: New York City; Sports, sports figures – Baseball
Reading Level: Grade 4   Interest Level: Grades 7–12

Football comes alive off screen for young passionate players and spectators as they follow the highlights of 60 years of Giant play. Past players star not only on the field but play a key role in the charting of many legendary events in sports history: Jim Thorpe, Tuffy Leemans, Bill Paschal, "Choo Choo" Roberts, Frank Gifford, Mel Triplett, Kyle Rote, Y. A. Tittle. Teenagers will recognize some of these former players from their sports records but others have name recognition because they are sportscasters today. This photograph-and-fact-filled text will draw young readers with such remarks as, "The 1934 title game between the Giants and the Bears is still known as the 'Sneakers Game' because the Giants surprised the Bears by wearing basketball shoes for better traction on that icy turf that day!" and "Did you know that in the early days of the NFL, most players were renewed—or cancelled—each week. It wasn't until 1930 that the practice of signing on a player for an entire year became the norm!" The 28 other titles in The NFL Today series include team portraits from the Atlanta Falcons to the Washington Redskins. Teenagers who live in the home team city will flock to this material.

259. Sachs, Marilyn. *Beach Towels.* Dutton, 1982. 76 pp. $11.95 (0-525-44003-8). **Fiction.**

Subjects: Friendship; Romance
Reading Level: Grade 2.4   Interest Level: Grades 7–10

It's summertime, and Lori and Phil are high school students who meet under the shade tree at the beach. He's tall and handsome but he always looks angry and won't even return Lori's smiles. Forced by the crowd to be near each other in the available shade, they see each other almost every day over a period of three weeks. Little by little they begin sharing lunch and their problems. Lori helps Phil to see that the girl he's hopelessly in love with no longer is interested in him and, in fact, his relationship with her had been based on little more than sex. Phil helps Lori get on with her life. She had withdrawn from all her friends and from thinking about anyone but herself since a recent car accident that left her recuperating in the hospital and her mother dead.

A sweet, touching, well-written story about friendship and caring and young love. Illustrations throughout.

260. **Sachs, Marilyn.** *Hello . . . WRONG Number.* **Scholastic, 1984. 106 pp. $2.50 (0-590-41570-0). Fiction.**

Subjects: Romance
Reading Level: Grades 1–2　　　　**Interest Level: Grades 7–9**

Angie has been crazy about Jim McCone for years and she almost had him. If only she hadn't acted so prudish while they were dancing! She calls him to apologize and realizes too late that she's reached the wrong number and has spoken to someone else named Jim. Angie keeps dialing her wrong number Jim, first, to make sure he won't spread around to the other high school students what he's inadvertently heard, then just to talk. The anonymity offered by the phone allows them to share parts of themselves that they might not have shared otherwise. Gradually they begin to know, like, and eventually love each other based solely on their phone conversations.

So, what's wrong? Why doesn't Jim agree to meet Angie? Her own insecurities tell her that it's because a tall, handsome, almost 18-year-old senior who's already a professional musician would be ashamed to be seen with her. But the real reason is that Jim is not the boy he has made himself out to be. He's only 16, he writes songs that he's too shy to sing in front of anyone, and he's very short. And, oh yes, he has a very large nose.

The moral, of course, is that what's on the inside is much more important than physical appearances. Told entirely in telephone dialogue. Well written; drawings throughout.

261. **Sanford, William, and Carl Green.** *Alabama.* **Crestwood House, 1986. 32 pp. $9.95 LB (0-89686-294-1). Nonfiction.**

Subjects: Biographies – Music; Music
Reading Level: Grades 4–5　　　　**Interest Level: Grades 7–12**

In 1969, cousins Randy Owen, Jeff Cook, and Teddy Gentry formed a band, dreaming of becoming a successful country group. After years of playing in bars and clubs, the band, called Alabama, finally played for the right people when they competed in a Nashville talent show in 1980. By 1981 they were receiving awards from their peers and had an album that sold over 1 million copies. Each succeeding year has brought more honors and impressive sales, making Alabama one of the most successful country bands of the era. Numerous photographs accompany the text.

262. **Sanford, William, and Carl Green.** *The Beach Boys.* **Crestwood House, 1986. 32 pp. $9.95 LB (0-89686-295-X). Nonfiction.**

Subjects: Biographies – Music; Music
Reading Level: Grades 4–5   Interest Level: Grades 7–12

Brothers Brian, Dennis, and Carl Wilson were only teenagers when they formed a group that would become the basis for a whole new style of 1960s music. The Beach Boys' sound appealed to the lighter side of a generation faced by rapid changes in the world. Their image and lyrics projected fun and wholesome values, using very basic themes to bring the feelings of surf, sand, and teenage love to the hearts of millions. After 25 years the Beach Boys are popular with two generations of listeners and are only getting better. Numerous photographs accompany the text.

263. **Sanford, William, and Carl Green.** *Bill Cosby.* **Crestwood House, 1986. 32 pp. $9.95 LB (0-89686-297-6). Nonfiction.**

Subjects: Biographies – Entertainers; Black Americans
Reading Level: Grades 4–5   Interest Level: Grades 7–12

For nearly 30 years Bill Cosby has been making America laugh by using his unique brand of humor to show the similarities in our lives. A man who is devoted to his family, Cosby gives the public a humorous view of his private life by recounting incidents from his childhood and marriage. As his talent has grown, Cosby has become not only a gifted stand-up comedian but a television powerhouse, with the most popular show on broadcast television. Numerous photographs accompany the text.

264. **Sanford, William, and Carl Green.** *Cyndi Lauper.* **Crestwood House, 1986. 32 pp. $9.95 LB (0-89686-300-X). Nonfiction.**

Subjects: Biographies – Music; Music – Rock stars; Women – Biographies
Reading Level: Grades 4–5   Interest Level: Grades 7–12

Cyndi Lauper has never conformed to anyone's standards except her own. While this is immediately obvious in her wardrobe, it is also clear in her music. Raised in Queens, New York, Lauper never fit in with the other kids and she used her music as an escape. After traveling throughout the country, Lauper returned to New York and began singing in clubs, first as part of a band and finally as a solo act. She has managed to carve out a niche for herself as one of rock music's most dynamic performers. Numerous photographs accompany the text.

265. **Sanford, William, and Carl Green.** *Hulk Hogan.* **Crestwood House, 1986. 32 pp. $9.95 LB (0-89686-299-2). Nonfiction.**
    Subjects: Biographies – Sports; Sports, sports figures – Wrestling
    Reading Level: Grades 4–5   Interest Level: Grades 7–12
    Hulk Hogan grew up in Venice Beach, California, where he was able to indulge in his two favorite pastimes: rock music and weight lifting. By the age of 21, Hulk was ready to move on to a more exciting life and decided to use his weight-lifting ability by becoming a professional wrestler. Although Hulk began his career as a "bad guy" named Sterling Golden, his fame began in 1982 when he was chosen for a part in *Rocky III* with Sylvester Stallone. After this role Hulk Hogan created his own groupies and product lines and gained popularity as one of wrestling's "good guys." Numerous photographs throughout.

266. **Sanford, William, and Carl Green.** *The Invisible Man.* **Crestwood House, 1987. 48 pp. $9.95 LB (0-89686-307-7); $4.95 paper (0-89686-372-7). Fiction.**
    Subjects: Monsters
    Reading Level: Grades 3–5   Interest Level: Grades 7–12
    The film classic *The Invisible Man* is based on the H. G. Wells novel, a story about a young scientist who discovers a drug that can make him invisible and thus has the illusion that he can take over the world. Sanford and Green use the technique of combining black-and-white frames from the film with an easy-to-read text to delight young readers. For other titles in the popular Monster series, see Ian Thorne in this chapter.

267. **Sanford, William, and Carl Green.** *Julian Lennon.* **Crestwood House, 1986. 32 pp. $9.95 LB (0-89686-301-8). Nonfiction.**
    Subjects: Biographies – Music; Music – Rock stars
    Reading Level: Grades 4–5   Interest Level: Grades 7–12
    Being the son of a world-famous musician had both good and bad points for Julian Lennon. Although he enjoyed the life-style he had as a child, when Julian decided he wanted to be a professional musician many people thought he was trying to use his father's name to get ahead. Once he finally found someone to produce an album for him, Julian proved to the world that while some of his talents may have been

inherited from his father, he is a very separate artist. Numerous photographs throughout.

268. **Sanford, William, and Carl Green.** *Michael J. Fox.* **Crestwood House, 1986. 32 pp. $9.95 LB (0-89686-298-4). Nonfiction.**
   Subjects: Biographies – Movies and television
   Reading Level: Grades 4–5   Interest Level: Grades 7–12

Michael J. Fox was born in Edmonton, Alberta, Canada, but has become the image of clean-cut American youth. Best known for his role as Alex Keaton on television's "Family Ties," Fox has also left a mark on the film industry in movies such as *Teen Wolf* and *Back to the Future.* Despite his successes Fox is a down-to-earth person who enjoys spending time with his friends and family, a quality that comes through in every character he portrays. Numerous photographs accompany the text.

269. **Sanford, William, and Carl Green.** *Stevie Wonder.* **Crestwood House, 1986. 32 pp. $9.95 LB (0-89686-296-8). Nonfiction.**
   Subjects: Biographies – Music; Black Americans; Music
   Reading Level: Grades 4–5   Interest Level: Grades 7–12

Blinded by an accident at birth, Stevie Wonder did not seem to have much of a future. One of five children born in a poor family, Stevie showed his musical talent at the age of two, and at nine he met the head of Hitsville, U.S.A., the future Motown. In 1963, when he was only 13, one of Stevie's songs sold 1 million copies and his success with Motown continued until 1971, when he left to go out on his own. Within a year he rejoined Motown, with full creative control over all of his music, and has gone on to become a rock legend. Numerous photographs accompany the text.

270. **Sanford, William, and Carl Green.** *Sylvester Stallone.* **Crestwood House, 1986. 32 pp. $9.95 LB (0-89686-304-2). Nonfiction.**
   Subjects: Biographies – Movies and television; Movies
   Reading Level: Grades 4–5   Interest Level: Grades 7–12

Sylvester Stallone may be a superstar, but it took a difficult childhood and years of hard work to make him the kind of man he is today. A child who was always getting into trouble, "Sly" eventually discovered a love for acting and writing. While trying to find acting jobs, he also worked at writing scripts for television and created his own "big break" in acting when he sold the script for the movie *Rocky.* By insisting on playing the starring role, Stallone made himself into a household name. After the *Rocky* sequels and his *Rambo* movies Stallone has become a true Hollywood powerhouse. Numerous photographs and interviews accompany the text.

271. **Schleifer, Jay.** *Everything You Need to Know about Teen Suicide.* **Rosen Group, 1988. 64 pp. $12.95 LB (0-8239-0812-7). Nonfiction.**
   Subjects: Suicide
   Reading Level: Grades 4–6   Interest Level: Grades 7–12
   Using excellent black-and-white and color photographs Schleifer examines the reasons why young people kill themselves. He discusses how to recognize the signs of suicidal behavior and the ways teenagers can help friends from becoming potential suicide victims. A glossary and a section on national organizations that help potential suicide victims round out the book.

272. **Selden, Neil.** *Night Driver.* **Scholastic, 1978. 127 pp. $2.95 paper (0-590-05227-6). Fiction.**
   Subjects: Crime stories; Humor
   Reading Level: Grades 3–4   Interest Level: Grades 8–12
   Joe's friends, Tully and Dixie, are always after him to stop driving his cab and find a safe job. Joe scoffs at them; in fact, he wishes the job was a little more exciting. One night his wish comes true. Some crooks are fighting over a valuable set of counterfeit money printing plates, and Joe finds himself caught in the middle. There are a couple of high-speed chases; a meeting with an unemployed, out-of-touch actor with a skinny dog; and a plainclothes detective who is a practical joker. Teenagers looking for a book full of action and appreciative of wise-guy humor will enjoy this book.

273. **Sheffield, Margaret.** *Life Blood: A New Image for Menstruation.* **Knopf, 1989. 44 pp. $14.95 (0-394-57065-0). Nonfiction.**
   Subjects: Health, health problems; Menstruation
   Reading Level: Grade 3+   Interest Level: Grades 7–12
   Beautiful Matisse-like drawings by Shelia Bewley give a dreamlike quality to the process of menstruation. The story of menstruation is told in matter-of-fact language, with paragraphs printed in narrow columns to resemble poetry. There is a comforting quality about this book that will help many young women ponder the meaning of their monthly period. A glossary of terms appends the text.

274. **Shuker, Nancy.** *Everything You Need to Know about an Alcoholic Parent.* Rosen Group, 1990. 64 pp. $12.95 LB (0-8239-1011-3). Nonfiction.

Subjects: Alcoholism; Family problems
Reading Level: Grades 4–6   Interest Level: Grades 7–12

Shuker offers advice on how to deal with an alcóholic parent and where to go for help. Living with an alcoholic parent is a difficult environment for most teens. The feelings of frustration and anger, as well as the everyday trite episodes, must be dealt with in a constructive fashion if the child is to develop and survive emotionally. With photographs of teenagers and parents in uncomfortable situations that show alcohol abuse, Shuker involves the high/low reader in the text. Coming to terms with the alcoholic parent and use of counseling are ways to meet the problem. A glossary and a list of helping organizations append the text.

275. **Shuker-Haines, Frances.** *Everything You Need to Know about Date Rape.* Rosen Group, 1990. 64 pp. $12.95 LB (0-8239-1013-X). Nonfiction.

Subjects: Rape; Women – Rape
Reading Level: Grades 4–6   Interest Level: Grades 7–12

Using realistic color and black-and-white photographs of teenagers in dating situations, the book attempts to debunk the myth that teenage girls, by their behavior and dress, provoke boys into rape. Shuker-Haines stresses behavior that is appropriate for women to express when aggressive actions by their dates start to overwhelm them. This is a good title for at-risk teenagers to use in discussion, and it clearly demonstrates the emotional and physical harm that teenage girls endure after suffering the effects of date rape. A glossary appends the text.

276. **Simonsen, Peggy.** *Becoming a Supervisor.* Scott, Foresman, Lifelong Learning Division, 1982. 64 pp. $3.45 paper (0-673-24143-2). Nonfiction.

Subjects: Jobs, job hunting; Supervisory work
Reading Level: Grade 4   Interest Level: Grades 9–12

This book will help teens understand that a supervisory position doesn't just mean more pay. There's a lot of work, and it's not necessarily as easy as it looks. This book clearly explains the different communication and management skills that are necessary, with charts and checklists to help the reader determine if he or she has these skills or will need to develop them. Simonsen helps the reader decide whether or not being a supervisor is something to consider and, if so, how to go about getting the job. Informative subheadings and enumerations organize the text. Includes a glossary of important terms.

277. Smith, Beverly. *The Long and Short of Mother Goose: The Long Book.* New Readers, 1990. 32 pp. $4.95 paper set (0-88336-983-4). Fiction.

Subjects: Nursery rhymes
Reading Level: Grades 2–3   Interest Level: Young children

Teenage mothers who are learning to read themselves and who are searching for material to read aloud to their children will appreciate this illustrated collection of Mother Goose rhymes with long vowel sounds. Also useful is *The Long and Short of Mother Goose: The Short Book* with short vowel sounds.

278. Sorrels, Roy. *A New Life.* New Readers, 1989. 64 pp. $3.50 paper (0-88336-200-7). Fiction.

Subjects: Accidents; Emergency care; Jobs, job hunting
Reading Level: Grade 3   Interest Level: Grades 7–12

Scott and Donna drive off to a secluded pond for a carefree afternoon of skating. While walking toward the pond they spot a trail of blood that leads them to an old man. They learn that the man was injured in a snowmobile accident while in search of medical care for a young pregnant woman. After reviving the old man they travel through a blizzard to his cabin, where Donna, a nurse-in-training, helps with the birth of the baby. Sorrels builds tension in this short tale of survival. Their brush with wilderness survival changes how Scott and Donna view their future career goals.

279. *Speaking Out on Health: An Anthology.* Literacy Volunteers of New York City, 1989. 64 pp. $2.95 paper (0-929631-08-0). Nonfiction.

Subjects: Disabilities; Health, health problems
Reading Level: Grades 4–5   Interest Level: Grades 7–12

This is an anthology of short essays about overcoming illness written by students enrolled in Literacy Programs in New York City. The writings are pure in form, substance, and emotional appeal. Although the students express themselves simply, these essays are from the heart. They cover illnesses that many have overcome, some resulting from birth defects (cerebral palsy); others are contagious illnesses (tuberculosis), gynecological problems, industrial accidents, and so on. Students will empathize with these brave people who have recovered from often prolonged illnesses and, having acquired the additional skill of reading, are well on their way to new fuller lives. This book ends with a list of organizations where people can get more information about the health issues raised in the text. This is a title in the New Writers' Voices series.

280. **Spies, Karen.** *Raffi: The Children's Voice.* **Dillon, 1989. 63 pp. $9.95 (0-87518-398-0). Nonfiction.**

Subjects: Biographies – Music; Canada; Music
Reading Level: Grades 3–4   Interest Level: Grades 7–12

One of the most popular and endearing children's performers of music today is Canadian artist Raffi. Born in Cairo, Egypt, of Turkish-Armenian parents, he and his family moved to Toronto, Canada, when he was a boy. In school he showed talent as a visual artist and musician. Eventually he chose to become a folk guitarist and began performing in clubs. Raffi was lured into performing for little children by his wife, Debi, who taught kindergarten. Now they are a team, making concert tours, videos, and best-selling albums. Much of Raffi's work focuses on caring for the environment. His album, "Singable Songs for the Very Young," has sold more than 700,000 copies. This is an excellent title to use in humanities programming in school and public libraries. Photographs.

281. **Stadelhofen, Marcie Miller.** *The Freedom Side.* **New Readers, 1989. 64 pp. $3.50 paper (0-88336-204-X). Fiction.**

Subjects: Black Americans; Slavery
Reading Level: Grade 3   Interest Level: Grades 7–12

When Becky Horn, a young black slave, hears that her mistress is planning to sell her, she risks her life to escape to Canada. As a runaway, Becky relies on the help of a white man who was sent by her father to escort her to the free state of Ohio. Pursued by her former owner, Becky almost gets caught along the way. Her strong will and courage to fight for freedom are an inspiration to all. Drawings.

282. **Stadelhofen, Marcie Miller.** *Last Chance for Freedom.* **New Readers, 1990. 95 pp. $3.50 paper (0-88336-206-6). Fiction.**

Subjects: Black Americans; Slavery
Reading Level: Grade 3+   Interest Level: Grades 7–12

Gregory, a runaway slave, risks his own freedom and a life with the woman he loves in order to help other slaves escape to Canada. Using the Underground Railroad, Gregory arrives in Maryland, where he meets John Brown and his raiders. When their plan to overtake an arsenal fails and Gregory is jailed, he is offered one last chance for freedom. In a dramatic rescue attempt, Gregory's fiancée, disguised as a white woman, crosses the border from Canada and helps him escape. Illustrations.

283. **Stark, Evan.** *Everything You Need to Know about Family Violence.* **Rosen Group, 1989. 64 pp. $12.95 LB (0-8239-0816-X). Nonfiction.**
   Subjects: Child abuse; Family problems; Women – Battered
   Reading Level: Grades 4–6   Interest Level: Grades 7–12

   Using color and black-and-white illustrations, Stark shows the fright that women and children experience when they are subjected to violence in the home. With reference to the first shelter for abused women, founded in London in 1971 by Erin Pizzey, Stark sets the stage for discussing the facts about women and child abuse and describes what victims of abuse are doing to stop it. A glossary and list of helping agencies append the text.

284. **Stark, Evan.** *Everything You Need to Know about Sexual Abuse.* **Rosen Group, 1988. 64 pp. $12.95 LB (0-8239-0814-3). Nonfiction.**
   Subjects: Child abuse; Family problems; Sexual abuse
   Reading Level: Grades 4–6   Interest Level: Grades 7–12

   Stark tackles a tough subject that many teenagers keep hidden forever. Sexual abuse can cripple young people emotionally. Stark's message to teenagers who read the accounts of incest and sexual abuse in this slim volume is that it is never bad to reveal the secret that you are being abused. Using very painful vignettes from the lives of teenagers who are being subjected to abusive situations, Stark suggests how and to whom teenagers can reach out to in order to lift this terrible burden. Black-and-white and color photographs break up the text. A glossary appends the text.

285. **Stewart, Gail.** *Coal Miners.* **Crestwood House, 1988. 48 pp. $10.95 LB (0-89686-395-6). Nonfiction.**
   Subjects: Coal mining; Jobs, job hunting
   Reading Level: Grades 4–6   Interest Level: Grades 7–10

   One of the most dangerous jobs in the eighteenth and nineteenth centuries was coal mining. Mine collapses, gas leaks, flooding, and lung disease made the lives of miners very hazardous, and often very short. After years of struggle the miners formed unions to help fight for safer conditions and better standards of living. As a result of these battles, conditions have improved, but coal mining is still a dangerous, if necessary, occupation. Numerous color photographs and a glossary/index accompany the text.

286. Stewart, Gail. *Off-Shore Oil Rig Workers.* Crestwood House, 1988. 48 pp. $10.95 LB (0-89686-397-2). Nonfiction.

Subjects: Jobs, job hunting; Oil rig workers
Reading Level: Grades 4–6   Interest Level: Grades 7–10

Drilling for oil has always been hard, dirty work requiring stamina and great physical reserves. Doing this work in the sea adds even more challenges and potential for danger. Off-shore workers live on their rigs for two weeks, working 12-hour shifts, and are then given two weeks on shore to relax. These breaks are necessary after dealing with the possibilities of fire, hurricanes, blowouts, and rig collapses. Although these events rarely occur, the life of an off-shore oil rig worker is difficult and certainly not for the faint-of-heart. Numerous color photographs and a glossary/index accompany the text.

287. Stewart, Gail. *Smokejumpers and Forest Firefighters.* Crestwood House, 1988. 48 pp. $10.95 LB (0-89686-398-0). Nonfiction.

Subjects: Environment; Firefighting
Reading Level: Grades 4–6   Interest Level: Grades 7–10

Forest fires are a potential disaster to many areas of the country and are usually stopped only through the efforts of dedicated groups of people who go into the heart of the fire to try to contain it. Every year hundreds of new firefighters are trained in the special skills needed to fight fires in the wilderness. Some are trained to fight at the outlying edges of the flames, while others are trained to parachute into dangerous areas for "spot" work. All of them work long shifts under dangerous conditions and must be in top physical condition at all times. Numerous color photographs and a glossary/index accompany the text.

288. Stewart, Gail. *Stuntpeople.* Crestwood House, 1988. 48 pp. $10.95 LB (0-89686-396-4). Nonfiction.

Subjects: Movies; Stuntpeople
Reading Level: Grades 4–6   Interest Level: Grades 7–10

We see them fall, burn, fight, get shot, and die, but we never see their faces and rarely know their names. The work that stuntpeople do is exciting and dangerous, but brings them little recognition from the public. Still, they practice their stunts constantly, always coming up with new ideas and mapping them out for maximum safety. This hard work pays off in exciting movies and television shows and brings them great personal satisfaction. Basic steps are outlined in this book for performing falls and car tricks, as well as burn scenes. Numerous color photographs and a glossary/index accompany the text.

289. **Stewart, Gail.** *Teen Suicide.* Crestwood House, 1988. 48 pp. $10.95 LB (0-89686-413-8). Nonfiction.

Subjects: Depression (mental); Suicide
Reading Level: Grade 4   Interest Level: Grades 7–12

The book begins with the suicide of an unhappy teenage boy and then goes on to examine the tragedy of suicide. The second leading cause of death for teenagers, suicide took 6,000 lives in 1987. Examination of the reasons for teenage suicide—low self-esteem to loss of one's center, parental conditional love, glamorization of death—gives a brief overview of the topic. The book then moves on to make suggestions to teenagers about what actions to take if they feel their friends are depressed and potentially suicidal. Sound advice on a serious contemporary issue. Color photographs. A glossary/index appends the text.

290. **Stewart, Jo.** *The Promise Ring.* Scholastic, 1979. 128 pp. $2.95 paper (0-590-05559-3). Fiction.

Subjects: Friendship; Jobs, job hunting; Romance
Reading Level: Grade 3   Interest Level: Grades 7–12

Growth and decision making for 17-year-old Cindy in job and friendship are the focuses of *The Promise Ring.* For Cindy, adjustment and success on her first job are complicated by her close ties with lazy and jealous roommates. Working as a salesperson in the Bottle House of Knott's Berry Farm is a job similar to many a position a young person might encounter the first time out for employment. But as Cindy seeks to manage on the job, her vicious roommates persist in placing her job in jeopardy by stealing her employee ID card and planting an expensive piece of stolen jewelry in her purse.

New friends that Cindy meets at Knott's Berry Farm are able to help her see the farce of relationships she has persisted in maintaining with high school friends she has long outgrown. Her immediate attraction to Matt, a manager of Knott's Berry Farm, not only adds romance to a predictable theme but also helps Cindy out of job problems. Although all the characters are high school graduates, the situations will appeal mainly to young teenage women.

291. **Stewart, Winnie.** *Night on 'Gator Creek.* New Readers, 1990. 64 pp. $3.50 paper (0-88336-215-5). Fiction.

Subjects: Adventure; Florida
Reading Level: Grades 3–4   Interest Level: Grades 7–12

Raised by his grandparents, Mattie learns to love the Florida wetlands and a life of camping and fishing. During their trips to 'Gator

Creek, Mattie and his grandfather commune with nature and share their innermost thoughts. Their idyllic existence ends abruptly when the boat that they use for fishing capsizes. Mattie, who is unable to rescue his grandfather, must fend off alligators and struggle against the rapids in order to remain alive. In his despair, Mattie recalls a hymn that his grandfather used to sing and finds the strength to survive. Illustrations.

292. **Stone, N. J.** *The Adventures of Shelley Holmes.* **Fearon, 1988. 80 pp. $3.90 paper (0-8224-6706-2). Fiction.**

Subjects: Crime stories; Mysteries
Reading Level: Grades 3–5   Interest Level: Grades 7–12

Two high school students, Sherlock (Shelley Holmes) and Jimmy Watson, set out to investigate the circumstances surrounding a serious beating of a football player and the mysterious thefts at a local college. When Shelley Holmes's brother is wrongly accused of beating another high school football player, she risks all to trap the thief who has implicated her brother in a possible homicide. Humor, romance, and vindication for her brother are the rewards in this slight mystery. Other titles in the Talespinner II series are *Bad Luck Gold, The Eye of Kali, Hard Road to Paradise, The Last Cowboy, Out of This World, The Poison Pen Mystery,* and *A Question of Freedom.*

293. **Streib, Daniel T.** *Ride Along.* **Scholastic, 1975. 90 pp. $2.95 paper (0-590-02995-9). Fiction.**

Subjects: Adventure; Police work
Reading Level: Grades 3–4   Interest Level: Grades 7–10

Steve Harris may be getting into more than he bargained for when he agrees to ride along with Officer Alvarez. His friends think he's selling out, and they're convinced that Steve will turn on them in the future. Steve's first day riding along is exciting and dangerous, and he faces the contempt of his friends while trying to direct traffic away from an accident. His integrity challenged, Steve almost gives in during an attempted burglary at the local store; he and his friend, Monster, are the near victims this time. Quick thinking and acting save the day for the two boys, and riding along suddenly becomes an interesting idea for Monster. Some exciting moments are highlighted with photographs.

294. **Sullivan, George.** *Here Come the Monster Trucks.* **Dutton, 1989. 64 pp. $14.95 (0-525-65005-9). Nonfiction.**

Subjects: Trucks
Reading Level: Grade 3   Interest Level: Grades 7–9

The text presents full-color photographs of Bigfoot, the first monster truck of the oversized wheel (44 inches in diameter) phenomenon, created by Bob Chandler in 1974. Since then, the craze of using large wheels on trucks to strengthen their car-crushing capacity has grown to the use of 100-inch wheels. Thousands of screaming fans in stadiums watch as these trucks crush rows of cars, jump cars, and engage in mud-bog competition. Many varieties of these oversized wheel vehicles exist today, with names such as Godzilla, Black Stallion, and Hercules II. Each of these gleaming trucks will capture the hearts of young teens.

295. **Sundquist, Nancy.** *A Changed Man.* **Fearon, 1988. 64 pp. $3.90 paper (0-8224-5344-4). Fiction.**

Subjects: Accidents; Mysteries
Reading Level: Grade 4   Interest Level: Grades 7–12

Sam Smith is driving down the Los Angeles Freeway, when after a crash he discovers that he is in the hospital and that 42 years of his life has disappeared. Reconstructing those lost years is an arduous experience. During this period he discovers that his wife is involved in a scheme with another man to use a stop-smoking cassette to create amnesia in Sam. When Sam comes to, he realizes that he has become a pawn in a romantic triangle designed to make him disappear on a business trip without a trace so that his wife could inherit his assets. Other titles in the Bestellers IV series are *Welcome to Skull Canyon, Dares, Blackbeard's Medal, Time's Reach, Trouble at Catskill Creek, The Cardiff Hill Mystery, Tomorrow's Child, Hong Kong Heat,* and *Follow the Whales.* Line drawings.

296. **Taylor, Barbara.** *Everything You Need to Know about AIDS.* **Rosen Group, 1988. 64 pp. $12.95 LB (0-8239-0809-7). Nonfiction.**

Subjects: AIDS; Health, health problems – AIDS; Sexually transmitted diseases
Reading Level: Grades 3–4   Interest Level: Grades 7–12

Taylor discusses the AIDS virus, its discovery, causes, transmission, treatment, and how to protect oneself from contracting the disease. The easy-to read format of this thin volume, filled with black-and-white and color photographs pertinent to the topic, makes it required reading for all teenagers who need to be educated about this preventable disease. A list of self-help organizations, a glossary, and an index append the text.

297. **Taylor, Barbara.** *Everything You Need to Know about Alcohol.* **Rosen Group, 1989. 64 pp. $12.95 LB (0-8239-0813-5). Nonfiction.**

Subjects: Accidents; Alcoholism; Peer pressure
Reading Level: Grades 4–6   Interest Level: Grades 7–12

Taylor discusses the effect of alcohol on the mind and body and directs those in jeopardy as to where to seek help. Taylor reveals some startling statistics about alcohol consumption in the United States: 100 million Americans drink occasionally, alcohol claims at least 100,000 lives, 50,000 deaths on highways can be attributed to alcohol, and 5,000 teenagers are killed and 130,000 are injured each year in drunk-driving accidents. Dealing with peer pressure to drink, learning to recognize alcoholism in family and friends, and when to turn to Alanon and Alateen are presented in an easy-to-read format. Includes black-and-white and color photographs of teenagers, a list of self-help organizations, a glossary, and an index.

298. **Teall, Kay M.** *TV Camera Three.* **Scholastic, 1978. 128 pp. $2.95 paper (0-590-05226-8). Fiction.**

Subjects: Jobs, job hunting; Television
Reading Level: Grade 3   Interest Level: Grades 9–12

Emily Steele and Lee Ann Stanley have been classmates all through school. Lee Ann has always excelled where good looks are concerned but is not keen on hard work. Emily has always felt like a nobody in Lee Ann's presence. After graduation, Emily lands a job as a trial cameraperson at the local television station. She is told by the station manager that although two young women were hired, only the best will be offered a permanent appointment. When Emily finds that her old-time rival, Lee Ann, is the other young woman, she is disgusted.

As the weeks of training continue, it is obvious to Emily that Lee Ann is up to her old tricks of letting other people do the hard work for her. Emily makes mistakes learning how to maneuver the camera and is often embarrassed by her own ignorance. Lee Ann, on the other hand, continues to flirt and lean on other staff members to carry off her difficult shots. A contemporary theme with a career setting attractive to many teenagers makes this a very popular high/low title.

299. **Thomas, Mark S.** *Braving a Blizzard.* **Fearon, 1987. 32 pp. $1.80 paper (0-8224-2918-7). Fiction.**

Subjects: Disasters; Women – Rights
Reading Level: Grades 4–5   Interest Level: Grades 7–12

Although *Braving a Blizzard* is a fictional account of one young woman's determination to vote in the first election (Nineteenth Amendment ratified in 1920; first election for women, 1924) in which women had the legal right to vote, the reader is quickly caught up in the woman's suffrage movement. Using Millicent as an example of a young woman braving blizzard conditions on her first hazardous journey to the polls, Thomas introduces reluctant teenage readers to actual events in history. An epilogue summarizes "The Facts" surrounding the fictional vignette. Other titles in the Flashback Disaster series are *Big-Top Tragedy,*

Black Sunday, Deadly Torrent (Johnstown flood, 1889), *Destruction at Dawn* (San Francisco earthquake, 1906), *Dreams of Fire* (*Apollo I*, 1967), *Idaho Inferno, Quake 8.1* (Mexico City, 1985), *Ship of Doom* (the *Titanic*), and *Twister!*

300. **Thorne, Ian.** *Creature from the Black Lagoon.* **Crestwood House, 1981. 48 pp. $9.95 LB (0-89686-187-2); $4.95 paper (0-89686-190-2). Nonfiction.**

Subjects: Monsters; Movies
Reading Level: Grades 3–5   Interest Level: Grades 7–12

Ian Thorne has taken the best monster films from late-night television and has retold the stories using photographs from the films to highlight a very easy-to-read and readable text. The Monster series also includes *The Deadly Mantis, It Came from Outer Space, Frankenstein Meets the Wolfman, The Wolfman, The Mummy, Godzilla, The Blob, Mad Scientists, Frankenstein, King Kong,* and *Dracula.* Background information on how each film was made, with photographs of the actors and descriptions of how the special effects were carried off, enhance each title. This series is essential for any library serving the poor reader. For additional titles in this genre see the Green and Sanford and Sanford and Green entries in this chapter.

301. **Turck, Mary.** *AIDS.* **Crestwood House, 1988. 48 pp. $10.95 LB (0-89686-412-X). Nonfiction.**

Subjects: AIDS; Health, health problems – AIDS; Sexually transmitted diseases
Reading Level: Grade 4   Interest Level: Grades 7–12

This no-nonsense approach to AIDS explains how to prevent the disease and discusses popular myths about it. There is a photograph of a condom, useful in preventing the virus, and photographs of needles. The text presents a frank and open discussion about homosexual transmission, prostitutes, and IV drug use. Real-life people with AIDS such as three brothers in Florida (who were banned from school because they were infected with the virus), babies of IV drug-using mothers, and those infected through homosexual contact bring the point home to even the most resistant teenager that AIDS is a fatal disease. A short chapter on AZT concludes the book. Includes a glossary/index.

302. **Turck, Mary.** *Alcohol and Tobacco.* **Crestwood House, 1988. 48 pp. $10.95 LB (0-89686-411-1). Nonfiction.**

Subjects: Alcoholism; Health, health problems – Smoking; Smoking
Reading Level: Grades 4–6   Interest Level: Grades 7–12

Explaining the origins and myths that surround alcohol and tobacco addictions, Turck uses examples of teenagers who, as early as the seventh grade, become alcoholics or who at the age of 10 become addicted to nicotine. Organizations such as Alcoholics Anonymous, Alateen, and Alanon are all described as invaluable aids both for the addicted individual and for friends and family. Teenagers learn about the warning signs of smoking or alcohol dependency so that they can seek help for early recovery. Color photographs. A glossary/index appends the text.

303. **Weber, Bruce.** *Sparky Anderson.* **Crestwood House, 1988. 48 pp. $10.95 LB (0-89686-379-4). Nonfiction.**

Subjects: Biographies – Sports; Sports, sports figures – Baseball
Reading Level: Grades 4–5   Interest Level: Grades 7–12

Sparky Anderson was brought up in a baseball household, the son of a semipro baseball player. One of his earliest dreams was to play professional baseball himself, and after six years in the minor leagues, Anderson got the call to move up to the Philadelphia Phillies as a second baseman. Unfortunately, his career as a player was not as illustrious as he had hoped, and he soon found himself back in the minor leagues. This disappointment led to the beginning of one of baseball's most successful all-time great major league managers. After leading teams to four World Series wins, Anderson is recognized as one of the most successful and popular managers in the game. Includes numerous photographs.

304. **Werner, Herma.** *The Dragster.* **Scholastic, 1978. 93 pp. $2.95 paper (0-590-09026-7). Fiction.**

Subjects: Automobiles; Sports, sports figures – Drag racing
Reading Level: Grades 2.5–2.9   Interest Level: Grades 9–12

Even though everyone else, including his friend, Zeke, thought that Greg had been ripped off, Greg knew that his 1969 Chevy would be ready for the National Hot Rod Association drag races in May. What he didn't know was how he would pay for all the parts the old car needed, and how he could get Eddie Connell off his back. Eddie was a cop and rather suspicious about the Chevy and Greg's "friend," Hank. Eddie was sure the car or its engine was "hot" and that there was some strange business going on down at Berry's junkyard. Greg wasn't going to turn anyone in to any cop, even if he did know something. Meanwhile, May was drawing closer and the car was not ready yet. Greg had to do some business with Hank and Berry after all, but what kind of payment did they mean? This is a well-written action story, and anyone interested in cars, young people, and good endings will enjoy following Greg and his adventures. Photographs.

305. **Werner, Herma.** *Rosina Torres, LPN.* Scholastic, 1979. 127 pp. $2.95 paper (0-590-35551-1). Fiction.

Subjects: Jobs, job hunting; Nursing
Reading Level: Grades 3–4   Interest Level: Grades 9–12

Rosina Torres is very excited on her first day of work as a licensed practical nurse at the biggest and best hospital in the city. Her problems begin when she is assigned to work under the toughest head nurse in the hospital, Mrs. Gilman. Rosina breaks the first rule of nursing by getting too involved with her patients: five-year-old Belle, who needs a heart operation; old Mr. Mitchell, critically injured in a car accident; and rich Mrs. Jefferson, in for a face-lift. However, Mrs. Gilman, though strict and by-the-book, recognizes that Rosina is a very good nurse with great potential and helps her strike the important balance between caring and overinvolvement that is necessary for all good nurses and doctors. An exciting, fast-paced story, highlighting an interesting career for young people. Photographs throughout.

306. **Westman, Paul.** *Jacques Cousteau: Free Flight Undersea.* Illus. by Reg Sandland. Dillon, 1980. 48 pp. $9.95 LB (0-87518-188-0). Nonfiction.

Subjects: Diving, underwater; Environment
Reading Level: Grades 2–3   Interest Level: Grades 7–12

Deep-sea rapture, high pressure at deep depths, and sharks are among the dangers faced by Jacques Cousteau in his undersea explorations. Cousteau invented the Aqua-lung, thus bringing scuba diving into existence. Cousteau has dedicated his entire life to unraveling the mysteries of the deep. This biography details the Conshelf experiments, the first experiments of underwater living, explorations of the *Calypso,* and Cousteau's efforts to rescue the oceans from pollution. A remarkable story of a remarkable life. Photographs and line drawings amplify the text.

307. **White, Dana.** *High-Rise Workers.* Crestwood House, 1988. 48 pp. $10.95 LB (0-89686-402-2). Nonfiction.

Subjects: Building and construction; Jobs, job hunting
Reading Level: Grades 4–5   Interest Level: Grades 6–10

We rarely think about the work they do, but high-rise workers affect our lives everyday. These men and women earn their wages by climbing on and constructing the metal skeletons that become our modern skyscrapers. Their jobs require great physical conditioning and nerves to match the steel they work with. Working in crews, or "gangs," these people have truly built our nation's cities. Numerous color photographs and a glossary/index accompany the text.

308. **Williams, Cecil, and Janice Mirikitani.** *I Have Something to Say about This Big Trouble.* **Glide Word Press, 1989. 124 pp. $9.95 (0-9622574-1-9). Nonfiction.**

Subjects: Literacy programs; Teenage problems
Reading Level: Grades 2–4   Interest Level: Grades 7–12

The best tools for literacy programs are materials written by the students themselves. In this collection of writings by young people enrolled in the Mary Agatha Furth Children's Program at Glide Memorial United Methodist Church in San Francisco, young people express their feelings about growing up in the desperate conditions that a crack-infested neighborhood produces. The reader sees glimmers of hope in the short pieces as the young writers warn of the dangers of drugs, express a desire to learn, speak warmly of their mothers and siblings, and reach for a way out of an environment saturated by the effects of drug abuse. Maya Angelou, in her foreword, comments: "It is amazing that our children do not hate us, do not gather together as one strongly knit and righteously indignant group and turn their backs on us and this decrepit world we offer them." Teenagers who share similar backgrounds will feel comforted by the hope that there is a way out.

309. **Wolhart, Dayna.** *Anorexia and Bulimia.* **Crestwood House, 1988. 48 pp. $10.95 LB (0-89686-416-2). Nonfiction.**

Subjects: Anorexia; Bulimia; Health, health problems – Eating disorders
Reading Level: Grades 4–6   Interest Level: Grades 7–12

Wolhart explains the differences between anorexia and bulimia using fictional examples of teenage girls who are suffering from the diseases. About one in every 200 to 250 American girls between the ages of 12 and 18 will get anorexia and the numbers are increasing. (Wolhart states that there is a set weight for each individual but those with eating disorders do not understand when they reach it and they diet on to extremes.) Wolhart cites low self-esteem as a characteristic of teenage anorectics and bulimics and stresses the value of the therapist/patient relationship in overcoming the illness. A comforting book that shows the way out of the pain and tragedy that come from the disorders. Color photographs. A glossary/index appends the text.

310. **Wood, Phyllis Anderson.** *Meet Me in the Park, Angie.* **Westminster John Knox, 1983. 116 pp. $11.95 (0-664-32710-9). Fiction.**

Subjects: Jobs, job hunting; Marriage, teenage
Reading Level: Grade 4   Interest Level: Grades 8–12

This is the story of the growth of a young married couple. Peter, 19 years old, is married to Angie, 18 years old, who is not emotionally equipped to deal with the harsher realities of life. He is a city gardener, she a counter girl at a roadside diner. After Angie is laid off, she finds it difficult to find work, even with a high school diploma. Interviewing for a position as a restaurant hostess, she naively discovers that the owner expects sexual favors in return for the job. Meanwhile, honest Peter is teamed up with a dishonest loafer, Manny. When Peter's supervisor asks about his partner's misconduct, Peter tells all. Manny, to get even, scares Angie into believing that they will be thrown out of their apartment for disregarding the "no pet" clause. Worse yet, he convinces the young wife that her husband is unfaithful.

All ends well. Angie grows up at the end and is about to enroll in a dog-grooming school. Peter obtains an offer as a landscape gardener for an apartment complex, the deal coming with free rent. They are looking forward to his entering college the next year so he can train as a landscape gardener. The emotional growth of the couple, especially that of Angie, is realistically described, including scenes of marital intimacy. The book should be well liked by older high school girls, although the happy ending will not convince teens that early marriage is condoned. No illustrations or photographs.

311. **Woods, Geraldine. *Jim Henson: From Puppets to Muppets*. Dillon, 1987. 62 pp. $9.95 LB (0-87518-348-4). Nonfiction.**
   Subjects: Biographies – Movies and television; Puppetry
   Reading Level: Grades 3–4   Interest Level: Grades 7–12
   A universe of imagination that has touched, influenced, and inspired generations was in the genius of one remarkable talent: Jim Henson. His innovative approach to the world of puppetry educated and entertained audiences numbering in the hundreds of millions. Almost as remarkable is the fact that despite wealth, power, and fame, Henson was a modest man who enjoyed the love and affection of his creative staff and family. He began his career over 30 years ago with a puppet reminiscent of "Kermit" on a television station in Washington, D.C. Although he loved puppetry he did not consider the craft seriously until he toured Europe and met "professional" puppeteers. Henson incorporated electronics and computer technology, always expanding his art form. Wonderful photographs of the Muppets throughout.

312. **Wulffson, Don. *More Incredible True Adventures*. Dutton, 1989. 111 pp. $12.95 (0-525-65000-8). Nonfiction.**
   Subjects: Adventure
   Reading Level: Grade 4   Interest Level: Grades 7–12
   All readers will be on the edge of their seats as they read these nine

true tales of survival. (The stories retain some of the excitement of a newsreel effect.) Each tale, 10 or 12 pages in length, pits the survivor against incredible odds—a teenager fighting off a grizzly bear attack, a soldier battling with a python in a Vietcong tunnel, a skydiver whose chute fails to open, explorers pursued by cannibals, a pilot landing a packed aircraft after the roof of the plane has blown off in midflight. Attractive black-and-white photographs complement the text.

10
Books for the Reluctant Reader

Joanne Rosario

As the vocational schools specialist for the New York Public Library, the major part of my job is visiting the dozen high schools in the area that prepare students for jobs in a vocational or technical area. The purpose of my visits is to encourage these students to become library users. Some of the students I meet in the course of the day are very bright, avid readers and regular library users—but most are not.

Many of the students I visit are reading below grade level and many do not see the value in reading at all. They view reading as a school-related task only. For these students, reading is often associated with difficulty, embarrassment, and failure; it is not something they do happily or willingly. These reluctant readers are my most important audience. These are the ones who will rarely visit the public library on their own. It will never occur to them to pick up a book and read just for fun. When I visit their classrooms I have an opportunity to change their minds with my booktalks.

I always start with a booktalk so that the class will know they are going to have a good time and that they will not be listening to a boring lecture on the Dewey decimal system—which is what many imagine when they are told a librarian is coming to talk to them. I like to begin with a mystery or adventure story to catch their interest. After the first booktalk, the room is quiet. Now I have everyone's attention.

At this point I give the students the basic information they need to get a library card, tell them where the closest library is located, and explain the services the library has to offer them. Once I have answered all the procedure-related questions, I end my presentation with as many booktalks as time will allow. Booktalking is the highlight of my class visit. It is the one part everyone usually enjoys. I always save time before the period ends for students to examine the books I have talked about because many are eager to look at them.

Booktalking is a successful technique to encourage reading. Three minutes is all it takes to say enough about a book so that someone else will want to read it. When choosing books to share with a group, select titles you have enjoyed yourself; it is difficult to make someone enthusiastic about a particular book if you don't feel that way yourself.

Always have a variety of books available. Mystery, humor, sports, adventure, and romance are all subjects that lend themselves to booktalks. Try to vary the reading level among the books so that there will be something for everyone in the group you are speaking to. Reluctant readers have been known to jump two grade levels for a book they really want to read, so don't be afraid to use good books that are above their level.

The following list of books is recommended for use with reluctant readers. It includes authors who are popular and easy to read, topics of interest to any teenager, and material that can be used for school assignments. Some of the titles have been published as children's books, but their subject matter and format will also appeal to teenagers. Many have been published for the general young adult market but are easy enough for even below-grade-level readers to understand and enjoy.

The reading level here generally ranges from fourth to eighth grade. These are more difficult to read than material published specifically as high interest–low reading level, but the fact that many of these look like "regular" books increases their acceptability to reluctant readers. When available, paperback editions have been listed because teenagers in general prefer paperbacks to hardcovers and this also increases the desirability of these books for reluctant readers.

When booktalking to groups of reluctant readers (or any other kind of reader) all that really matters is that you communicate the pleasure books give you and the idea that the books you are talking about will give your listeners pleasure, also.

313. **Aaseng, Nathan.** *The Rejects.* **Lerner, 1989. 80 pp. $9.95 (0-8225-0677-7). Nonfiction.**

Subjects: Entrepreneurs

The stories of nine entrepreneurs who ignored the negative advice of experts and went on to succeed with their ideas for new products. The chapters on Xerox, Monopoly, and Orville Redenbacher are most appealing.

314. **Abbe, Kathryn M., and Frances M. Gill.** *Twins on Twins.* **Crown, 1980. 190 pp. $17.95 (0-517-54149-1); $11.95 paper (0-517-55761-4). Nonfiction.**

Subjects: Twins

Includes twins who model, twins who play basketball, and twins who married twins. Also has information on the International Twins Association and a section on the biology of twinning.

315. **Alvarez, Mark.** *The Official Baseball Hall of Fame Answer Book.* **Simon & Schuster, 1989. 95 pp. $6.95 paper (0-671-67377-7). Nonfiction.**

Subjects: Sports, sports figures – Baseball

The questions that young baseball fans often ask are the ones included in this entertaining trivia book. The text is sprinkled with photographs that add to the enjoyment.

316. **Ames, Lee J.** *Draw Fifty Famous Faces.* **Doubleday, 1978. 64 pp. $9.95 paper (0-385-13218-2). Nonfiction.**

Subjects: Drawing

A book without words giving step-by-step instructions for anyone with a pencil on how to draw. This is one in a very popular series that also includes *Draw Fifty Monsters, Creepy Creatures, Superheroes, Dragons,* and *Draw Fifty Famous Cartoons.*

317. **Ashabranner, Brent, and Paul Conklin.** *Born to the Land.* **Putnam, 1989. 134 pp. $14.95 (0-399-21716-9). Nonfiction.**

Subjects: Southwest (U.S.)

In words and pictures Ashabranner and Conklin introduce us to the people of Deming, New Mexico, a farming and ranching community. The text is not overly easy, but the wonderful photographs make the book very accessible to poor readers.

318. **Asher, Sandy.** *Everything Is Not Enough.* **Delacorte, 1987. 155 pp. $14.95 (0-385-29530-8); $2.75 paper (0-440-20002-4). Fiction.**

Subjects: Jobs, job hunting

Seventeen-year-old Michael breaks away from the comfortable life his parents provide for him when he takes a job as a busboy at a beach resort.

319. **Avi.** *Something Upstairs.* **Orchard Books, 1988. 120 pp. $11.95 (0-531-05782-8). Fiction.**

Subjects: Ghost stories; Mysteries

A strange stain on the floor of his new bedroom draws Kenny into a story of a 200-year-old murder with a ghost that demands his help and a sinister presence that may trap him in the past.

320. **Ballard, Robert D.** *Exploring the Titanic.* **Scholastic, 1988. 64 pp. $14.95 (0-590-41953-6). Nonfiction.**

Subjects: Adventure; Disasters

The leader of the expedition that located the ship uses color photographs and diagrams to show how it was done.

321. **Beckett, James.** *Official 1990 Price Guide to Football Cards.* **House of Collectibles, 1989. 435 pp. $5.95 paper (0-87637-800-9). Nonfiction.**

Subjects: Sports, sports figures – Football

Information on how to collect, obtain, preserve, and invest in football cards. Includes information on pricing of cards from 1950 to 1988.

322. **Bennett, Jay.** *The Haunted One.* **Watts, 1987. 176 pp. $12.95 (0-531-15059-3); Fawcett $2.95 paper (0-449-70314-2). Fiction.**

Subjects: Ghost stories; Mysteries

Eighteen-year-old Paul Barrett is having the perfect summer. He's a lifeguard on the Jersey shore, and the prettiest girl on the beach is his. When boredom sets in at the end of summer, a fatal error in judgment turns the perfect summer into a nightmare.

323. **Blackwood, Gary L.** *Wild Timothy.* **Atheneum, 1987. 153 pp. $12.95 (0-689-31352-7). Fiction.**

Subjects: Adventure

When Tim goes into the forest for firewood, he loses his sense of direction. His parents can't find him and go to seek help when their jeep battery dies. Alone and inexperienced, Tim manages to survive for three weeks. This entertaining survival story has lots of appeal.

324. **Blume, Judy.** *Forever.* **Bradbury, 1975. 216 pp. $12.95 (0-02-711030-3); Pocket Books $3.50 paper (0-671-53225-1). Fiction.**

Subjects: Romance

The story of a first love that doesn't have to last forever.

325. **Brittain, Bill.** *The Fantastic Freshman.* **Harper, 1988. 160 pp. $11.70 (0-06-020798-3). Fiction.**

Subjects: School

When Stanley's wish to be important at school instead of just a lowly freshman comes true, he discovers that being ordinary also has its advantages.

326. Brown, Fern. *Teen Guide to Childbirth.* **Watts, 1988. 62 pp. $11.90 (0-531-10573-3). Nonfiction.**

Subjects: Pregnancy and parenthood

A concise, easy-to-read book about childbirth from late pregnancy to postdelivery. Brief descriptions of Lamaze and Leboyer methods are included, as are descriptions of a hospital birth, birthing center, and a home birth. A good overview for teens.

327. Browne, David. *Crack and Cocaine.* **Gloucester, 1987. 32 pp. $11.90 (0-531-17047-0). Nonfiction.**

Subjects: Drug abuse

A large-format book with photographs on every double spread that gives basic information on crack and cocaine use. Includes where and how it is grown and manufactured, the dealers, the users, the effects, and treatments.

328. Bunting, Eve. *Someone Is Hiding on Alcatraz Island.* **Clarion, 1984. 136 pp. $12.95 (0-89919-219-X); Berkley $2.75 paper (0-425-10294-7). Fiction.**

Subjects: Gangs

Danny saves an old woman from being mugged by Priest's brother. Priest belongs to the Outlaws, the toughest gang in Danny's school. The Outlaws want revenge. Danny hopes to hide on Alcatraz Island, but the gang follows him there and locks him in a cell. Nobody has ever escaped from Alcatraz. How can Danny?

329. Bunting, Eve. *A Sudden Silence.* **Harcourt, 1988. 112 pp. $13.95 (0-15-282058-2). Fiction.**

Subjects: Crime stories; Disabilities

Consumed by guilt when his deaf younger brother is killed by a hit-and-run driver as they walked home from a party, Jesse spends his summer trying to locate the killer.

330. Bunting, Eve. *Will You Be My Posslq?* **Harcourt, 1987. 181 pp. $12.95 (0-15-297399-0). Fiction.**

Subjects: Health, health problems – Cancer; Romance

When Kyle Pendleton asks UCLA freshman Jamie McLaughlin to be his POSSLQ, she doesn't know what the word means—"Persons of the opposite sex sharing living quarters." Jamie finds Kyle very attractive, but this is to be strictly a financial relationship. Can Jamie handle it, and can she trust Kyle with the secret of her struggle with cancer?

331. Calvert, Patricia. *Stranger, You and I.* **Scribner, 1987. 152 pp. $12.95 (0-684-18896-1); Avon $2.50 paper (0-380-70600-8). Fiction.**

Subjects: Pregnancy and parenthood; Romance

When Hugh's best friend, Zee, begins to act like a girl instead of a tomboy, he is attracted to her. When he asks her out on a date she tells him she is pregnant and has told no one else.

332. Carter, Alden R. *Sheila's Dying.* **Putnam, 1987. 207 pp. $13.95 (0-399-21405-4). Fiction.**

Subjects: Death; Health, health problems – Cancer

Just when Jerry Kincaid decides it would be best to break up with his girlfriend, Sheila, he learns that she has cancer. He doesn't desert her, and supports her to the end. Her sharp-tongued friend, Bonnie, whom Jerry has never liked, comes to mean more to him than he'd ever thought possible.

333. Christopher, Matt. *Tackle without a Team.* **Little, Brown, 1989. 145 pp. $12.95 (0-316-14067-8). Fiction.**

Subjects: Drug abuse; Sports, sports figures – Football

Scott is kicked off his high school football team when marijuana is discovered in his duffle bag. He's been framed and is determined to discover who did it.

334. Cohen, Daniel. *The Headless Roommate & Other Tales of Terror.* **Evans, 1988. 128 pp. $11.95 (0-87131-327-8). Fiction.**

Subjects: Horror stories; Short stories

Humorous and horrific short stories and urban folktales people swear are true.

335. Cohen, Daniel, and Susan Cohen. *How to Get Started in Video.* **Watts, 1986. 128 pp. $12.90 (0-531-10250-5). Nonfiction.**

Subjects: Jobs, job hunting; Videos

This guide tells how to work in video either on the production side or the performing side. Included are interviews with people who have been successful in the field.

336. Cole, Brock. *The Goats.* **Farrar, 1987. 184 pp. $11.95 (0-374-32678-9). Fiction.**

Subjects: Adventure

Thirteen-year-old Laura and Howie are left alone and naked on an island by kids at their camp. This practical joke backfires when Laura and Howie take control of the situation and get themselves out of their predicament.

337. **Cooney, Caroline B.** *The Girl Who Invented Romance.* **Bantam, 1987. 167 pp. $13.95 (0-553-05473-2). Fiction.**

Subjects: Romance

Sixteen-year-old Kelly has never been kissed or even been on a date. She dreams of romance and creates a board game by that name to help herself learn the rules of love.

338. **Dalton, Stephen.** *Split Second: The World of High Speed Photography.* **Salem House, 1985. 144 pp. $21.95 (0-88162-063-7). Nonfiction.**

Subjects: Photography

How photographers achieve the special effects we see in ads and on record covers, as well as information on how scientists use high-speed cameras to study movement of birds and insects that cannot be seen by the naked eye.

339. **Darling, David J.** *The Microchip Revolution.* **Dillon, 1986. 80 pp. $11.95 (0-87518-313-1). Nonfiction.**

Subjects: Computers

Many diagrams, drawings, and photographs illustrate the text about how microchip technology has already changed our world and will continue to do so.

340. **Davis, Jenny.** *Sex Education.* **Orchard Books, 1988. 150 pp. $13.95 (0-531-05756-9). Fiction.**

Subjects: Pregnancy and parenthood; Sex education

Livvie and David, ninth graders, have a class assignment to "care about someone" and they chose a young couple who are expecting a baby. Their choice leads to tragedy.

341. **Deaver, Julie Reece.** *Say Goodnight, Gracie.* **Harper, 1988. 214 pp. $12.89 (0-06-021419-8). Fiction.**

Subjects: Death; Friendship

Morgan's best friend, Jimmy, is killed by a drunk driver. She must deal with her grief and learn to live without the person who'd been part of her life since their mothers met in the maternity hospital.

342. Drimmer, Frederick. *Born Different.* **Atheneum, 1988. 182 pp. $13.95 (0-689-31360-8). Nonfiction.**

Subjects: Disabilities

The true stories of people born with incredible handicaps who nevertheless struggled to live a life with happiness and human dignity. Tom Thumb, the Elephant Man, and the Siamese twins are included.

343. Duncan, Lois. *Don't Look Behind You.* **Delacorte, 1989. 179 pp. $14.95 (0-385-29739-4). Fiction.**

Subjects: Friendship; Moving (relocation)

When April's father becomes a government witness, her life is turned upside down. The family is relocated and all are given new identities, but April can't accept giving up her friends, her boyfriend, and everything else she liked about her life. But is there a way to get back?

344. Duncan, Lois. *Locked in Time.* **Little, Brown, 1985. 240 pp. $12.95 (0-316-19555-3); Dell $2.95 paper (0-440-94942-4). Fiction.**

Subjects: Mysteries; Stepfamilies

When Nore goes to visit her father and his new wife in her southern plantation-style house everything seems normal. Slowly Nore comes to realize her new relatives aren't quite what they seem to be, and that knowledge puts Nore and her father in great danger.

345. Dygard, Thomas J. *Halfback Tough.* **Morrow, 1986. 224 pp. $12.95 (0-688-05925-2); Penguin $3.95 paper (0-14-034113-7). Fiction.**

Subjects: Friendship; Sports, sports figures – Football

Joe Atkins had been in trouble in his old school—smoking, drinking, cutting class. Now in his new school he has made the football team and become a star. Could he leave his old self behind when his old "friends"come back for him?

346. Edwards, Harvey. *The Art of Dance.* **Little, Brown, 1989. 144 pp. $35.00 (0-8212-1734-8). Nonfiction.**

Subjects: Dancing

Beautiful black-and-white and color photographs of the behind-the-scenes world of classical and modern dance. Edwards illuminates the hard work, hours of practice, and discipline it takes to be a dancer.

347. **Elsman, Max.** *How to Get Your First Job.* **Crown, 1985. 153 pp. $4.95 paper (0-517-55739-8). Nonfiction.**

Subjects: Jobs, job hunting

Good information, not only on how to go about a job search, how to handle interviews, and what to do once you've got the job, but also on career planning for the future.

348. **Ferris, Jean.** *Invincible Summer.* **Farrar, 1987. 176 pp. $12.95 (0-374-33642-3); Avon $2.75 paper (0-380-70619-9). Fiction.**

Subjects: Health, health problems – Leukemia; Romance

Robin is 17 and in love with Rick. Unfortunately, they meet in a hospital where both are being treated for leukemia. Their friendship and love help them through the tragedy their disease brings.

349. **Francis, Neil.** *Super Flyers.* **Addison-Wesley, 1988. 80 pp. $6.95 paper (0-201-14519-7). Nonfiction.**

Subjects: Airplanes

Learn all about aerodynamics painlessly by making paper gliders, helicopters, parachutes, and kites.

350. **Glenn, Mel.** *Back to Class.* **Clarion, 1988. 112 pp. $13.95 (0-89919-656-X). Nonfiction.**

Subjects: School

Free verse poetry, with accompanying photographs, tell the stories of high school teachers and their students with humor, charm, and honesty.

351. **Gordon, Sol.** *When Living Hurts.* **Union of American Hebrew Congregations, 1985. 127 pp. $8.95 paper (0-8074-0310-5). Nonfiction.**

Subjects: Depression (mental); Suicide

An attractive book that presents ways that a teen can help someone who is lonely, depressed, or suicidal—even if that person is himself.

352. **Gorman, Carol.** *Chelsey and the Green-haired Kid.* **Houghton, 1987. 110 pp. $12.95 (0-395-41854-2). Fiction.**

Subjects: Crime stories; Mysteries

Chelsey, a 13-year-old paraplegic, is convinced that the fatal accident she witnessed at the basketball game was murder. She and her friend Jack (who has green hair) join forces to find the killer.

353. **Grillone, Lisa, and Joseph Gennero.** *Small Worlds Close Up.* **Crown, 1987. 64 pp. $12.95 (0-517-53289-1); $4.95 paper (0-517-56347-9). Nonfiction.**

Subjects: Microscopes

Guess what is revealed to us by photography and the electron microscope? Pictures include a crystal of salt, a piece of cork, and the foot of a fruit fly.

354. **Gunning, Thomas G.** *Strange Mysteries.* **Putnam, 1987. 95 pp. $9.95 (0-396-09038-9). Nonfiction.**

Subjects: Mysteries

A variety of true tales that tell of lighthouse keepers who vanish, buried treasure that is never recovered, a dolphin that guides ships through dangerous waters, and other mysteries.

355. **Harrar, George, and Linda Harrar.** *Signs of the Apes, Songs of the Whales.* **Simon & Schuster, 1989. 48 pp. $14.95 (0-671-67748-9). Nonfiction.**

Subjects: Animals

Filled with color photographs, diagrams, and charts, this book describes experiments in which apes and dolphins have been taught aspects of human language. How these experiments have contributed to our understanding of animal intelligence is also discussed.

356. **Haven, Susan.** *Maybe I'll Move to the Lost and Found.* **Putnam, 1988. 158 pp. $13.95 (0-399-21509-3); Archway $2.75 paper (0-671-67402-1). Fiction.**

Subjects: Divorce; Family problems

Gilly is always losing things. She is also close to losing her cool in trying to deal with her parents' breakup and her father's new girlfriend.

357. **Hawks, Robert.** *This Stranger My Father.* **Houghton, 1988. 228 pp. $13.95 (0-395-44089-0). Fiction.**

Subjects: Family problems; Spy stories

Patty becomes a fugitive when it is revealed that her father has been hiding from the police for more than 20 years after being accused of selling secrets to the Soviets.

358. **Head, Ann.** *Mr. and Mrs. BoJo Jones.* **Putnam, 1967. 192 pp. $9.95 (0-399-10562-X); NAL $3.50 paper (0-451-16319-2). Fiction.**

Subjects: Marriage, teenage; Pregnancy and parenthood

A classic story of teenage pregnancy and marriage that, although a bit outdated in language and style, remains a favorite of this type of literature.

359. Hein, Karen, and Theresa Foy DiGeronimo. *AIDS: Trading Fears for Facts*. Consumer Reports Books, 1989. 196 pp. $3.95 paper (0-89043-269-4). Nonfiction.

Subjects: AIDS; Health, health problems – AIDS

A clear presentation of AIDS information aims specifically at teens. Various approaches—straight narrative, case studies, diagrams, questions, and answers—are used to ensure that young adults get the facts.

360. Hermes, Patricia. *A Time to Listen*. Harcourt, 1987. 132 pp. $12.95 (0-15-288196-4). Nonfiction.

Subjects: Depression (mental); Suicide

Interviews with teens who have attempted suicide, parents and friends of suicide victims, as well as practicing psychologists reveal the warning signs of teenage suicide, some causes of depression, and how to get help.

361. Hinton, S. E. *The Outsiders*. Dell, 1968. 156 pp. $3.95 paper (0-440-96769-4). Fiction.

Subjects: Gangs

Written by a teenager, this novel of gang life has become a classic in teenage literature.

362. Hinton, S. E. *Taming the Star Runner*. Delacorte, 1988. 181 pp. $14.95 (0-440-50058-3). Fiction.

Subjects: Sports, sports figures – Horseback riding; Stepfamilies

When Travis can't get along with his stepfather, he's sent to live on his uncle's ranch where a friendship with a girl who gives riding lessons and is trying to tame a wild horse helps him cope with his problems.

363. Hopper, Nancy. *Wake Me When the Band Starts Playing*. Lodestar, 1988. 117 pp. $13.95 (0-525-67244-3). Fiction.

Subjects: Health, health problems – Obesity; Sports, sports figures – Swimming

Overweight and out of shape, Mike is forced by his mother and doctor to join the school swim team. In time he gains confidence, loses some weight, and becomes more of a participant and less of a mere observer in his own life.

364. Howe, Norma. *In with the Out Crowd*. Houghton, 1986. 196 pp. $12.95 (0-395-40490-8); Avon $2.50 paper (0-380-70472-2). Fiction.

Subjects: Friendship; Teenage problems

Robin, 16, is in her junior year in high school when she realizes she no longer wants to be with the "in" group at school. Who are her friends—especially her boyfriend, Bill, who is pressuring her about sex? Who will she hang out with then, and how will she spend her time?

365. **Isberg, Emily.** *Peak Performance.* **Simon & Schuster, 1989. 48 pp. $14.95 (0-671-67750-0); $5.95 paper (0-671-67745-4). Nonfiction.**

Subjects: Sports, sports figures

Describes the ways in which scientific advances have contributed to athletic performance, focusing on sports medicine and the work of the U.S. Olympic Training Centers. A companion video is also available.

366. **James, Elizabeth, and Carol Barkin.** *How to Write a Term Paper.* **Lothrop, 1980. 96 pp. $3.95 paper (0-688-41951-8). Nonfiction.**

Subjects: Writing

From topic selection to outline development, this is an easy-to-read guide to all the steps needed to organize and produce a term paper.

367. **Janeczko, Paul B.** *This Delicious Day.* **Watts, 1987. 81 pp. $11.95 (0-531-05724-0). Nonfiction.**

Subjects: Poetry

Sixty-five short poems by many different authors. Each helps us taste the delights of life with all its many flavors.

368. **Lauber, Patricia.** *Lost Star: Story of Amelia Earhart.* **Scholastic, 1988. 106 pp. $10.95 (0-590-41615-4). Nonfiction.**

Subjects: Biographies – Aviators; Women – Biographies

The life story of one of aviation's most famous pioneers, who was lost in an attempt to circle the globe. Includes black-and-white photographs.

369. **Levitin, Sonia.** *Incident at Loring Groves.* **Dial, 1988. 192 pp. $13.95 (0-8037-0455-0). Fiction.**

Subjects: Crime stories; Peer pressure

When Cassidy and Ken discover the body of a missing classmate while attending a party in a park outside town, they allow group pressure to keep them silent.

370. **Levy, Marilyn.** *Touching.* **Fawcett, 1988. 176 pp. $2.95 paper (0-449-70267-7). Fiction.**

Subjects: Alcoholism; Family problems

Sixteen-year-old Eve can't stand her alcoholic father, especially after he embarrasses her in front of a teacher and her friends. With the support of her first boyfriend and other friends, she learns how to deal with being the child of an alcoholic.

371. **Lukes, Bonnie L.** *How to Be a Reasonably Thin Teenage Girl.* **Macmillan, 1986. 96 pp. $12.95 (0-689-31269-5). Nonfiction.**
Subjects: Health, health problems – Obesity
A humorous yet sensible approach to losing weight. Good advice on exercising, counting calories, and psychological tips to help one stay on track.

372. **McKie, Robin.** *Energy.* **Hampstead, 1989. 45 pp. $12.90 (0-531-19509-0). Nonfiction.**
Subjects: Energy sources
A well-written, profusely illustrated book that surveys the current state of research and development in energy science. Covers conventional energy sources, such as oil, coal, nuclear, and solar, and some unconventional sources, such as tidal, geothermal, and sunflower oil.

373. **MacLean, John.** *Mac.* **Houghton, 1987. 175 pp. $12.95 (0-395-43080-1); Avon $2.75 paper (0-380-70700-4). Fiction.**
Subjects: Child abuse; Sexual abuse
Fourteen-year-old Mac has a good life with good grades, a spot on the soccer team, and a pretty girl named Jenny. Then he is sexually assaulted by a doctor during a physical and he almost loses everything.

374. **McWhirter, Norris.** *Guinness Book of World Records.* **Sterling, 1989. 446 pp. $16.95 (0-8069-0276-0). Nonfiction.**
Subjects: World records
Enjoyed as a browsing item by all ages, this compendium of records throughout history is especially appealing to trivia lovers.

375. **Madaras, Lynda.** *The What's Happening to My Body? Book for Boys.* **Newmarket, 1987. 251 pp. $9.95 paper (0-937858-99-4). Nonfiction.**
Subjects: Health, health problems – Sexually transmitted diseases; Sex education
An excellent guide to puberty for boys. Includes information on physical and emotional changes, romance and sexual feelings, the facts of intercourse, pregnancy, and childbirth, and sexually transmitted diseases, including AIDS.

376. **Madaras, Lynda.** *The What's Happening to My Body? Book for Girls.* **Newmarket, 1987. 269 pp. $9.95 paper (0-937858-98-6). Nonfiction.**

Subjects: Health, health problems – Sexually transmitted diseases; Sex education

This excellent guide to puberty for girls includes information on physical and emotional changes, sex, pregnancy, and birth control, and sexually transmitted diseases, including AIDS.

377. **Males, Carolyn, and Roberta Feigen.** *Life after High School.* **Messner, 1986. 163 pp. $11.29 (0-671-54664-3). Nonfiction.**

Subjects: Jobs, job hunting

Using various exercises to help the reader determine his or her interests and skills, the authors then go on to discuss how to create a résumé, how to interview, and how to update career plans as priorities change over the years.

378. **Mallory, Kenneth, and Andrea Conley.** *Rescue of the Stranded Whales.* **Simon & Schuster, 1989. 64 pp. $14.95 (0-671-67122-7). Nonfiction.**

Subjects: Animals

A true story about three pilot whales that were stranded on Cape Cod and rescued by scientists from New England Aquarium. They were released after a six-month stay at the aquarium's Animal Care Center, the first successful release of its kind.

379. **Maurer, Richard.** *Junk in Space.* **Simon & Schuster, 1989. 48 pp. $14.95 (0-671-67768-3). Nonfiction.**

Subjects: Space exploration

Describes space trash—from mislaid cameras and tools to abandoned satellites and moon vehicles—and includes sections on how they got there, potential hazards to navigation, orbits, and the like.

380. **Mayo, Gretchen Will.** *Star Tales.* **Walker, 1987. 96 pp. $11.95 (0-8027-6672-2). Nonfiction.**

Subjects: Astronomy; Native Americans

Stories about the stars, the moon, and the night sky collected from many North American Indian tribes.

381. **Mazer, Harry.** *City Light.* **Scholastic, 1988. 192 pp. $12.95 (0-590-40511-X); $2.75 paper (0-590-40515-2). Fiction.**

Subjects: Romance

When his girlfriend, Julie, leaves him, 17-year-old George is devastated. He chases after her but can't win her back. When he tries to pick up the pieces and start life over again, a friendship begun over a computer enables George to be happy again.

382. **Meigs, James B., and Jennifer Stern.** *Make Your Own Music Video.* **Watts, 1986. 96 pp. $10.40 (0-531-10215-7). Nonfiction.**
Subjects: Music; Videos

An easy to follow step-by-step guide that beginners can use to create a video of their own.

383. **Miklowitz, Gloria D.** *Goodbye Tomorrow.* **Delacorte, 1987. 138 pp. $13.95 (0-385-29562-6). Fiction.**
Subjects: AIDS; Health, health problems – AIDS

Alex is in a near-fatal accident and must have blood transfusions. A year later he has become infected with AIDS and has ARC (AIDS related complex). The emotional changes Alex, his sister, Christy, and his girlfriend, Shannon, go through are realistic, as are problems with school and the media as the fear spreads.

384. **Miller-Lachmann, Lyn.** *Hiding Places.* **Square One Publishers, 1987. 205 pp. $4.95 paper (0-938961-00-4). Fiction.**
Subjects: Moving (relocation); Teenage problems

Teenage Mark keeps all his pain and heartache locked inside. A move to New York City gives him the chance he needs to let his feelings out and to let others into his life.

385. **Miner, Jane Claypool.** *Young Parents.* **Messner, 1985. 160 pp. $9.79 (0-671-49848-7). Nonfiction.**
Subjects: Pregnancy and parenthood

For unmarried pregnant teens, this book provides a clear picture of the choices they must make. Interviews with girls who have been through it add realism without being judgmental.

386. **Myers, Walter Dean.** *Crystal.* **Viking Penguin, 1987. 198 pp. $12.95 paper (0-670-80426-6). Fiction.**
Subjects: Jobs, job hunting; Modeling

For a teenage girl from Brooklyn, a career as a high fashion model is a dream come true. Yet there is a lot of pressure in this business, from opportunistic agents to overbearing photographers, and Crystal must find a way to reconcile it all with her life as a normal teenager.

387. **Myers, Walter Dean.** *Scorpions.* **Harper, 1988. 224 pp. $12.70 (0-06-024364-3). Fiction.**

Subjects: Gangs; Teenage problems

Jamal and Tito live in Harlem and are struggling to get good grades and stay out of the way of the bigger, tougher kids at school. Jamal is given a gun by members of his brother's gang who want him to join now that Randy is in prison. Tito uses the gun to defend Jamal and a gang member dies.

388. **Nixon, Joan Lowery.** *Secret, Silent Screams.* **Delacorte, 1988. 180 pp. $14.95 (0-440-50059-1). Fiction.**

Subjects: Death; Suicide

Everyone agrees that Barry's death is the latest in a string of suicides at Farrington Park High School except his friend and neighbor, Marti. Her investigation puts her own life in danger.

389. **O'Dell, Scott.** *My Name Is Not Angelica.* **Houghton, 1989. 130 pp. $14.95 (0-395-51061-9). Fiction.**

Subjects: Black Americans; Slavery

The story of the slave rebellion of 1733 on the island of St. John in the Virgin Islands is told by Raisha, a Senegalese girl, who is a body slave of a planter's wife.

390. **Paulsen, Gary.** *Hatchet.* **Macmillan, 1987. 195 pp. $12.95 (0-02-770130-1). Fiction.**

Subjects: Adventure

When the plane taking him to spend time with his divorced father crashes in the Canadian wilderness, Brian is left with only the hatchet his mother had given him before he left home.

391. **Phifer, Kate Gilbert.** *Tall and Small.* **Walker, 1987. 87 pp. $11.95 (0-8027-6684-6). Nonfiction.**

Subjects: Health, health problems – Stature; Teenage problems

Teens like to fit in, so it is hard on them to be taller or much shorter than average. This book includes some interesting facts about height and hints on how to feel good about yourself.

392. **Pipkin, Turk.** *Be a Clown.* **Workman, 1989. 112 pp. $8.95 paper (0-89480-347-6). Nonfiction.**

Subjects: Clowns

A handbook for clownmanship, including makeup, funny faces, props, costumes, juggling, walking, and stunts.

393. *Reader's Digest Illustrated Book of Dogs*. Rev. ed. Reader's Digest, 1989. 384 pp. $21.95 (0-89577-340-6). Nonfiction.

Subjects: Animals; Pets

An alphabetical list of dog breeds that includes information on how to identify and classify dogs. A section on you and your dog helps you to choose the right dog for you.

394. Reit, Seymour. *Behind Rebel Lines*. Harcourt, 1988. 102 pp. $12.95 (0-15-200416-5). Nonfiction.

Subjects: War, war stories; Women – Biographies

True story of a woman who disguised herself as a man to enlist in the Union Army and was so successful in her deception that she was asked to cross enemy lines to gather information for her superiors, who never suspected she was a woman.

395. Richter, Elizabeth. *Losing Someone You Love: When a Brother or Sister Dies*. Putnam, 1986. 80 pp. $12.95 (0-399-21243-4). Nonfiction.

Subjects: Death; Family problems

In very brief chapters 16 young people between the ages of 10 and 24 talk about their feelings after the death of a brother or sister.

396. Ride, Sally, with Susan Okie. *To Space and Back*. Lothrop, 1986. 96 pp. $16.95 (0-688-06159-1). Nonfiction.

Subjects: Astronauts; Women – Biographies

Large size, large print, and filled with color photographs from NASA, Sally Ride's book is a very accessible work about the daily routines of shuttle astronauts.

397. Schmitt, Lois. *Smart Spending*. Macmillan, 1989. 102 pp. $11.95 (0-684-19035-4). Nonfiction.

Subjects: Consumer education

How teenagers can recognize and avoid consumer traps is discussed in this informative book. Misleading advertising, consumer fraud, product safety, fad diets, effective complaining, and more are discussed.

398. Shaw, Diana. *Gone Hollywood*. Little, Brown, 1988. 143 pp. $12.95 (0-316-78343-9). Fiction.

Subjects: Movies

Teenage Carter Colburn joins her director father in Hollywood just as the teenage star of the show he's working on disappears. If Carter can find Dory West, the show won't be cancelled and she won't be sent home to her mother.

399. **Silverstein, Herma.** *Mad, Mad Monday.* **Lodestar, 1988. 128 pp. $12.95 (0-525-67239-7). Fiction.**

Subjects: Ghost stories; Romance

Fourteen-year-old Miranda wants to catch her school heartthrob with a magic spell. Instead, she conjures up a 17-year-old ghost who died in 1958.

400. **Sleator, William.** *Duplicate.* **Dutton, 1988. 160 pp. $12.95 (0-525-44390-8). Fiction.**

Subjects: Fantasy

When he finds a machine that can copy living things, David replicates himself, thinking that he can send his double to do all his unpleasant tasks. But his duplicate has ideas of its own.

401. **Sullivan, George.** *Big League Spring Training.* **Henry Holt, 1989. 118 pp. $14.95 (0-8050-0838-1). Nonfiction.**

Subjects: Sports, sports figures – Baseball

How spring training started, what the managers hope to accomplish during this time, and what the players' routine is when down in Florida or out in Arizona. Numerous black-and-white photographs show spring training activities.

402. **Vedral, Joyce.** *My Parents Are Driving Me Crazy.* **Ballantine, 1986. 160 pp. $2.95 paper (0-345-33011-0). Nonfiction.**

Subjects: Family problems

To help teens cope with the age-old problem of confusing parental behavior and to deal constructively with the frustration, impatience, and anger intergenerational clashes can generate.

403. **Ventura, Piero.** *Michelangelo's World.* **Putnam, 1989. 44 pp. $13.95 (0-399-21593-X). Nonfiction.**

Subjects: Drawing

This large-size book, charmingly illustrated with Ventura's cartoonlike drawings, gives a great deal of information about Michelangelo, the spirit of his time, and the troubles he faced.

404. **Wachter, Oralee.** *Sex, Drugs and AIDS.* **Bantam, 1987. 80 pp. $3.95 paper (0-553-34454-4). Nonfiction.**

Subjects: AIDS; Health, health problems – AIDS

Based on the award-winning film starring Rae Dawn Chong, Wachter's book is very easy to read and illustrated with stills from the film. Included are facts about the disease, safe sex, teen attitudes, and a question-and-answer section.

405. **Walker, Paul Robert.** *Pride of Puerto Rico: Life of Roberto Clemente.* **Harcourt, 1988. 135 pp. $11.95 (0-15-200562-5). Nonfiction.**

Subjects: Biographies – Sports; Hispanic Americans

Star right fielder for the Pittsburgh Pirates, Clemente lost his life on a mercy mission to Nicaragua when his plane, carrying relief supplies to earthquake victims, crashed. Overcoming prejudice off and on the playing field, he was an inspiration to Puerto Ricans.

406. **Ward, Brian R.** *Smoking and Health.* **Watts, 1986. 48 pp. $12.40 (0-531-10180-0). Nonfiction.**

Subjects: Health, health problems – Smoking; Smoking

Color charts, diagrams, and other illustrative materials make this a good introduction to the facts about smoking, the history of tobacco, the tobacco industry, and the health risks.

407. **Williams-Garcia, Rita.** *Blue Tights.* **Dutton, 1988. 138 pp. $12.95 (0-525-67234-6). Fiction.**

Subjects: Sexuality; Teenagers

Fifteen-year-old Joyce Collins, a New York City teenager, is searching for her identity and struggling with her emerging sexuality. Her performance in an African dance troupe enables her to center her true talents, find romance with J'Had, and meet real friends for the first time.

408. **Wirths, Claudine G., and Mary Bowman-Kruhm.** *I Hate School! How to Hang In and When to Drop Out.* **Crowell, 1987. 115 pp. $11.95 (0-690-04556-5); Harper $7.95 paper (0-06-446054-1). Nonfiction.**

Subjects: School

A self-help book for students who are having trouble with school. Written by two teachers. There is plenty of good advice on getting a handle on schoolwork, and the importance of knowing when to drop out and having a plan for what to do after leaving school.

409. **Wolff, Virginia Euwer.** *Probably Still Nick Swansen.* **Henry Holt, 1988. 144 pp. $13.95 (0-8050-0701-6). Fiction.**

Subjects: Romance; School

Nick Swansen is in Special Ed, but he wants the same things most other high school students want, including a date for the prom.

410. **Wulffson, Don L.** *Incredible True Adventures.* **Putnam, 1986. 112 pp. $8.95 (0-396-08799-X). Nonfiction.**

Subjects: Adventure

An easy-to-read collection of true adventures, from being caught inside a tornado to surviving in hostile jungles, violent seas, and arctic cold.

411. **Zable, Rona S.** *Love at the Laundromat.* **Bantam, 1988. 160 pp. $2.95 paper (0-553-27225-X). Fiction.**

Subjects: Romance

Jo's widowed mother is a talented artist who decides to buy a laundromat since she has never held a regular job. Jo thinks this is awful, until she falls for a college student who does his laundry there.

412. **Zeinert, Karen.** *Salem Witchcraft Trials.* **Watts, 1989. 95 pp. $11.90 (0-531-106-73-X). Nonfiction.**

Subjects: American history; Witchcraft

An easy-reading book with good historical background on the Massachusetts colony and how seriously witchcraft was taken there. It also offers an explanation of the behavior of the women.

Appendix I:
Core Collection Publishers

Ellen V. LiBretto

Addison-Wesley
Addison-Wesley Publishing Co., Inc.
One Jacob Way
Reading, MA 01867

Archway
Division of Simon and Schuster, Inc.
1230 Ave. of the Americas
New York, NY 10020

Atheneum. *See* Macmillan

Avon
Avon Books
105 Madison Ave.
New York, NY 10016

Ballantine
Ballantine Books, Inc.
201 E. 50 St.
New York, NY 10022

Bantam
Bantam Books, Inc.
666 Fifth Ave.
New York, NY 10103

Berkley
Berkley Publishing Group
200 Madison Ave.
New York, NY 10016

Book-Lab
Annmaur Corp.
500 74 St.
North Bergen, NJ 07047

Bradbury
Bradbury Press
866 Third Ave.
New York, NY 10022

Cambridge
Cambridge Adult Education (Prentice
    Hall)
1230 Ave. of the Americas
New York, NY 10020

Clarion
Clarion Books
52 Vanderbilt Ave.
New York, NY 10017

Consumer Reports Books
51 E. 42 St.
Suite 800
New York, NY 10017

Creative Education
Creative Education, Inc.
Box 227, 123 S. Broad St.
Mankato, MN 56001

Crestwood House
Crestwood House, Inc.
866 Third Ave.
New York, NY 10022

Crowell
Thomas Y. Crowell, Co.
10 E. 53 St.
New York, NY 10022

Crown
Crown Publishers, Inc.
225 Park Ave. S.
New York, NY 10003

Delacorte
Delacorte Press
One Dag Hammarskjold Plaza
245 E. 47 St.
New York, NY 10017

Dell
Dell Publishing Co.
666 Fifth Ave.
New York, NY 10103

Diabetes Center, Inc.
DCI Publishing
13911 Ridgedale Dr.
Minnetonka, MN 55343

Dial. *See* Doubleday

Dillon
Dillon Press, Inc.
242 Portland Ave. S.
Minneapolis, MN 55415

Dodd
Dodd, Mead & Co.
71 Fifth Ave.
New York, NY 10003

Doubleday
Doubleday & Co., Inc.
666 Fifth Ave.
New York, NY 10103

Dutton
E. P. Dutton
2 Park Ave.
New York, NY 10016

East End Literacy Press
265 Gerrard St.
Toronto, Ontario M5A 2G3, Canada

EMC
EMC Corp.
300 York Ave.
St. Paul, MN 55101

Evans
M. Evans & Co., Inc.
216 E. 49 St.
New York, NY 10017

Farrar
Farrar, Straus & Giroux, Inc.
19 Union Square W.
New York, NY 10003

Fawcett
Fawcett Book Group
201 E. 50 St.
New York, NY 10022

Fearon
Fearon Education
500 Harbor Blvd.
Belmont, CA 94002

Glide Word Press
330 Ellis St.
San Francisco, CA 94102

Gloucester. *See* Watts

Hampstead. *See* Watts

Harcourt
Harcourt Brace Jovanovich, Inc.
1250 Sixth Ave.
San Diego, CA 92101

Harper
Harper & Row, Publishers, Inc.
10 E. 53 St.
New York, NY 10022

Henry Holt
Henry Holt & Co.
115 W. 18 St.
New York, NY 10011

Houghton
Houghton Mifflin Co.
One Beacon St.
Boston, MA 02108

House of Collectibles
201 E. 50 St.
New York, NY 10022

Janesville Literacy Council
17 S. River St.
Janesville, WI 53545

Janus Books
Janus Book Publishers, Inc.
2501 Industrial Parkway W.
Haywood, CA 94545

Just Us Books
301 Main St., Suite 22–24
Orange, NJ 07050

Kern Adult Literacy Council
401 18 St.
Bakersfield, CA 93301

Knopf
Alfred A. Knopf, Inc.
201 E. 50 St.
New York, NY 10022

Lerner
Lerner Publications Co.
241 First Ave. N.
Minneapolis, MN 55401

Lippincott
J. B. Lippincott Co.
E. Washington Sq.
Philadelphia, PA 19105

Literacy Volunteers of New York City
666 Broadway, Suite 520
New York, NY 10012

Literary Council of Alaska
833 Third Ave.
Fairbanks, AK 99701

Little, Brown
Little, Brown & Co.
34 Beacon St.
Boston, MA 02108

Lodestar
Lodestar Books
2 Park Ave.
New York, NY 10016

Lothrop
Lothrop, Lee & Shepard Books
105 Madison Ave.
New York, NY 10016

M. Evans. *See* Evans

Macmillan
Macmillan Publishing Co., Inc.
866 Third Ave.
New York, NY 10022

Messner
Julian Messner
Simon & Schuster International
    Group
Prentice Hall Bldg.
190 Sylvan Ave.
Englewood Cliffs, NJ 07632

Morning Glory Press
6595 J San Haroldo Way
Buena Park, CA 90620-3748

Morrow
William Morrow & Co., Inc.
105 Madison Ave.
New York, NY 10016

NAL (New American Library). *See*
    Penguin

New Readers
New Readers Press
Box 131
Syracuse, NY 13210

Newmarket
Newmarket Press
18 E. 48 St.
New York, NY 10017

Orchard Books
387 Park Ave. S.
New York, NY 10016

Oxford University Press, Inc.
200 Madison Ave.
New York, NY 10016

Penguin
Penguin Books
375 Hudson St.
New York, NY 10014

Pocket Books. *See* Simon & Schuster

Putnam
The Putnam Publishing Group
200 Madison Ave.
New York, NY 10016

Reader's Digest
Reader's Digest Press
200 Park Ave.
New York, NY 10166

Rosen Group
The Rosen Publishing Group, Inc.
29 E. 21 St.
New York, NY 10010

Salem House. *See* Harper

Scarf
Scarf Press
58 E. 83 St.
New York, NY 10028

Scholastic
730 Broadway
New York, NY 10003

Scott, Foresman, Lifelong Learning Di-
    vision
1900 E. Lake Ave.
Glenview, IL 60025

Scribner
Charles Scribner's Sons
866 Third Ave.
New York, NY 10022

Simon & Schuster
1230 Ave. of the Americas
New York, NY 10020

Square One Publishers
Box 4385
Madison, WI 53711

Turman Publishing
Turman Publishing Co.
200 W. Mercer
Seattle, WA 98119

Union of American Hebrew Congregations
838 Fifth Ave.
New York, NY 10021

Viking Penguin
40 W. 23 St.
New York, NY 10010

Walker
Walker & Co.
720 Fifth Ave.
New York, NY 10019

Watts
Franklin Watts, Inc.
387 Park Ave. S.
New York, NY 10016

Westminster John Knox
925 Chestnut St.
Philadelphia, PA 19107

Workman
Workman Publishing Co., Inc.
708 Broadway
New York, NY 10003

Appendix II:
Bibliographies and Sources
of Current Reviews

Patsy H. Perritt

BIBLIOGRAPHIES

The Best: High/Low Books for Reluctant Readers. **Marianne Laino Pilla. Libraries Unlimited, 1990. 125 pp. paper $11.50. ISBN 0-87287-532-6.**
Available in book form or on disk for Apple and IBM computers, these in-print titles for grades 3–12 include reading and interest levels; book version contains indexes by reading level and subject; the disk may be used to produce printed reading lists by theme or reading level and can be customized to fit a library's collection. (Apple for Appleworks, $16.00; IBM-ASCII files, $16.50; Mac for Microsoft Works, $17.00.)

The Best in Children's Books: The University of Chicago Guide to Children's Literature 1979–1984. **Zena Sutherland, ed. University of Chicago Press, 1986. 511 pp. $35.00. ISBN 0-226-78060-0.**
Includes reviews of titles selected for outstanding literary quality from those already published in the *Bulletin of the Center for Children's Books.* A reading level index is arranged in order of increasing difficulty. All reading levels are determined by the *Bulletin* advisory committee, not by a specific formula.

Easy Reading: Book Series and Periodicals for Less Able Readers, **2nd ed. Randall J. Ryder, Bonnie G. Graves, and Michael F. Graves. International Reading Association, 1989. 96 pp. $8.75; $6.00 for IRA members. ISBN 0-87207-234-7.**

Descriptive and evaluative reviews of 44 book series and 15 periodicals written especially for those who have difficulty reading materials written for their age level in grades 4 through 12; reading and interest level index.

Easy-to-Read Books for Teenagers. **New York Public Library, Office of the Branch Libraries, 1989. 20 pp. $1.50 plus mailing costs of $1.00 (1–5 copies), $1.25 (6–10 copies), $1.50 (bulk). ISBN 0-87104-699-7.**

A list of fiction and nonfiction titles popular with New York City teens; no reading levels are given, but those titles with readability in the first- to fourth-grade range are noted.

Elementary School Library Collection: A Guide to Books and Other Media, **16th ed. Lois Winkel, ed. Brodart, 1988. $99.95. ISBN 0-87272-092-6.**

Lists selected multimedia titles for preschool through sixth grade. Interest levels are indicated and reading ability levels are assigned for books using the Spache Readability Formula for grades 1 and 2 and the Fry Graph for third grade and higher. Special appendixes list books for independent reading at first and second grades on levels 1.1, 1.2, 2.1, and 2.2 using the Spache Readability Formula.

High Interest–Easy Reading for Junior and Senior High School Students, **5th ed. Dorothy Matthews, ed. National Council of Teachers of English, 1988. 115 pp. paper $6.95. ISBN 0-8141-2096-2.**

Annotates books for readers who haven't found material that interests them; descriptions of series of books. No exact grade levels are indicated. In previous editions all titles have been tested for readability and none are above eighth-grade level.

Reaching the Reluctant Teen Reader. **Judith Druse, 5200 W. 20 Terr., #120, Topeka, KS 66604. $1.00.**

Camera-ready masters or floppy disks compatible with Appleworks on the Apple IIe (128 K required) of "Retrospective Title List of Books Chosen by the American Library Association for the Reluctant Reader 1982–89" and other materials prepared by the YASD/ALA Recommended Books for the Reluctant Young Adult Reader Committee.

Reader Development Bibliography. **Vickie Collins, ed. 1990. Contact the Free Library of Philadelphia, Office of Work with Adults and Young Adults.**

Lists over 350 inexpensive titles written on or below the eighth-grade reading level that were selected for use in the Philadelphia Reader Development Program; a new section lists materials appropriate for English as a Second Language. Includes comments about each book's content; author, series, and subject indexes. Reading levels were determined by the Gunning Fog Index of Readability.

Recommended Books for the Reluctant Young Adult Reader. **American Library Association, annual. $1.00 (quantity discounts available).**

Annotated book titles selected annually by the Young Adult Services Division Recommended Books for the Reluctant Reader Committee (formerly the High Interest/Low Literacy Level Materials Evaluation Committee) for their popularity with teens and readability on or below the sixth-grade level as calculated by the Fry Readability Scale; published each year in a spring issue of *Booklist.*

Through the Eyes of a Child: An Introduction to Children's Literature, **2nd ed. Donna E. Norton. Merrill, 1987. 691 pp. $34.95. ISBN 0-675-20725-8.**

A children's literature textbook that has thousands of titles noted by interest age level and reading grade level as determined by the Fry Readability Graph. The Fry is explained and a sample calculation given in an appendix.

SOURCES OF CURRENT REVIEWS

The Book Report. **Linworth. 5/yr. $35.**

Extensive review section on materials for secondary school libraries; reviewers note appeal for reluctant readers. Occasional articles specifically related to serving poor readers, such as "Reluctant Readers: The Librarian's Greatest Challenge" (January/February 1988).

Booklist. **American Library Association. Bimonthly. $56.**

A column, "Easy Reading," for easy-to-read books appropriate for beginning readers and older children with reading problems no longer includes Fry Readability listings; grade level indications encompass both reading and interest levels; published several times a year.

Kliatt Young Adult Paperback Book Guide. **Kliatt. 8/yr. $33.**

Reviews of paperback editions of titles recommended for ages 12–19. A code indicates that the book is low reading level and that the size of print and the vocabulary are not demanding.

School Library Journal. **R. R. Bowker. Monthly except July and August. $59.**

Reviews note suitability of books for poor or reluctant readers; no readability levels given. Columns on paperback teen romances and Spanish books are published several times a year. Articles such as "Characterizations in High-Interest/Low-Vocabulary Level Fiction" (February 1987) offer additional professional information.

Voice of Youth Advocates (VOYA). **Scarecrow. Bimonthly/April–February. $27.**

Reviewers often call attention to the general reading level, although no special designations are given; many small press items are reviewed or noted.

Although the following publications do not review high/low materials in quantity, they often include articles related to poor readers and provide short reviews, notices, and descriptions of appropriate materials. They are written from the perspective of the reading teacher or the English teacher.

The *ALAN Review* is a publication of the Assembly on Literature for Adolescents of the National Council of Teachers of English. Three issues a year cost $15 and subscribers do not have to belong to NCTE. Book reviews are printed in a clip and file format in each issue. Often a review will indicate whether a work would be good for a poor reader. No reading levels are given.

The *Journal of Reading* is the International Reading Association periodical related to the teaching of reading at the secondary school, college, and adult levels. Articles such as "Year Long Motivation in the 8th Grade 'Reluctant' Class" (December 1987), "Profiles of and Instructional Strategies for Adult Disabled Readers" (April 1988), "Implementing the Reading Workshop with Middle School LD Readers" (May 1989), and selected titles in the "Reviews" section are useful. The *Journal* is published eight times a year and the $30 IRA membership fee includes one subscription.

SIGNAL is the newsletter of the International Reading Association's Special Interest Group of Literature for the Adolescent Reader. It is published nine times a year and includes clip and file reviews of books for teens, often noting that the title would be appropriate for a poor or reluctant reader. Membership is $10 for members of the IRA and $12 for a nonmember.

DIRECTORY OF SOURCES

American Library Association
50 E. Huron St.
Chicago, IL 60611

Bowker, R. R.
245 W. 17 St.
New York, NY. 10011

Brodart Co.
500 Arch St.
Williamsport, PA 17705

Free Library of Philadelphia
Logan Square
Philadelphia, PA 19103

International Reading Association
800 Barksdale Rd.
Box 8139
Newark, DE 19714-8139

Kliatt Paperback Book Guide
425 Watertown St.
Newton, MA 02158

Libraries Unlimited, Inc.
Box 3988
Englewood, CO 80155

Linworth Publishing Co.
5701 N. High St., Suite One
Worthington, OH 43085

Merrill Publishing Co.
1300 Alum Creek
Columbus, OH 43216

National Council of Teachers of English
1111 Kenyon Rd.
Urbana, IL 61801

New York Public Library
Office of the Branch Libraries
455 Fifth St.
New York, NY 10016

Scarecrow Press
VOYA
52 Liberty St.
Metuchen, NJ 08840

School Library Journal
249 W. 17 St.
New York, NY 10011

SIGNAL. See International Reading Association

University of Chicago Press
5801 S. Ellis Ave.
Chicago, IL 60637

VOYA. See Scarecrow Press

Contributors

Jean M. Casey is Assistant Professor, School of Education, California State University, Long Beach.

Julie M. T. Chan is Coordinator, English Language Arts, Orange County, Department of Education.

Milton Goldman teaches reading in the content area at the University of California, Los Angeles, and is Reading Coordinator at Alexander Hamilton High School, Los Angeles.

Sandra Goldman teaches remedial reading and English at Alexander Hamilton High School, Los Angeles.

Ellen V. LiBretto is Young Adult Consultant, Queens Borough Public Library, Jamaica, New York.

Lyn Miller-Lachmann is an author of books for teenagers and the founder of Square One Publishers/Stamp Out Sheep Press.

Sandra Payne is Supervising Young Adult Specialist at the New York Public Library for the Borough of Staten Island.

Patsy H. Perritt is Associate Professor, School of Library and Information Science, Louisiana State University.

Marianne Laino Pilla is the author of *The Best: High/Low Books for Reluctant Readers in Grades 3–12*, forthcoming from Libraries Unlimited. She is currently Children's Librarian at Upper Dublin Public Library in Dresher, Pennsylvania.

Joanne Rosario is Vocational Schools Specialist for the New York Public Library.

Jean F. Rossman is Reading Consultant, East Lyme Junior High School, East Lyme, Connecticut.

Louise Spain is Professor and Coordinator of Media Services, Library Media Resources Center, La Guardia Community College, Long Island City, New York.

Author Index

This index includes all authors found in Part III, "The Core Collection." Numerals refer to entry numbers in Part III.

Title Index

This index includes all book titles found in Part III, "The Core Collection." Numerals refer to entry numbers in Part III.

Subject Index

Numerals refer to entry numbers in Part III. When numerals are preceded by "p" or "pp" references are to page numbers in Chapters 1–8.